Strat to Action

The KAIZEN™ method for turning Strategy into Action

Strat to Action

The KAIZEN™ method for turning Strategy into Action

Alberto Bastos and Charlie Sharman

MADRID · LONDON · MEXICO · NEW YORK · MILAN · TORONTO
LISBOA · NUEVA DELHI · SAN FRANCISCO · SIDNEY ·
SAN JUAN · SINGAPUR · CHICAGO · SEUL

Strat to Action

The KAIZEN™ method for turning Strategy into Action

McGraw-Hill/Interamericana de España, S.L.
Basauri, 17
Building Valrealty (A), 1.st floor
28023 Aravaca (Madrid)

ISBN 978-84-486-1990-9
MHID 978-000850204-1
Legal Deposit: M-37107-2019

Authors: Alberto Bastos / Charlie Sharman
Editor: Cristina Sánchez Sainz-Trápaga
Higher Ed & Prof Manager: Norberto Rosas Gómez
Director South Europe: Álvaro García Tejeda
Design and illustrations: Patrícia Ferreira
Senior advisor: Fernando Pinto
Translation from the book in Portuguese: Strat to Action. O método KAIZEN™ de levar a estratégia à prática. ISBN 9789892088167 © 2018 All rights reserved by Kaizen Institute
Translation and technical review: Rita Alves
Proof reading: David M. Woolford
Interior amendments: barnaTec®
Printer: Liber Digital, S.L.
0213456789 - 2423222120

IMPRESO EN ESPAÑA - PRINTED IN SPAIN

I dedicate this introductory note to my friend Charlie Sharman, who I consider to be a world reference in Lean. His knowledge in this area began in the 1970s, in Japan, where he had the opportunity to learn how to use KAIZEN™ as a way to eliminate waste. He led operations at benchmark companies such as Johnson Controls and Danaher, where he took the position of Vice President of Operations in Europe.

In "Strat to Action," the authors guide the reader through a three-year Lean transformation journey conducted by Hoshin Planning (also called Policy Deployment or Strategy Deployment). This is probably "the" core process used by Danaher in conducting its transformation processes and achieving exceptional results. And Danaher is, perhaps, the best example of how to achieve real results through the Lean approach. The success of Danaher is based on the DBS - Danaher Business System, which has, in its essence, KAIZEN™. This system requires that all levels of management actively participate in the implementation of continuous improvement, led by the CEO.

Chapter after chapter, the authors take the reader through a journey of transformation using the tools of Breakthrough KAIZEN™ and the Daily KAIZEN™.

The reader will get the chance to see how the strategy turns into action, through Hoshin's application, to focus on truly meaningful Breakthroughs, aligning the management team and delivering superior performance. The importance of keeping the gains is also emphasised, as we can often fall into the temptation to return to old habits; hence the need to use Daily KAIZEN™ to ensure that new standards are incorporated into the day-to-day business.

The Chapter on the Culture of Countermeasures describes the real underlying power of KAIZEN™, when disseminated throughout the company to continuously boost improvement.

Finally, the reader will be introduced to "Nagamichi KAIZEN™", or KAIZEN™ long path... A 10 to 15 year journey to build a truly powerful and lasting Lean culture. As I mentioned earlier, "KAIZEN™" is intensive leadership, and "Strat to Action" is the complete guide for leaders who are determined to win.

George Koenigsaecker

George Koenigsaecker is a member of the Board of Directors of the Shingo Prize. He has held, among other duties, the role of President of the Tool Group at Danaher Corp., where he developed and implemented the Danaher Business System. In 2009 he published the book "Leading The Lean Enterprise Transformation". Koenigsaecker graduated from the Harvard Business School.

Index

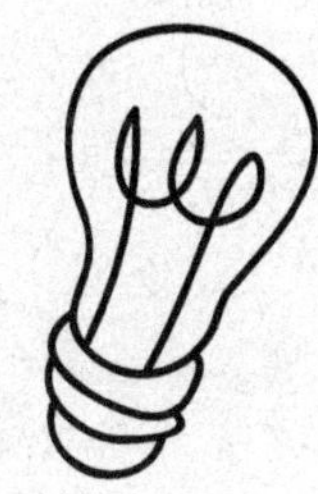

4. Breakthrough KAIZEN™

5. The Daily KAIZEN™

6. Countermeasure Culture

Index

Preface

It is with great honour and pleasure that I witness another Kaizen's Institute Western Europe book edition. This book is a set of tips and guidelines about how every organisation can improve, being profit-branch or not, in the industrial, commercial, logistics and services sectors.

Here we present a KAIZEN™ Management Model (KAIZEN™ Business System) in a very simple and clear way, as in the endowment of a very pragmatic KAIZEN™ model.

The goal is to change for the better and do it in a sustainable and continuous way. Step by step, the vision is to build a solid capacity to lead the organisation and its employees to the next performance level.

Strat to Action is about a very common story in the daily life of organisations, where a new CEO wants to change the organisation's course, wants to define what are the steps, successes and failures of a 3-year journey, by applying a KAIZEN™ management method to define strategy and by implementing it through the breakthrough results achieved.

In fact, the subtitles of some chapters translate the text richness by starting with "If you're not growing, you're dying". Also, the description of the "need to change for the better", by implementing a "great strategy that can be summarised in one single page".

The changing for the better vision defines how we must "plan objectives that are hard to achieve", because "with great results come great changes". Objectives are defined in a very scientific way for which players can deploy and apply them at the point of impact".

"Create awareness to sustain and empower results", to "build a culture of effective counter-measures" and "Not even the best action plan is free from deviations" are examples of the detailed subjects for you to understand the influence of KAIZEN techniques.

The Strat to Action review (or Hoshin as it is frequently called in the book) is a measure to monitorise regular results, to allow quick reactions and to better plan adjustments and corrections in view of deviations. Also, the sales effort increase is becoming more complex. To put Hoshin on the right path, we need to listen to the VOC (Voice of the Customer) and to implement KAIZEN™ in sales: "When clients speak, we listen" - should be our motto, a way of thinking very well described in this book.

This book is also about "How to budget without effort" and about the connection between Hoshin and Budget. Once again, we conclude that ambition and simplification generate results, as waste elimination in every process is the key to success.

Peter Drucker once said that "Culture eats strategy for breakfast" and, indeed, this is exactly it. What is the use of having a great strategy if culture barriers prevent its appliance? Although a great improvement might be fundamental, the lack of a great strategy will always stop an organisation from expressing its mission and vision completely, even if in KAIZEN™ we always fight for an improvement strategy and culture.

This book is a very important contribution for a deep understanding of what the KAIZEN™ Management System is, of how we can implement it and how we could lead an organisation to be the Best in Class. I am certain that this book will be read over and over again, as always happens with best-sellers.

I hope that the reader will be capable of applying these ideas to put their organisation on the right path, the one of standards and Continuous Improvement.

In conclusion, allow me to thank my colleagues Alberto Bastos and Charlie Sharman for the amazing work with this 3-year ALFA journey description as well as the **Strat to Action** overview that started with average results and has achieved Dantotsu results (by far the best in the sector).

Euclides A. Coimbra
Senior Partner & Managing Director
Kaizen Institute Western Europe

A dying star

If you're not growing, you're dying

If you're not growing, you're dying - in business, you are either moving forward or backwards.

Most leaders know where they want to lead their organisation to and have a long-term vision in mind - their dream!

The problem arises when, due to communication failures, the "small powers" installed, the "accumulated fat" in processes and incipient control systems fail to lead the organisation by defining and implementing the strategic priorities to achieve the Vision.

Leaders usually seek consensus in deciding what is a priority, but resources end up being dispersed in secondary projects because of the prevalence of personal goals instead of the overall objectives.

The search for ideal conditions and the perfect solution leads to procrastination of implementation, while resistance to change brings together more "not to do" arguments. All these are obstacles that create bewilderment, strain and discouragement in teams, which makes it difficult to carry out the designed strategy and take the organisation forward.

Aware of these difficulties, at Kaizen Institute we developed the "Strat to Action" methodology. This enhances the communication of the strategic objectives, ensures the alignment and prioritisation of what is most critical to execute, with involvement at all levels, and emphasises the achievement of results.

We seek to help leaders make their dreams come true!

1.1 When everything is new

It was his first day at Alfa's. Everything was new. The location, the machines, the product, the teams, the culture and the challenges. Now, he was going to be a CEO for the first time, and he felt anxious.

It was raining, heavily. On the way to the company he thought about the speech he would deliver at the meeting with the Executive Committee members. He had only had contact with the Finance Director prior to signing his contract.

He arrived at the company's headquarters. He drove slowly past reception. After all the normal security procedures the security guard showed him his parking place and he parked his car equally aligned between the two lines that bounded the parking area - he had always been a perfectionist even when he was a child, almost obsessive with numbers and puzzles.

He went to the reception desk where the receptionist was already waiting for him, ready to escort him to the Executive Committee room. When he entered, everyone was seated. Some of them on the tablet, others on the phone, and the rest lost in thought. As soon as the receptionist announced his arrival, the new CEO felt all eyes focused on him, but that did not disturb him in the least.

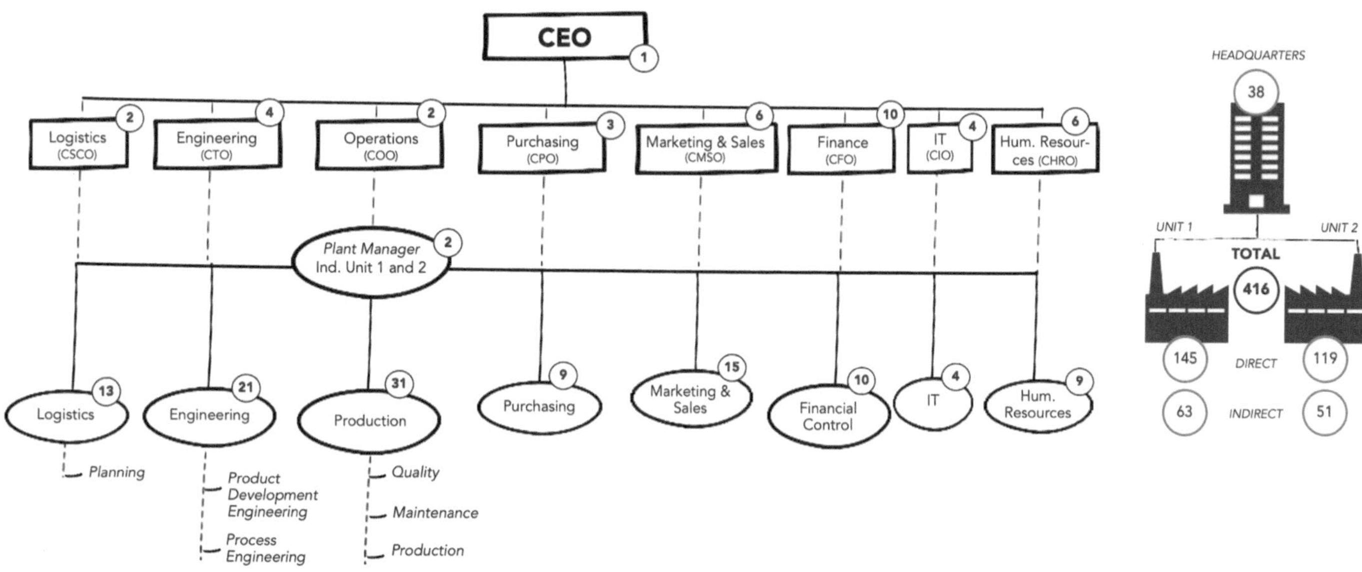

ALFA's organisational structure, Year 0

One by one he greeted all the members of his new team, they all introduced themselves swiftly during the handshakes.

The Financial Director was in his mid-thirties. He had an MBA in Economics and had been working in the company ever since he had left university. He was the son of the former Logistics Director who had retired a few years earlier. According to a previous meeting, he seemed to be a very capable guy, determined to give the organisation a new approach.

The Operations Director was a Mechanical Engineer in his 60s with many years of experience. He had only ever worked in Alpha company, as man and boy. The new CEO had already been warned about his bad temper as well as his difficulty in accepting differing opinions from his own.

The Marketing and Sales Director was a tall man in his 50s. He had started at Alfa 15 years ago. After several years of company growth, the situation had reversed in the last few years. The spirit of the team was rather low due to many customer complaints resulting from delays and quality issues.

The Human Resources Director, a woman in her 50s, had been working at Alfa for two years. She had felt frustrated from the beginning, as all she had been doing was dismissal and recruitment procedures. These circumstances had prevented her from being focused on talent management, training initiatives, development of activities to support job stability, and team building organisation.

Other members of the Executive Committee were the Logistic & Materials Director, the Engineering Director, the Purchasing Director, and the IT Director, all of them part of a younger generation. They all expected the new CEO would give the company a new direction.

The CEO already knew Alpha's historical background. The company was a group of two industrial plants and traditionally recognised as market leader. Throughout its four decades of trading it had maintained a sound image in the industry, standing out for its know-how, quality and reliability, a steady path over the years, only more recently slowed.

The new CEO thanked the team for having introduced themselves and made a short summary of his academic and professional career. He began by explaining to the audience that in the following weeks it would be essential that he would spend the necessary time in both industrial plants, in order to get to know the teams better, as well as the manufacturing procedures and processes, and to understand the company's culture. He mentioned that he would collect some essential data in order to be able to evaluate the company's current economic and financial condition as well as conduct a study of the competitors. He asked everyone present to support him during these early times and said that he would be available to discuss any matter and to help with any problem. The CEO announced that the meeting was over, and they all left the room, leaving a feeling of concern behind as to the changes they were already anticipating.

The new CEO's early days were completely absorbing, if a little slow in getting the data. He called the leaders of all the teams to his office, one by one. This was an old routine he had used in his previous company, he wanted to get to know each of his team members. He spoke to each one of them, trying to understand their expectations, and then joined them in their department to get to know all the elements of his extended team and to have them know him a little better. He wanted them to speak freely about the processes and what "pain" they felt daily. He repeated several times that he would always be open to discuss ideas or problems and that he would remain available for them to come and talk. Obviously reporting lines were in place, but he needed to know the employees' thoughts better.

At the end of the 2nd week, the CEO visited the two industrial units and their managers. He had invested his time in understanding the differences between them, the shared problems, and the production flow. His experience allowed him to see some important improvement opportunities in several processes, which would easily generate some quick wins.

It was in the 3rd week that the CEO decided to focus on preparing his findings. One of the key lessons he would never forget from his Kaizen coach was "talk with data". Using the company standard data with his own observations he prepared a reasoned Benchmark analysis mainly focused on Alpha's economic and financial performance, as well as those of its competitors.

Quite soon after he had prepared the report, the CEO scheduled a meeting with the Executive Committee to submit his analysis. The scope was clear: to set the course of the organisation for the next 3 years. At that moment, it was already possible for him to discuss and define Alfa's strategic objectives to deliver the shareholders expectations. He was certain that time was of essence, they needed to start the improvement journey towards excellence as soon as possible, as he had promised the shareholders.

1.2 The Benchmark

At the beginning of the meeting, the discomfort in the room was quite obvious. The CEO started by presenting the economic and financial indicators, as well as the market analysis. Although everyone had already noticed that things were not going so well as before, everything was becoming more and more real as the presentation proceeded.

1.2.1 Dimension and Market Share

The presented results were for the whole group. Separately, the two plants were in different locations and had different dimensions, number of employees and In Year 0, plant 1 achieved a turnover of 45788 million euros and plant 2 achieved 33826 million euros.

COMPANY	SALES (M€)	% MARKET SHARE
Alfa	79 614	21%
Beta	69 264	18%
Zeta	39 253	10%
Gama	35 738	10%
Delta	29 944	8%
Sigma	26 304	7%
Other	94 883	25%
Full market value	**375 000**	**100%**

Dimension and market share, Year 0

1.2.2 Competitive Positioning

When compared to its competitors, Alfa was the largest in terms of sales. It stood out due to its high differentiation through the use of engineering innovation. Technology was the company's main distinction with the largest volume of engineered products on the market. The high costs associated to this strategy were completely unsustainable for Alfa in the short to medium term.

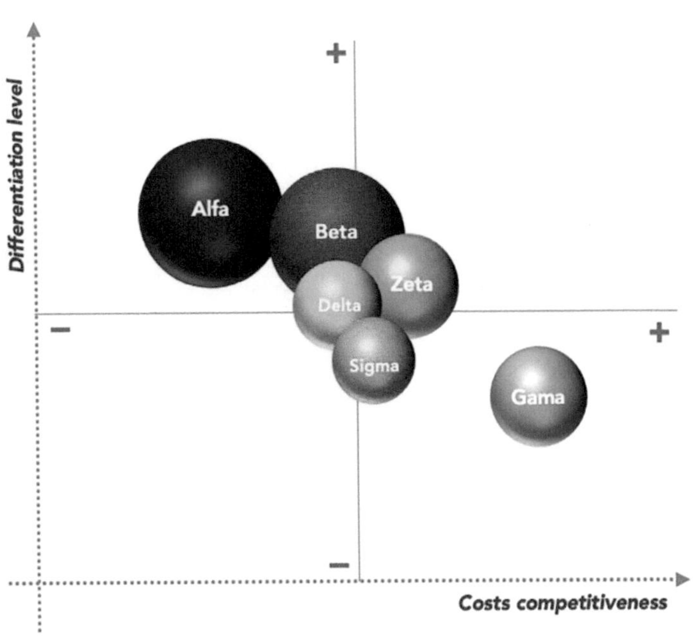

Competitive positioning, Year 0

1.2.3 Sales and Net Results

At the time of the analysis, ALFA had the highest sales volume and the lowest profitability when compared to its competitors. The declining trend was unchanged as the company had tried unsuccessfully to reduce its high costs and its main competitors had been progressively increasing market share and profitability.

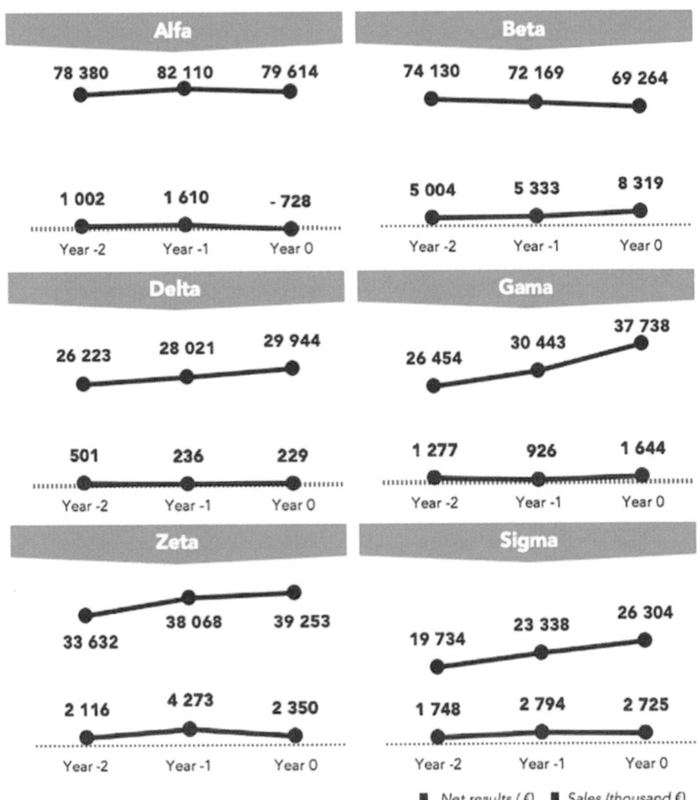

Sales and net results evolution, Years -2, -1 and 0

1.2.4 EBITDA

ALFA's EBITDA[1] 3 year trend showed a year on year reduction in results with the last year 0 having achieved 2.9% EBITDA, while its main competitor, Beta, had achieved an EBITDA of 12.7%.

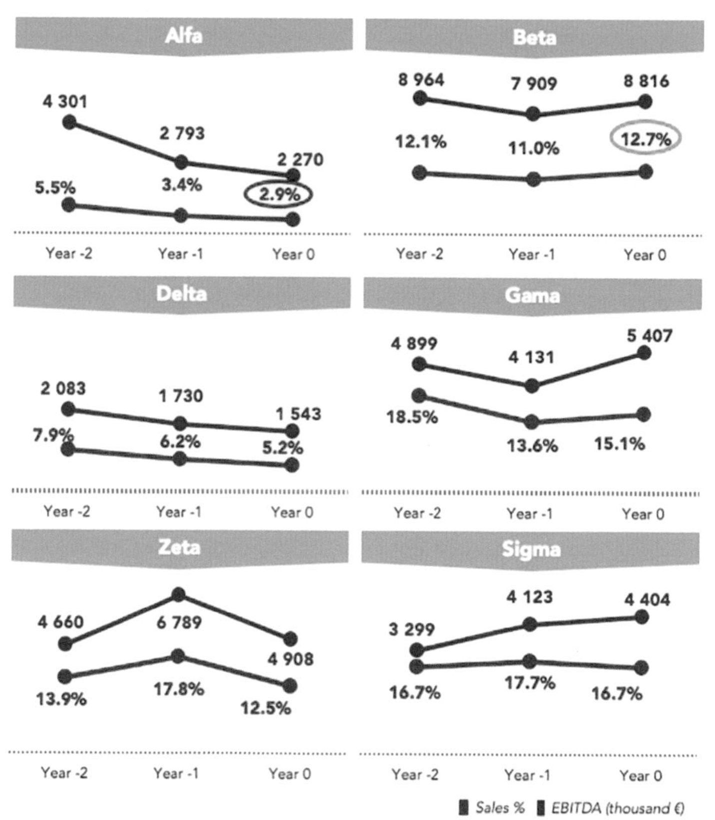

EBITDA evolution, Years -2, -1 and 0

1.2.5 Free Cash Flow and ROCE

As a result of its low performance levels and recent investments, ALFA's free cash flow[2] and profitability of capital employed (ROCE), had fallen below acceptable minimums, to 545 thousand euros. Its main competitor, Beta, had reached 10.6 million euros and 15.2%, with every other competitor having obtained ROCE values above 10%.

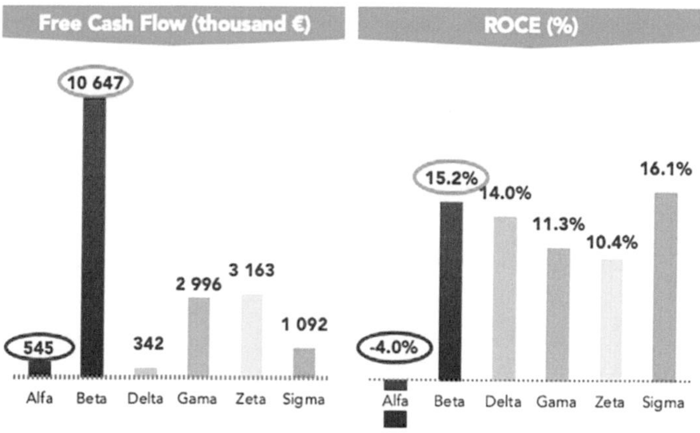

Free cash flow and ROCE evolution, Years 0

1.2.6 Personnel Expenses

The expenses per employee were significantly higher than those from the other players, and the trend over the last 3 years had been increasing. It should be noted that the average cost per

1 EBITDA: Earnings before Interest, Taxes, Depreciation and Amortisation

2 Free cash flow: EBIT - taxes, depreciation, amortisation - Capex: working capital variance

3 ROCE: Return on capital employed; EBIT (current asset/liability)

employee in Alfa, in the last year, was € 30000, while the average of its competitors was around € 22000, part of this cost relying on non-recurring costs of damages (about € 1 million).

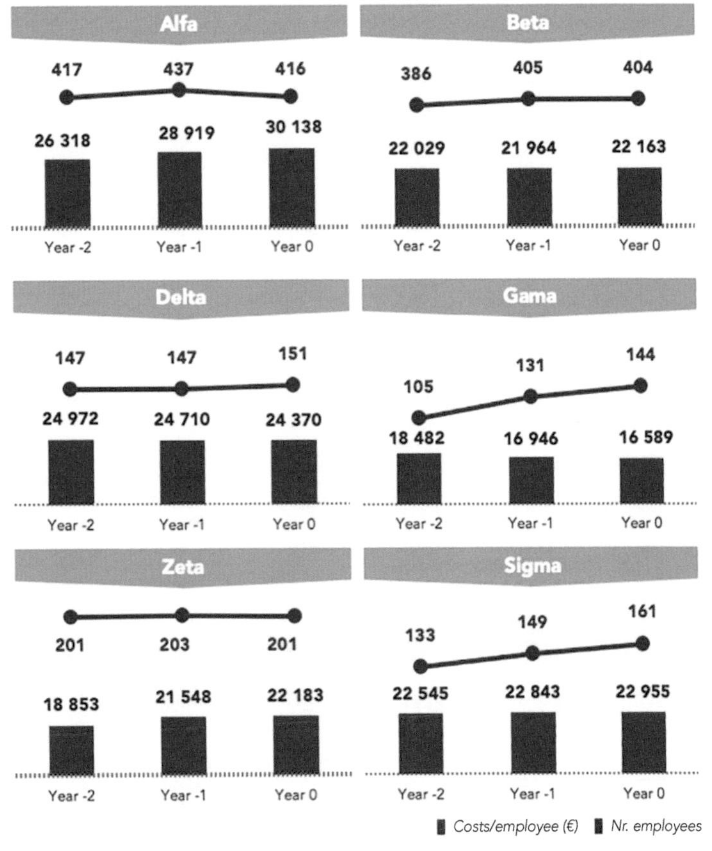

Personnel expenses evolution regarding Years -2, -1 and 0

1.2.7 Comparison of the Main Ratios for Year 0

ALFA had a gross margin value of 36.5%, the lowest of the competition. External services accounted for 17.7% of total sales, contrasting with the 15% achieved by its main competitor.

As already mentioned, a significant differential was noted in the company's staff costs, with a value on sales of 15.7% in the last year, while the average of its competitors was around 11.5%.

Inventory had increased with the higher complexity and with customers demanding smaller batches, leading to inventory turnover of 6.0, this being the lowest of any of its direct competitors.

The low EBITDA of 2.9% and EBIT[4] at -0.9% was a very real threat to the company. That could also be seen in the Balance Sheet: the company showed substantial risk in that it had a very low level (22.2%) of net debt on the EBTIDA of 8.1, when good practices recommend a value of no more than two.

For more detailed data, refer to Appendix 2.

4 EBIT: Earnings before Interest and Taxes

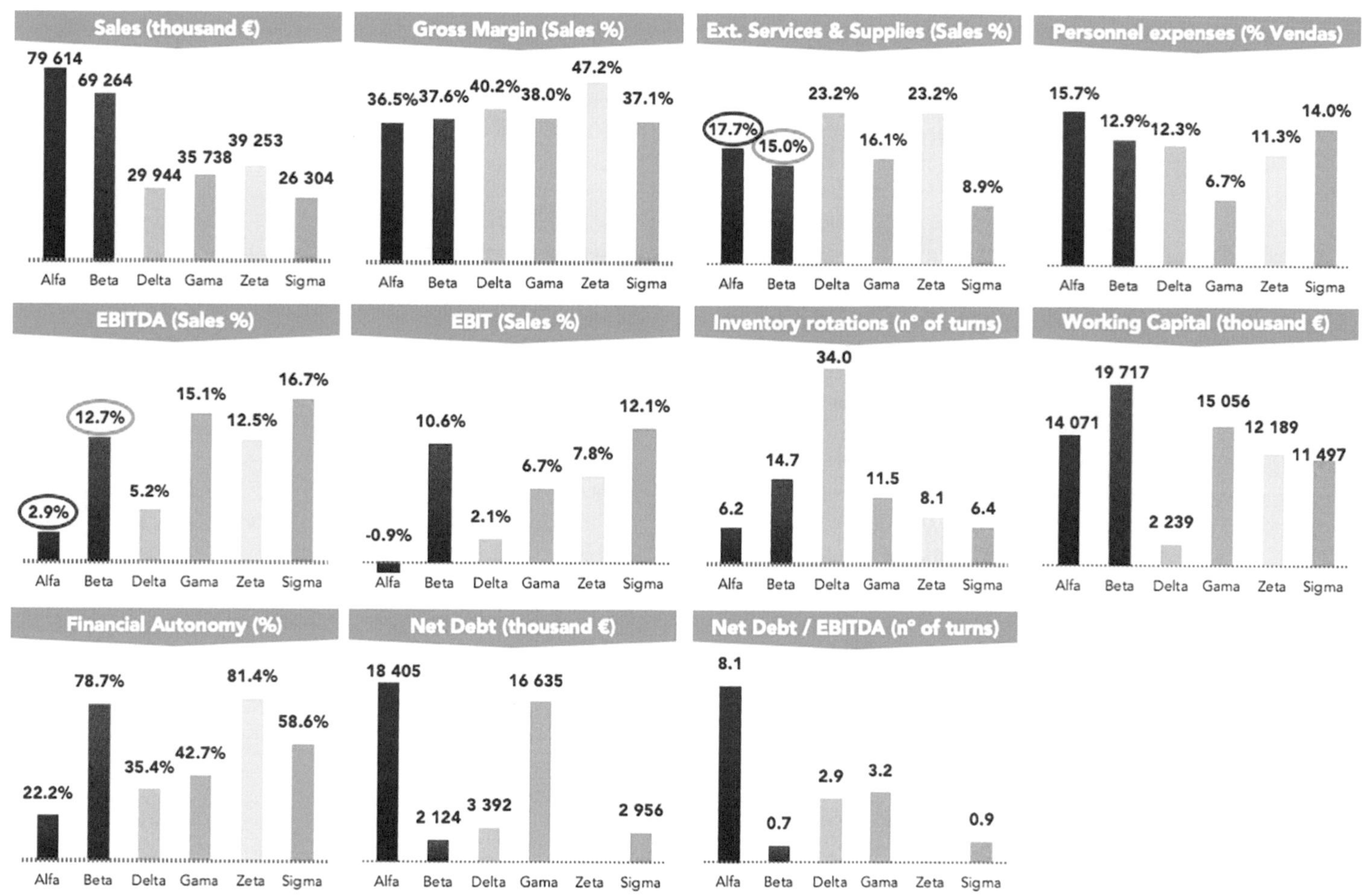

Key financial ratios comparison, Year 0

1.3 The first decision

Several comments were heard among the members of the Executive Committee during the benchmark presentation, as well as an exchange of accusations among some of them. The team was edgy regarding the submitted results. Nobody was pleased to conclude that the company was "in trouble". Everybody realised that they had no understanding of the competitors' performance, and they were not aware that the risks were so high. They feared that the ideas of the new element could change the "home" they had once known.

The CEO pointed to the flipchart and started an exercise with the team for them to agree what the objectives should be. The exercise was quite simple: from the Benchmark analysis, they should identify which competitor presented the best performance for each indicator, this being Alpha's next new goal. The Financial Director confirmed the company data vs the best competitor's data used in the benchmark:

1. Cost of raw material from 63.5% to 52.8% of sales.
2. Cost of bought in service from 17.7% to 8.9% of sales.
3. Staff costs from 15.7% to 6.7% of sales.
4. Inventory rotation from 6.2 to 34 times.

Then, based on these objectives, the team was asked to calculate the corresponding gains in EBITDA. After some quick calculations, this information was added to the flipchart:

1. Cost of raw material from 63.5% to 52.8%
   €8.5 million euros.
2. Cost of bought in service from 17.7% to 8.9%
   €7 million euros.
3. Staff costs from 15.7% to 6.7%
   €7.2 million euros.
4. Inventory rotation from 6.2 to 34 times
   €10.6 million euros.

With this information given, the CEO calculated the projection of the new EBITDA for ALFA, assuming all objectives would be achieved. Under these conditions, it was possible to achieve an in EBITDA of 25 million, or even better, 22.7 million over the current 2.3 million EBITDA. They added an additional 10.6 million in cash flow, resulting from the reduction of working capital. After this conclusion, the CEO addressed his speech to the Financial Director, by asking:
"So, what do you think about 25 million euros in EBITDA?"

"Honestly, I see it as utopian. We cannot expect to be the Best-in-Class on all indicators!" the Financial Director replied, slightly angry.

The CEO answered promptly:
"Of course, we have to focus, but that should not prevent us from being ambitious."

"Particularly because our shareholders are less demanding!" the Financial Director said, reminding the team of the shareholders' expectations for the next 3 years:

- 7.5% of EBITDA on sales.
- 12% of Growth on sales (market growth + 2%/year).
- Free Cash Flow at least equal to EBIT.

It was then that the Operations Director felt that he had just made an ally, so he decided to intervene:

"I also do not think it makes any sense to compare our conditions with the conditions of our competitors! They do not make the same products we do, nor do they have our technical skills. If we fail to pay a decent salary to our people, as a preview of what will be proposed after this meeting, we will surely lose the best technicians and increase demotivation. And then you can be sure that productivity will drop and delays in deliveries will be even greater!" He continued, even more angry, addressing the CEO directly "Excuse me, but have you visited the plants of any of our competitors?"

The CEO asked everyone to calm down. He mentioned that as he already said, he had been in the field for as long as possible over the recent weeks. But, of course, he had not had the opportunity to visit ALFA's competitors, nor had this ever been one of his priorities. The numbers spoke for themselves and the waste associated with Alpha's internal processes was obvious, the CEO needed no further evidence. He needed to push the team to "get to work".

After the Operations Manager had relaxed a bit, the CEO continued: "Neither you nor I have a clear understanding of what the objectives need to be for ALFA. What is clear is that we are very far from the competition in every indicator, and this should be a warning. My vision is to redefine the whole strategy of this company and I know we have to do it together."

A sense of shock and confusion was felt by the team. A few seconds later without any comment, the CEO proceeded.
"OK everyone, the only way to turn things around depends on our commitment". Some members of the Executive Committee looked at each other, shrugging their shoulders. "What I consider to be important at this stage is that each of you are aware of your role and that of your people in this challenge. We must improve our level of service and on being recognised for being a quality provider for our customers, as we have been in the past. I do not want to see unmotivated teams with no participation in decisions and with successive complaints, instead of looking for solutions. I believe that ALFA needs to totaly change its behavior and develop a continuous improvement culture. We all have relevance here and we all have our responsibilies."

When he was asked how they should do this, he talked about his KAIZEN™ experience and how this had changed his leadership perspective. At that time, he felt like a leader focused on continuous improvement, believing that this was the "only way" of really changing an organisation. He discussed the **KAIZEN™ principles and approach** as an essential part of any management process:

1. **Value** - specify value according to the customer's vision.
2. **Value Streams** - waste identification in all phases.
3. **Create flow and eliminate MUDA (japanese word for "waste")** - implement of actions to eliminate waste and improve flow in processes (refer to Appendix 2 to 7, Muda Model Analysis).
4. **A pull system implementation** - to produce only what is "pulled" by the client.
5. **The pursuit of perfection** - improve processes through continuous elimination of MUDA[5].

5 MUDA: Japanese word meaning waste, everything that does not add value to the customer (internal or external).

Although this approach seemed very simple, these were new terms for most Executive Committee members. In spite of believing in the continuous improvement concept, their efforts were focused on solving daily emergencies, with the teams gathered for hours and without a pre-defined agenda. They did not feel the need to involve employees in decisions, and the problem solving did not involve any cause or effect analysis, it was driven by instinct and gut feelings.

The team remained tense, and unsure where the CEO's speech would take them to.

"It is not an easy situation we are living today. We do not know exactly what to do next. I am sure we are all very committed, but we need help." the Financial Director claimed.

"We've been losing clients almost every day!" the Marketing Director confessed "Do you really believe that everyone's commitment to solve problems will be enough to solve something that we already perceived to be structural?"

The CEO decided to end the drama and regained the control of the meeting:
"I know we're in a complicated situation, and nothing I've said makes any difference. We need to redefine the true direction of this company through clear initiatives in the short, medium and long term. We need experts who can support us in the design and implementation of how to create change, who can help us turn our Strategy into Action."

The CEO reinforced the relevance of working together with a skilled coach at this stage.

Having said that, The Financial Director commented:
"As you remember, Consultants X, who were here two years ago, took 9 weeks to suggest an improvement strategy. They presented us a very detailed study about indicators and general benchmark analysis of the sector, as well as the macro trends at European level. It was a global report with all the guidelines for the way forward, which further enhanced the long-term benefits, proven from scenario analyses and simulations."

"They sold us a 'turnkey' project, but the car was still not built" the Operations Director said, while smiling.

"Effective transformation, that is what we called the plan that would be managed internally. And that was the problem... We stopped right there." the Financial Director concluded.

Despite this initial reluctance everyone ended up agreeing to an external intervention that would help deliver the transformation everyone recognised as necessary.

"I suggest that we ask Kaizen Institute for help. I have already worked with them twice, and always achieved good results. They are practical and deliver results, individuals who do not rest until they reach the goals they have set themselves! And, in addition to helping us design a future solution, they support us in the implementation phase." The CEO said to everyone "Does anyone have anything to add to what I am proposing?"

None of the members of the Executive Committee opposed this option. They were even curious to see the proposal that would be made. The meeting ended soon after. Slowly, everyone left the room as they exchanged impressions about the loss of another customer.

Later that afternoon, the CEO contacted the Kaizen Institute and the proposal came a few days later.

1.3.1 The Offer

After a visit and processes evaluation, Kaizen Institute presented an Offer to the CEO, who was pleasantly surprised. Expectations were good. Key productivity and quality improvement and lead time reductions were identified as key opportunities to ensure a high level of customer service. On the other hand, Alpha could not afford to forget the marketing changes necessary to improve Sales and New Product Development processes.

Based on the experience in similar projects, Kaizen Institute was prepared to target 50% inventory reduction, 30% increase in productivity, 30% in occupation reduction and 20% in costs reduction.

By sharing the proposal with the other Executive Committee members, some directors seemed shocked by the figures presented.

"Here we go again with those consultants that claim to be able to increase productivity by 30%." the Operations Director said, clearly annoyed.

"You are completely right. How can they reduce inventory by 50% this seems like utopia to me!" the Logistics Manager seemed discouraged.

"Yes, but that is exactly what is exciting about this Offer. What Kaizen Institute is suggesting is a process that will force us to design solutions to achieve these goals. In fact, these goals have to stop being the consultants' goals and need to become our own! If we can do that, then we will succeed, I'm quite sure of that." the CEO said.

The KAIZEN™ implementation is focused on coaching the organisation's leaders, enabling them to identify the wastes in their own processes and mastering the appropriate tools to eliminate these wastes in a radical way.

The first KAIZEN™ Event (refer to concept in 3.2.4) was carried out with the mandatory participation of the entire Executive Committee and other key elements from the different areas of the company, for ALFA's future vision design. In turn, the second step was to translate this vision into strategic objectives to be achieved in the coming years.

The next chapter begins by describing the key concepts associated with the Strat to Action process.

Strat to Action

The KAIZEN™ method for turning Strategy into Action

There are many challenges when in business, but waiting for results to improve can be very frustrating. Organisations are more alert than ever to ever-changing market demands, trying to be one step ahead of their competitors. The new method of converting "Strat to Action" at last turns this risk of doing nothing into an opportunity to outperform your competitors.

"Strat to Action" is a methodology that creates alignment, ensuring the whole company focuses on what is important; we call these the significant few breakthroughs. This new method is applied to align individual goals and resources throughout the organisation so that everyone knows their responsibilities regarding the organisation's improvement priorities. The process starts by defining the strategy and ends with clearly describing the changes that are needed at the point of impact, the place where the real improvement is delivered by recognising the root causes and implementing solutions. By separating the significant few over the many, "Strat to Action" creates a process that can deliver breakthrough performance quickly.

This chapter presents the "Strat to Action" process main steps and highlights its key role in delivering effective results in any organisation. It also shows "How" Kaizen is used to deliver the improvement priorities in a well-organised and structured way being carried out at the different levels of the organisation.

2.1 The Importance of Alignment

In the absence of a structured change process it is common to see different managers each with a different view of what has to be done and how it should be implemented. Consequently, each one chooses different priorities. So, without alignment we see important decisions being postponed, thus preventing the organisation from achieving its full growth potential.

In view of this, it is necessary to ensure agreement between decision-makers when defining the strategic direction and priorities of the organisation. In fact, this is the first step of "Strat to Action" - to agree the significant few breakthrough objectives which can then be deployed as improvement priorities; this directly links the Strategy to the point of impact or where the real action will be taken.

2.2 The "Strat to Action" Process

"Strat to Action" is a KAIZEN™ methodology for implementing the strategy of an organisation and ensuring the alignment of all the people engaged, from the top to the point of impact. This process consists of annual cycles that take place in **Planning** and **Review** stages, often referred to as **Hoshin Planning** and **Hoshin Review**, respectively.

Hoshin Planning defines Breakthrough Objectives for the next 3 to 5 years based on the organisation's strategic priorities using data gathered from the voice of the customer and Enterprise Value Stream Analysis (refer to 2.3). The 3 to 5 year goals are then transformed into Annual Breakthrough Goals and organised into a matrix that will be deployed to every level of the organisation.

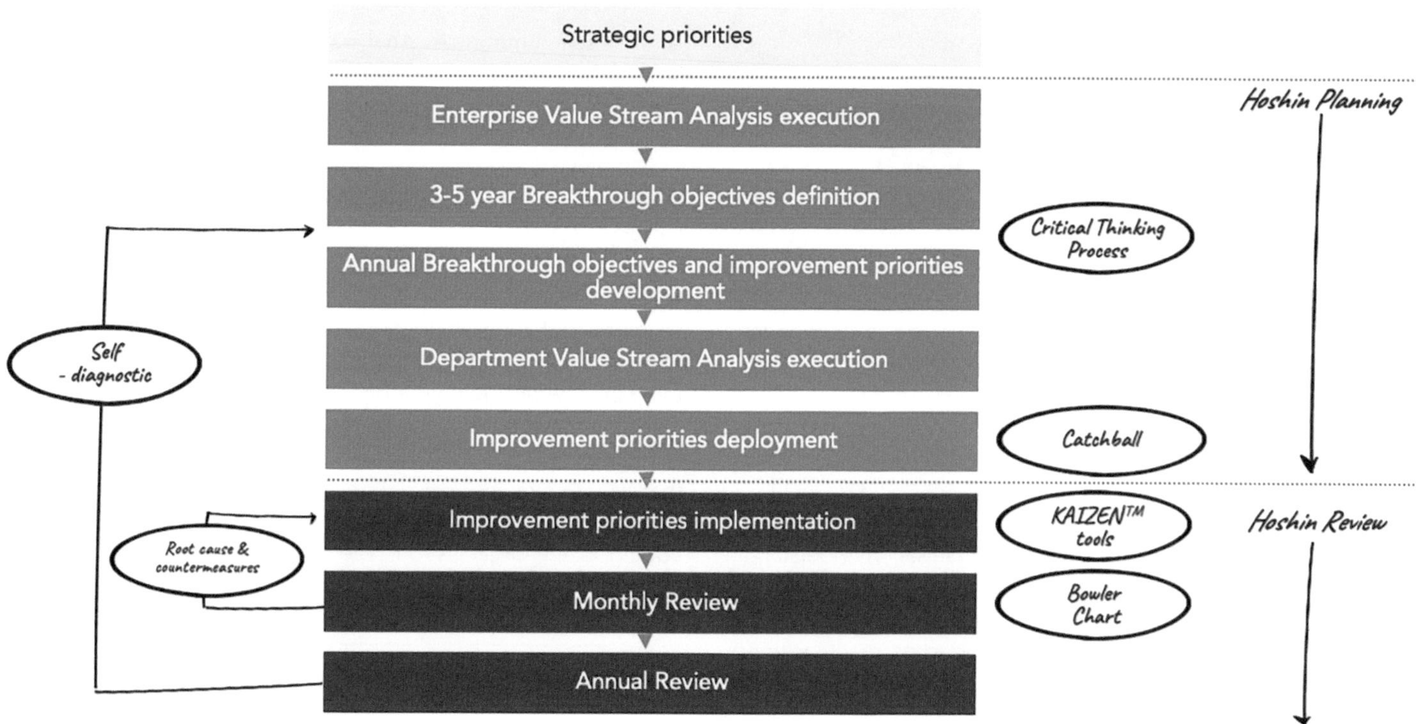

To be able to visualise the changes necessary to deliver the improvement priorities across the organisation the first step is to build Value Stream Maps (refer to 2.4). This will help to identify high priority improvement opportunities that will deliver the strategic objectives.

The **Hoshin Review**, in turn, includes monthly reviews to monitor the progress the effect of implementing the individual action plans created from the Value Stream Analysis, also using countermeasures to correct deviations from the defined objectives.

2.3 Enterprise Value Stream Analysis

The Enterprise Value Stream Analysis is a KAIZEN™ Event that aims to make all activities performed in the organisation visible to identify waste in the product/service. The best way to do this is to map every task, from order arrival up to the delivery of the product/ service to the end-customer.

In an industrial organisation such as ALFA, the Enterprise Value Stream Analysis maps all the material and information flows, making it clear when these flows are interrupted. Whenever a flow is interrupted, we know that we are not adding value but generating waste. It is essential that everyone in the organisation understands which activities add value and which do not in the eyes of the customer. Only then does the full extent of the waste become visible. Studies have shown that in world class manufacturing organisations 300 minutes are needed to add 1 minute of added value, with the most common organisations having a ratio of 10 000 minutes or more to add 1 minute of value. At first, you will think this number is incredibly wrong and you will say 'my organisation will have a much more efficient ratio', but when you compare the real processing time vs how long it takes to deliver the product or service to the customer, the reality sinks in.

After the Current State has been mapped and the data confirmed, then the team can design the Future State that has removed substantial amounts of waste with the necessary action plans to deliver the results.

The Kaizen Enterprise Analysis aims to analyse the entire organisation through an 11-step process that leads to the design of a Breakthrough Vision for the future.

1. DEFINING VALUE

The first stage of the process aims to define the added value in the organisation. It starts by answering the question - "What is the customer willing to pay for the service or product?". This study must be considered in Gemba[1] through direct observation of activities, including work measurement of tasks, times, inventory and necessary stocks and other necessities. Only by following the workflow and rework loops can an accurate current state be mapped. If we consult the quality manual or sit in the meeting-room, we will deliver a totally unreal situation. It is essential that we capture the real data no matter how ugly they are. This understanding is fundamental to realise the extent of non-value adding in the organisation. The following paragraphs will detail these steps in the order they occur.

1 GEMBA: Japanese word literally means "the real place". It refers to the place where the value is added.

2. MAPPING MATERIALS FLOW

The purpose of mapping the material flow is to identify all the steps in the current process, highlighting everything that may interrupt the flow. This analysis is called the 'current state mapping'. It does not map the Quality Manual or what people think, but what is actually happening in practice. It is usual to map the material flow and then the information flow.

3. MAPPING INFORMATION FLOW

This step maps the lines of communication and information shared between the different areas of the organisation starting from the customer request to the confirmed delivery of the product or service. In all value streams we need to trigger in the correct work sequence, as this links the planning to the physical work, and this may happen at many different points in the value stream. The most important thing is to clearly identify where the handovers are; it is usually at the fringes where we find many different hand offs, decisions and rework loops.

4. ADDING DATA TO EACH PROCESS STEP

This adds data to each process step that you have mapped, highlighting the data showing the organisation's ability to deliver on time, overspending valuable resources, creating scrap and rework. Presenting these data will quickly show where the productivity gains are. Remember most of the realised waste can be seen as productivity of labour or materials used, in addition a clear picture of the amount of inventory opportunities will appear for lead-time reduction and increasing free cash flow. Finally, we see how investment into large centralised equipment "dinosaurs" have reduced flexibility and have added high levels of nonvalue adding activity. The future state will create the challenges in designing smaller, simpler and more flexible equipment.

At the end of this stage the Map will identify the high levels of waste which are:

- "Where are the losses?"
- "Where are the errors and the rework?"
- "Where are the people?"
- "Where is the inventory?"
- "Where is the money?"

5. DEVISING THE VISION

This is where creativity takes on special relevance. Here, the team must place itself in the fictional scenario of running a small business starving for sales and money, operating in a "garage". Most small businesses are very good at creating low-cost or no cost solutions in order to solve day-to-day problems as they have neither the time nor the money to waste on meetings and long studies. This exercise shows that improvement and waste elimination can be achieved by implementing simple, practical and innovative solutions, that do not kill profitability. With this in mind the team starts to challenge paradigms and design solutions that include only what is strictly necessary to produce Excellent Quality, Low Cost and High Delivery performance. These small changes when added together will deliver substantial competitive advantage.

6. IDENTIFYING VALUE STREAMS

Keeping the creative mindset, teams detail knowledge of the value stream mapping but, still in the concept of "garage", they can start looking at simpler, more efficient ways to flow materials and information, typically by product and customer, in order to simplify flow and reduce lead time, which will give greater flexibility and will allow us to build a further vision of the ideal Value Stream. At this time, it may not yet be possible to define exactly how to get there, but this step shows the direction of the Vision and creates opportunities to identify important Breakthroughs.

7. CHOSSING NATURAL GROUPS

In general, where we mix different types of groups, we will interrupt the flow. Most things that can flow easily are typically interrupted by the few that cannot. It is the segregation need which makes ABC Analysis the simplest and most effective tool for improving Quality, Cost and Delivery. In KAIZEN™, products or services are usually described as follows:

- ***Runners*** - 80% of the sales volume and 20% of the mix.
- ***Repeaters*** - 15% of the sales volume and 30% of the mix.
- ***Strangers*** - 5% of the sales volume and 50% of the mix.

Many organisations use the same value streams for large groups of products with little or no understanding that a high-volume low-variety cannot be mixed with a low-volume high-variety product, it's like oil and water, they cannot be mixed as one contaminates the other. When this occurs, we are adding unnecessary management complexity. This separation requires a very difficult planning exercise, often unclear and almost unmanageable, with high levels of errors and uncertainty. Being able to separate Runners, Repeaters and Strangers is an absolutely necessary discipline for the organisation to be able to maximise its Value Stream design.

8. CHANGING PARADIGMS

A paradigm is a model, a rule, or a habit that influences the way human beings interpret a given situation. Paradigms can be the very source of waste deeply rooted in corporate culture. Teams need to be open-minded in order to identify and break their own paradigms, adopting a pioneering role regarding the new way of thinking or performing.

Within the Value Stream Mapping many deep-rooted Beliefs and Behaviours will be characterised as, "we always did it that way", a simple clue to challenge the waste and break a paradigm; or "you don't understand, our business is different"; in fact, it isn't, that paradigm has just been created. This step is very important in building a continuously challenging improving organisation. You must go through the identification of the main paradigms that can lead to difficulties in the implementation of the ideal Vision and make them visible and break them down with zero tolerance. Some of the Paradigms are so deep-rooted that, in order to break them, the team must believe they will destroy the company and this is the ultimate challenge.

The implementation of an ideal state often breaks old paradigms and adds new paradigms with a positive effect, such as Unit Flow vs Large Batches, Pull vs Push, or Zero Defects vs Acceptable Quality Levels. The ideal state will start to change the way of thinking, but it may still be difficult to realise. However, the team cannot place barriers that prevent change, but rather think "Why not now? Why not assume the new paradigms right now?" Many of the disruptive concepts and ideas developed in the ideal state will still be far from immediate implementation, but all energy and knowledge must go in that direction.

9. DEVELOPING THE IDEAL STATE

The Ideal State is a state where there is no waste. There are no constraints regarding the design of the Ideal State as the goal is not to be practical. It is assumed that anything is possible and that there are no resource limitations. In this state, the team builds a picture of perfect flow, World Class Quality, Lowest cost and 100% on time delivery.

Despite being utopian, thinking like this can be useful, as it allows the identification of some design concepts and principles that can be encouraged and started in the current state plans, from small acorns large oak trees grow.

10. DEVELOPPING FUTURE STATE
The future state describes what the team wants to achieve in the next 6 to 12 months. Its development must start from the customer's needs, focusing on the most relevant opportunities. The team should question key factors for the construction of the future situation, such as:

- "What is the lead time required by the customer?"
- "Are customers reducing the batch size?"
- "Where can we create flow and integrate operations?"
- "Is the equipment suited to the needs?"
- "Where can we improve efficiency/productivity?"
- "What is the planning model to be implemented?"
- "What is the process stage where we are going to launch the customer's demand?"
- Are customers demanding discounts? How can we protect our Margin?

In the future state there is waste remaining. It takes many cycles of Value Stream Mapping to create a world class process. That is why there is the crucial need to repeat the focus on this waste, and a continuous effort to eliminate it.

11. TRACKING BENEFITS FROM KAIZEN™ EVENTS
Profitability is of the essence for any business. For this reason, it is necessary to calculate all the gains to be achieved with the future state implementation. To support the future state, we need to monitor Key Performance Indicators (KPIs) to track benefits, expressed in monetary units, whenever possible.

The KAIZEN™ Enterprise Analysis is an essential input to build the Hoshin Planning. It is through this process that it is possible to see how to realise the Strategy and Breakthrough Objectives for the future.

2.4 Department Value Stream Analysis

In order to have a more effective deployment in terms of Improvement Priorities, there is the need to perform a detailed analysis of the processes involved through the identification of opportunities for breakthroughs, optimisation and acceleration. This is a crucial stage in Hoshin Planning as it forces leaders and their teams to think that Breakthrough Objectives will only be achieved when sub-processes are really improved.

2.5 The Daily KAIZEN™ Lasting Effect

"Strat to Action" is the implementation of two improvement processes - Breakthrough KAIZEN™ and Daily KAIZEN™. The former develops breakthrough objectives allowing the organisation to step change in performance. On the other hand, these results are only sustained if a Daily KAIZEN™ program is implemented, which converts the new way of working into standardised work. This "Daily Management" adopts these new standards as the daily work. Long-term sustainability is guaranteed by making this the best way of working today, reinforced through systematic and regular training and follow-up, becoming "people's habits". It is said that we need 27 consecutive days for habits to become the new standard; it is necessary that we understand this "Daily Kaizen" constantly checking the standard every day.

The following chart shows how Hoshin can support the implementation of these two KAIZEN™ approaches and multiplies the results achieved year after year, until the strategic objectives are reached.

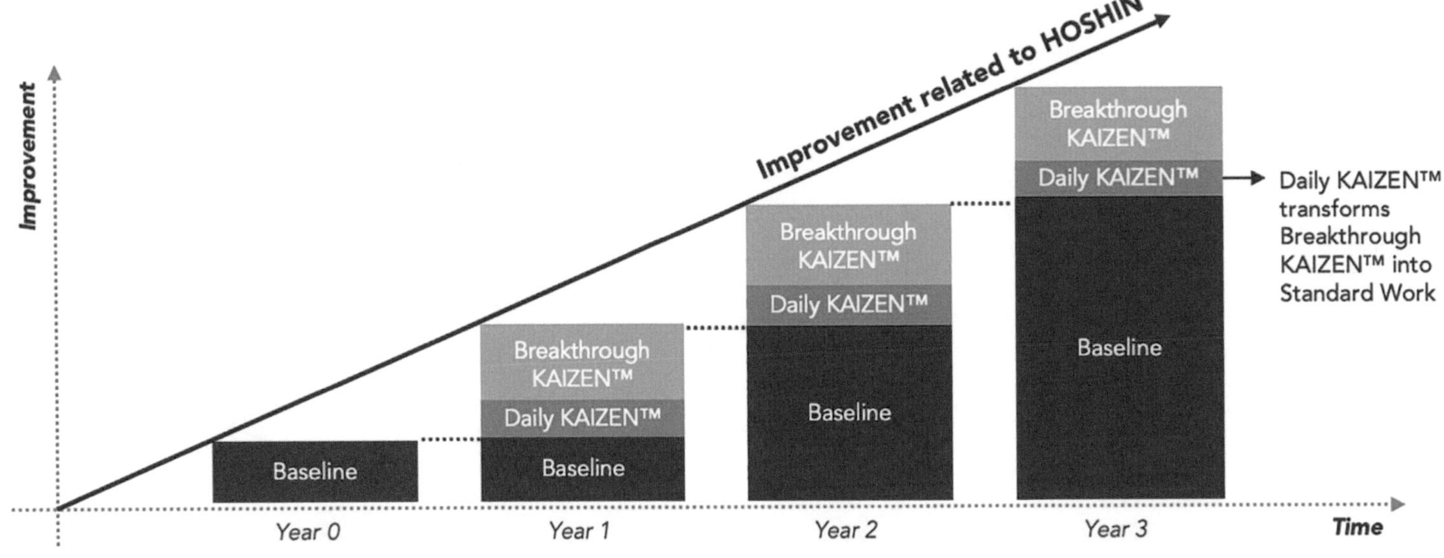

2.6 The Breakthrough KAIZEN™ Multiplying Effect

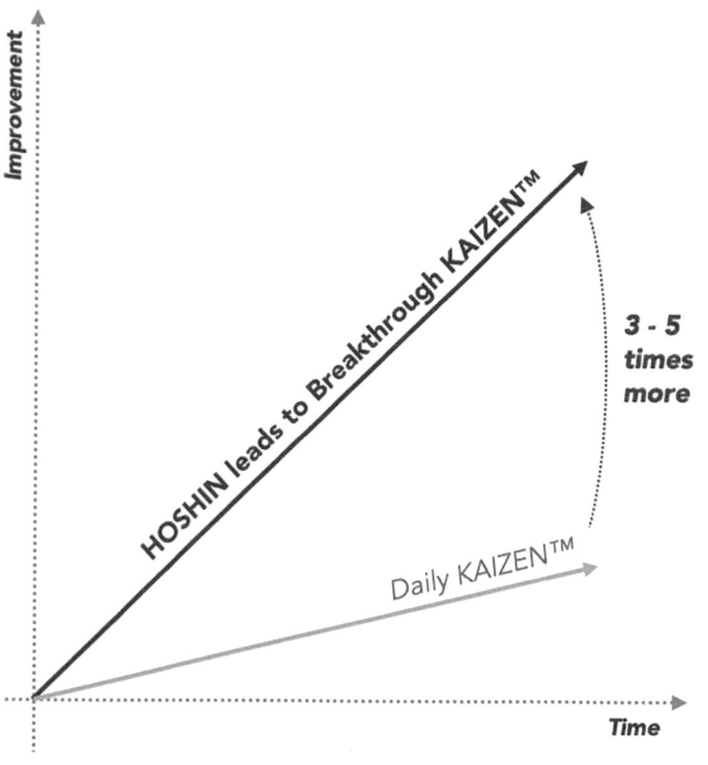

Many organisations are only applying KAIZEN™ tools in a random way, and Daily KAIZEN™ is their improvement strategy, so they hardly ever see the impact on their financial performance. Daily KAIZEN™ obtained results get lost in the 'noise' of the organisation. It is very important that you use Breakthrough KAIZEN™, together with Daily KAIZEN™, to keep multiplying the results 3 to 5 times compared to the traditional approach to improvement.

The first intensive work session organised by Kaizen Institute at ALFA's was the Enterprise Value Stream Analysis. This activity was fundamental for managers to "learn to see" the waste in their organisation, and how aggressive they should be in defining improvement goals. The construction of the matrix that summarises the 3 to 5 year objectives was the next stage, with the participation of the entire Board of Directors.

Before deploying to the second level of the organisational structure, Department Value Stream Analysis were performed, focused on Operations, Logistics, Marketing and Sales, and Engineering. Only from here on, the deployment to the level where Action Plans would be triggered was launched. This process is described in the next chapter.

Hoshin Planning

The Strategy on One Single Page

Is it possible to put the strategy of an organisation onto one single page? Yes, it is.

In KAIZEN™ we call this tool the X Matrix and it is used for this purpose. It is included in the Hoshin Planning process and allows you to break your Strategy down into Strategic Objectives in a visual format on one single page. In the second phase, it also serves as an input for deploying the strategy to lower levels of the organisation.

This chapter introduces the X Matrix, detailing its construction step by step and showing all the fundamental concepts for the correct definition of its content.

3.1 The X Matrix Structure

The CEO's X Matrix is built first, and it is commonly referred to as the Level 1 X Matrix. It describes the top-level objectives of the organisation. These objectives must be achieved through the implementation of Level 1 Improvement Priorities, which are assigned to the person in charge who will build their own unfolding matrix, called the Level 2 Matrix. It separates the specific breakthroughs to be applied to the correct areas to achieve the goals defined in each improvement priority. This process of unfolding creates accountability and alignment at the various levels of the organisation to achieve the results for the planned time scale.

The construction of the Matrix entails the answer to 5 key questions:

1. "What do you want to achieve in 3 to 5 years?"
2. "How far do you want to go in the first year? "
3. "How are you going to do it?"
4. "How will you measure success?"
5. "Who is responsible?"

These 5 questions are what gives the matrix its distinctive "X" shape, by splitting the matrix into 4 quadrants: in the **South**, there is the 3 to 5 year Breakthrough; in the **West**, the 1 Year Breakthrough objectives; Improvement Priorities are in the **North**; and in the **East**, the targets to improve. A dot is placed at the intersections of the matrix (full black dots or open dots) that identifies them so you can follow a single objective through the 4 quadrants. In addition, on the right side of the Matrix, you can find those responsible for carrying out each of the appropriate initiatives. This is where you will see the open dot being needed to denote secondary responsible.

Each phase of the Matrix building is further explained in greater detail.

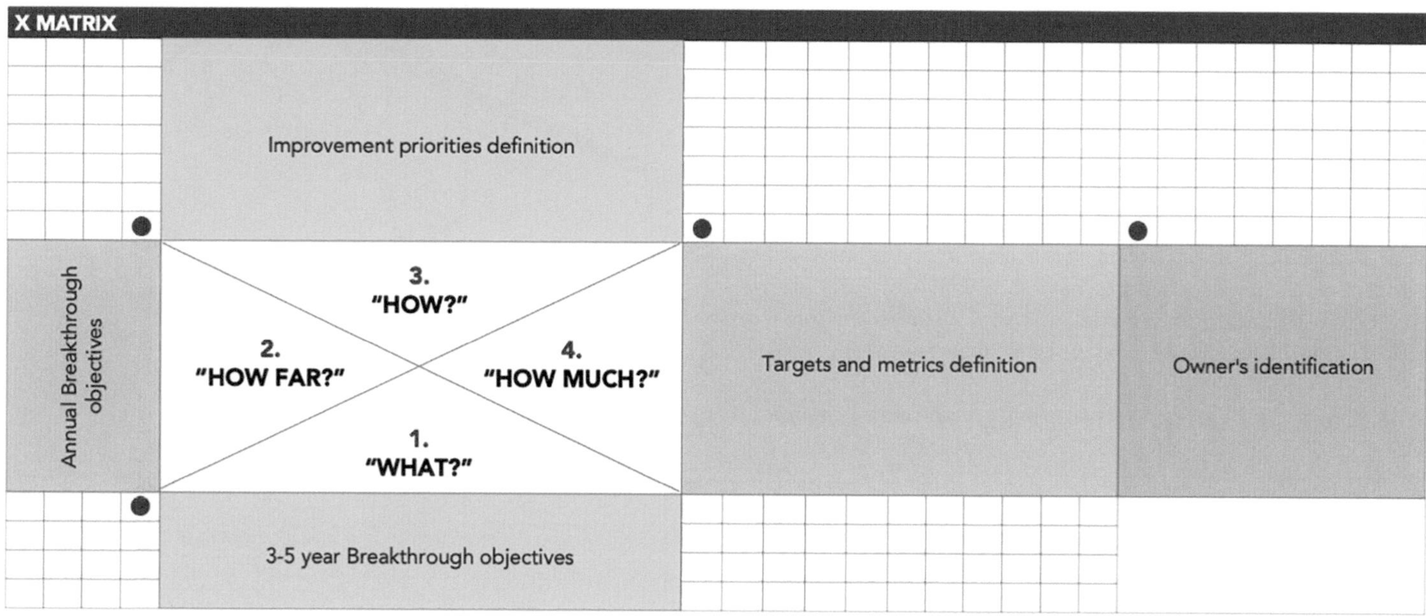

X Matrix structure

3.2 The Meaning of Stretching the Goals

The time had come to define what ALFA's strategic goals were. It was essential to ensure alignment among the top team as well as to trigger deployment in the different levels of the organisation.

The KAIZEN™ consultant was already in the room when the CEO and his team arrived. After a brief introduction to Hoshin Planning, he went on to explain the first fundamental concept.

The only way to make the problems of an organisation visible is to STRETCH its improvement objectives. This has two basic benefits: **(1)** it creates an assurance to deliver commitment to the Executive Committee, and **(2)** it breaks the internal paradigms wide open.

"What are ALFA's strategic goals?" The consultant asked.

"We had a great discussion on this matter only last month." The CEO smiled at his colleagues. "And the truth is that we haven't reached any conclusion! The only thing that is clear in our minds are the requirements of the shareholders. Our sector is growing 2% per year and our shareholders expect us to grow at least 2% above the market. Only in this way we can earn the share we have been losing in recent years. In the case of EBITDA, the scenario is similar. Our results have been between 3 to 4%, but the truth is that, historically, the company already reached 7.5%. We must reverse this trend in EBITDA and at least return to 7.5% in the next 3 years."

The consultant then questioned the top team:
"So, assuming that we define these as our goals, what might happen is this: by expecting to have an EBITDA of 7.5%, do we run the risk of staying on the sideline? Would it make any sense to STRETCH our goals above what we have been asked for?"

"But, the greater the commitment, the greater is the chance of non-compliance!" The HR Director answered, while some of her colleagues nodded in agreement.

"Before we move on with this discussion, I am going to introduce you a new paradigm about how to define the organisation´s goals." The consultant continued. "The Best in Class organisations **STRECTH** their goals and transform them into their **Breakthrough Objectives**. These organisations raise their targets to ensure the commitment to their shareholders is always delivered. In fact, organisations raise the bar and challenge themselves to go further." The consultant went on, while walking around: "What is the minimum EBITDA we are expecting?" Almost immediately the CEO answered €6.7 million and the consultant kept on: "Achieving an EBITDA of €6.7 million in the next three years is not a Breakthrough Objective. Do you know why? Because this value has already been achieved in the past! It is our duty to achieve it! A Breakthrough Objective should be something impossible to achieve regarding our current condition. Only by thinking in that way is it possible to identify what is preventing us from growing and what needs to be drastically improved within our organisation. Otherwise, we will remain with the same weaknesses."

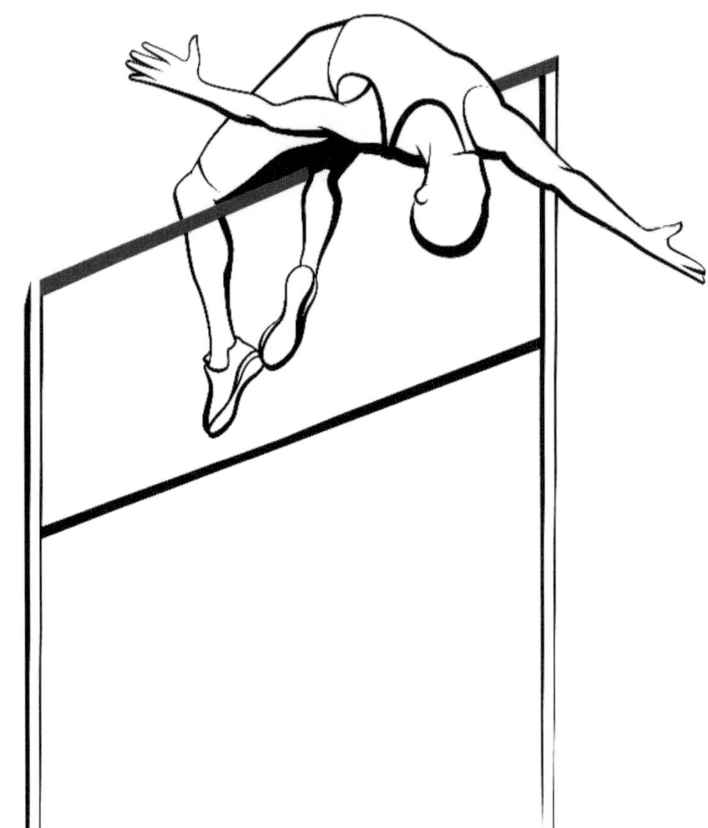

The CEO replied:
"I get your point. Instead of establishing a Breakthrough Objective, that doesn't need to identify the what, where and how, we must improve to achieve the target. It is like performing this exercise in a way that is contrary to our traditional thinking."

"Well done, that's it! Now, let me ask you: what is preventing us from reaching 10 million in EBITDA? What do we need to change in this organisation to deliver 10 million to the shareholders in 3 years?" The consultant asked.

"I understand the process you want to follow, but before we move on, I would like to be sure that under taking this or any other commitment will not put more pressure on my people. I have a serious problem regarding internal motivation, and I want my team to be motivated to improve, without being suffocated by overambitious objectives."

Everyone in the room seemed to breathe a sigh of relief after the CEO's intervention.

"No, that is not what we meant by STRETCHING the goals. This methodology does not put the pressure on people, but rather on the process. This will force the organisation to adapt and improve its processes. The truth is that, by putting a goal above the expected minimum, we shall be working to achieve much more than that. By stretching we will exceed the budget, which reduces the pressure of delivering the budget. The commitment we have to the shareholders is different from our internal goals." The consultant concluded.

In an even more relaxed atmosphere, the consultant informed them that it was about time for a coffee break.

3.3 Level 1 X Matrix

"Let's build our L1 X Matrix. Let's fix it on the wall and fill it in, step by step, as we all agree together. We must start by defining our 3-5 year Breakthrough Objectives." Said the consultant to all the Executive Committee.

Even before the session restarted, the HR Director informed everyone that she would have to leave for three hours in the afternoon. She mentioned that she had to conduct interviews for the position of IT manager, since the last person had resigned the previous month. In response, the consultant said that it was crucial for all the team to participate in this event, so that they would all be fully engaged in the common objective. She recognised the logic and the CEO, feeling uncomfortable with her suggestion asked her to manage her agenda in order to be present, since these sessions were of the highest priority for everyone in the team. In view of his insistence, she decided to stay.

3.3.1 South Box - 3 to 5 years Breakthrough Objectives

"The first decision we need to make is: Do we want to set objectives for the next 3, 4 or 5 years?" The consultant asked.

"3 years! Nobody is going to give me 5 years to achieve results." The CEO laughed.

"So, let's focus on what we must do in the next 3 years. What are we going to improve?" Asked the consultant, encouraging the team "What should be our main goal for the next 3 years?"

"We have to grow the business, of course! We cannot continue to lose share. This has been happening for years!" Replied the CEO without hesitation.

"But do you think this to be our Breakthrough goal?" The consultant did not seem to agree with the CEO.

"I would say yes... Well, that sums up everything we have to do." Replied the CEO, with some uncertainty.

"Ok, let me challenge you then. If our goal is making ALFA grow, it is most likely that we don't know what to do, since it's very difficult to realise where to focus and what should indeed be implemented to get there. But if, on the other hand, we question what prevents us from growing, we will easily begin to identify reasons, in other words, processes that do not work or that do not yet exist." The consultant took a short break to reemphasise this issue "Can we then consider growth as a strategic objective? No. Growth is mandatory. In an increasingly competitive market, either we grow or we die. If we focus only on growth, it is very difficult to outline a clear Action Plan. We have to look from growth from another direction." Everyone in the audience seemed to be curious "In KAIZEN™ we have a fundamental principle: consistent processes lead to expected results. So I ask you: What prevents us from growing? What needs to change significantly in the eyes of the customers? Is it low quality? Is it costs? Is it on time delivery? Do we launch new products too late? Or are all these factors together keeping us from growing? Thinking about what stops us from growing allows us to internalise growth and analysis of our internal processes."

"Well, answering your questions, I would say that ALFA's competitors are currently stronger and with better results than we have achieved. They have lower costs, better quality, and start releasing new products with shorter lead times than we are capable of, something where we were effectively the best at many years ago. If we revisit the vision we have built, we realise that there are several opportunities for improvement in our organisation. From cost reduction to quality improvement and reduced Time to Market, resulting in faster delivery times and better customer service. All this will certainly give us the growth we need." Concluded the CEO, looking at his team.

"That's it!", exclaimed the consultant."I think we all are in the right mindset now to start building the Level 1 Matrix. Let's return to the discussion we had this morning about how much we need to stretch the value of ALFA's EBITDA." The consultant paused "Is EBITDA a cause or an effect?"

After a few seconds of silence in the room, the CEO replied: "An effect, I would say because it is a consequence of improving all other indicators."

"That is correct." The consultant said. "So, can we all agree that increasing EBITDA will force us to drastically reduce costs, improve quality and service levels?" Everyone in the room agreed. "But despite being an effect, it is the indicator that best incorporates the Breakthroughs that we must achieve reducing costs and improving quality, so we must put it into the matrix."

This way, the team quickly agreed that EBTIDA should be the first Breakthrough Objective to put into the South Box.

"We discussed this morning whether 10 million EBITDA would be a challenging goal. The truth is that putting the goal at 10 million we have drastically increased the probability of delivering the 6.7 million required. But is it enough to STRETCH the organisation and to identify which processes are broken, turning them into our improvement priority? So, everyone, what should our Breakthrough Objective for EBITDA be?"

"If we impose an ambitious growth of 20% in sales, we must obtain an EBITDA of at least €12 million euros. And before you ask me, I'll explain why. As you can remember from my benchmark analysis, Best in Class organisations in this industry generate 12% to 15% EBITDA. This means that by reaching €12 million euros in three years, we will be matching the levels of the best competitors. Although this seems impossible to us today, in fact, from what I have understood, this is exactly what we have to do." Explained the CEO.

"Agreed!, said the consultant," The question we all must ask is: What is impossible today, if we could achieve it, that would drastically change the way we do things at ALFA's? That is, what are the new paradigms we have to discover to move to a new level of performance?" The consultant paused and restarted after a few seconds. "If we all agree, we can add the €12 million EBITDA into the South Box."

The consultant, using the example of EBITDA, explained how the objectives should be described in the matrix, highlighting that they would have to indicate what was intended to be improved, their starting point, the objective to be achieved and how long it was intended to reach that objective:

Objective **from X to Y** by **Z years** EBITDA **from € 2.3** million t**o € 12** million € **by year 3**

After updating the Matrix, the consultant continued the exercise:

"To get this progress in the result what is the first thing that we need to change in this company? Remember that we are always seeing through the eyes of the customer! What do we have to change dramatically from the customers' perspective?"

"If we want to do something disruptive, then we need to deliver what we promise!" The Sales and Marketing Director commented "In my opinion, this is what is preventing us from selling more. Customers are buying from us because they cannot get our products from our competitors."

"Let's talk with data. What is our Delivery performance in terms of keeping our word, that is, delivery satisfaction? If you remember, in Enterprise Value Stream Analysis we concluded that this value was low but that we were not measuring it accurately by line items delivered" The consultant replied."Have we been able to figure this out yet?"

"On Time Deliver" or OTD is an indicator that measures the percentage of orders delivered on time, and there are two levels of measurement, **(1) OTD (P)** to Promise after agreeing with the customer. **(2) OTD (R)** to Request this is the requested delivery that the customer expects, the second measure is the true measure of Delivery Performance.

The Logistics Director explained that the measurement was not solid. Internally it was very difficult to implement OTD in ALFA, since there were different opinions about the correct concept to follow. Some wanted to measure the service level versus the date agreed with the customer while others chose to measure performance against internally established lead time.

However, for some of its most important customers, ALFA was measuring OTD in terms of delivery time and quality, based on the contractual conditions agreed for the lead time. For these, the performance was around 75%. However, for the others, the team perception was that the results would be even lower.

Looking ahead to the beginning of a new discussion centred on OTD, the consultant introduced another fundamental KAIZEN™ concept, the **Market-In vs. Product-Out.**

MARKET-IN VS. PRODUCT-OUT

In the **Product-Out** scenario, the organisation can sell everything it produces, since the level of demand is higher than the level of supply. A product-out business is typically associated with a large market share, where there is little or no competition and very little choice for the end-user, so all products sell easily. In addition, these are sold with high profitability and no worries regarding quality or delivery. In this context, the company defines its own standards. This type of attitude leads to a scenario in which the organisation delivers only what it can, regardless of the end-users' expectations, and with a low priority on value to the customer.

In the **Market-In**, the organisation is focused on the customer's satisfaction, applying solid processes to meet their expectations. This kind of business understands its marketplace and values aggressive competition, whilst constantly measuring customer satisfaction in Quality, Delivery and Cost:

- ***Quality*** - since the objective of every organisation is zero defects, this is a parameter that is no longer a differentiator. Customers expect high quality, it's the entry level and is mandatory, poor quality will lead to loss of customers and shrinking market share.

- ***Cost*** - price is determined by the market, which means that, in order to be profitable, organisations need to continually reduce costs by constantly eliminating processes' waste and not passing on price increases.

- ***Delivery*** - the real differentiation is made in the delivery performance; the target is 100% on time deliveries. After cost, this is the parameter most highly differentiating Alpha over its competitors. This is a key differentiator and it can be quantified in Cash, Lead time, and customer satisfaction.

Back to the discussion, the consultant addressed the audience: "I think that nobody doubts that we need to see OTD as one of our Breakthrough Objectives."

"Absolutely! Let's consider the current OTD to be 75% and, in order to be disruptive enough, I think we have to aim to reach at least 90%... What do you think?" Asked the CEO, teasing the team.

"I think it is possible, but this will lead to an increase in the value of internal stocks." The Logistics Director seemed a bit lost in his thoughts.

"That would be true if we did nothing to improve flows and the planning method. If we take a look at Enterprise Value Stream Analysis, we realise that by implementing a Pull Planning Model and creating flow in the production processes we will be able to ensure an OTD of more than 90% with half the current stock in finished goods and WIP" Explained the consultant.

"That's exactly what we designed as a Vision!" Said the CEO "For that reason, we should add another breakthrough for inventory reduction. And in this case, I think the 50% reduction is challenging enough. We cannot aim to improve OTD and increase stocks, otherwise it would be easy. I remind you all that the shareholders are expecting us to improve free cash flow at least equaling EBIT. We cannot expect to be given more money for investments in the short run."

The consultant concluded: "Let's put the free cash flow objective in the Matrix. This should include, besides stock reduction, pushing out Payables and pulling in Receivables. Finally, we should look at CAPEX and review the spending based on the future state value stream. I know we have a proposal for more Warehousing and high bay racking, maybe we can solve this problem by reducing Raw, WIP and Finished Goods Materials."

The Financial Director turned to the flipchart and with a few quick calculations, he concluded: "By reducing our stock of 12.9 to 6.4 million in 3 years and by improving terms of Payables and Receivables to market values added to our operational improvement targets, we should aim for a free cash flow of 10 million. This would seem to be Disruptive and a Breakthrough in three years!"

The Matrix was updated again. By then, the discussion was remaining focused on the need to add more QCD objectives, but they unanimously agreed to focus on delivering the significant few and resisted the temptation to keep adding more.

The consultant continued with the exercise: "So, what about innovation? Don't we need a breakthrough in innovation?"

"As you know, we've always been at the forefront in launching innovative products. We triggered the great technological advances in the market. When customers are looking for more complex or innovative products different from the rest, they come to us first!" The Director of Engineering said.

The Sales Director decided to intervene in the discussion: "That may be true, but customers only know when they ask for a new product, they never know when they will receive it. Our lead time is in fact very high. Sometimes we spend years until we can put a new product on the market."

"We must talk with data! In two weeks from now we are going to map our New Product Development process, the average delivery time of our latest developments is 50 weeks. But you are talking about years..." The Engineering Director raised his voice "And if you don't remember, during the KAIZEN™ Enterprise Analysis discussion we have pointed to a lead time reduction target of 30 weeks!"

The discussion got heated so the consultant intervened to get some alignment among those present: "So, do you all agree that reducing time from 50 to 30 weeks will STRETCH our development processes, making us think outside the box and challenging ourselves to improve dramatically?"

"In the previous KAIZEN™ session I participated in, it was clear to me that we are outdated in terms of product development methodologies. We will have to completely change our processes, from ideation processes to the application of the new Set Based Engineering tools, completely redesigning our Stage Gates model with Lean Project Management tools." The Engineering Director was convinced of what had to be done and he took the opportunity to demonstrate his knowledge regarding these tools (please refer to the concepts explained in appendix 4)."

The team agreed with the objective outlined and updated the South Box of the X Matrix again. Finally, it was filled in.

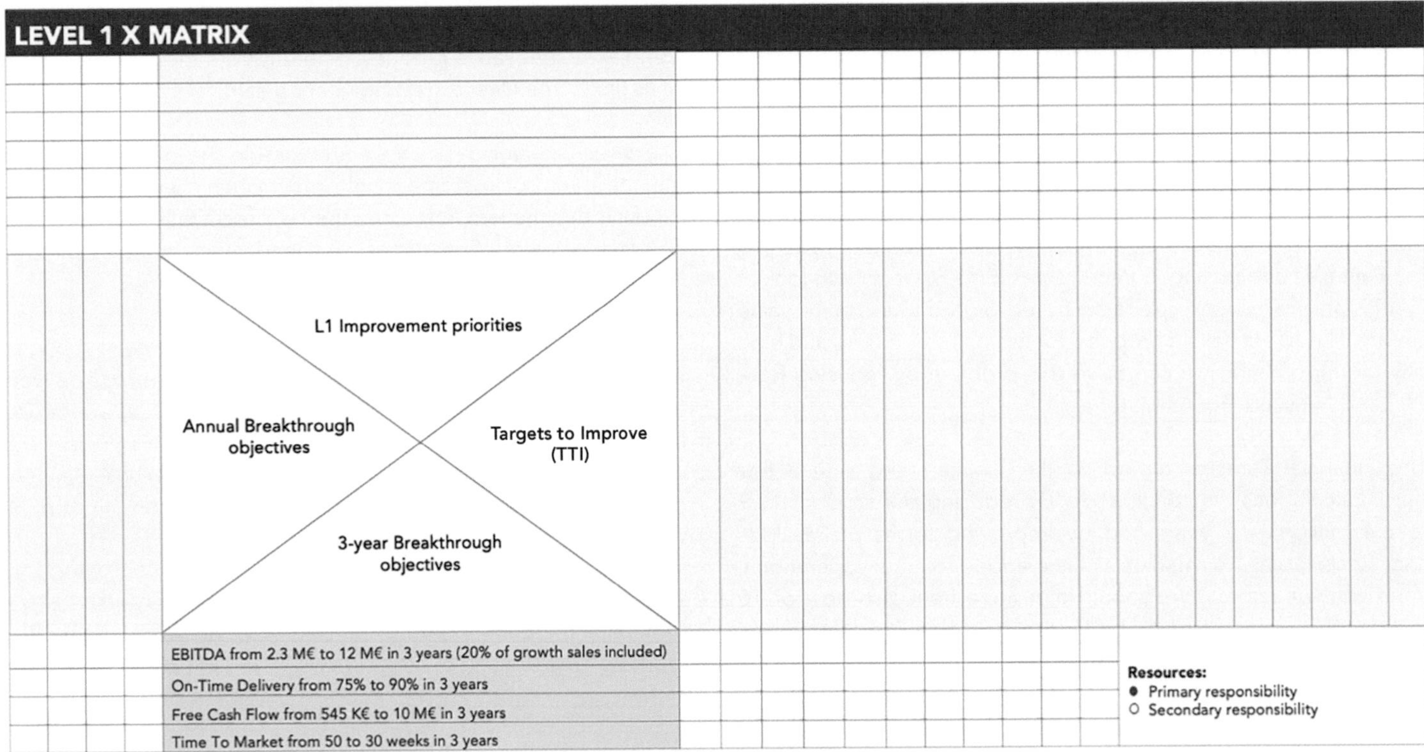

South box of the level 1 X Matrix, Year 1

"In fact, we ended up with 4 Breakthrough Objectives in our Matrix, which is a good number as a rule 'less is more' in order to be sure that we focus on what is really critical." After a short pause the consultant guided the team towards a conclusion. "The discussion thread that we have been following is called **Critical Thinking Process**. It is essential to understanding the importance of STRETCHING the goals. When President Kennedy announced to the world that he would put a man on the moon in seven years, trust me, he had no idea of how he would do it. The only thing he knew was that he would have to get there because the commitment was already made."

The 'Critical Thinking Process' is a 5-step approach to thinking, to define the organisation's objectives, which promotes the discussion and consequent alignment of all those involved. The company is constantly challenged to commit to disruptive goals, asking itself what processes will prevent us from achieving that result.

CRITICAL THINKING PROCESS

Step 1: "WHAT"
3-5 year Breakthrough objectives

Step 2: "HOW FAR"
Annual Breakthrough objectives definition

Step 3: "HOW"
Key processes identification

Step 4: "HOW MUCH"
Metrics definition

Step 5: "WHO"
Resources identification

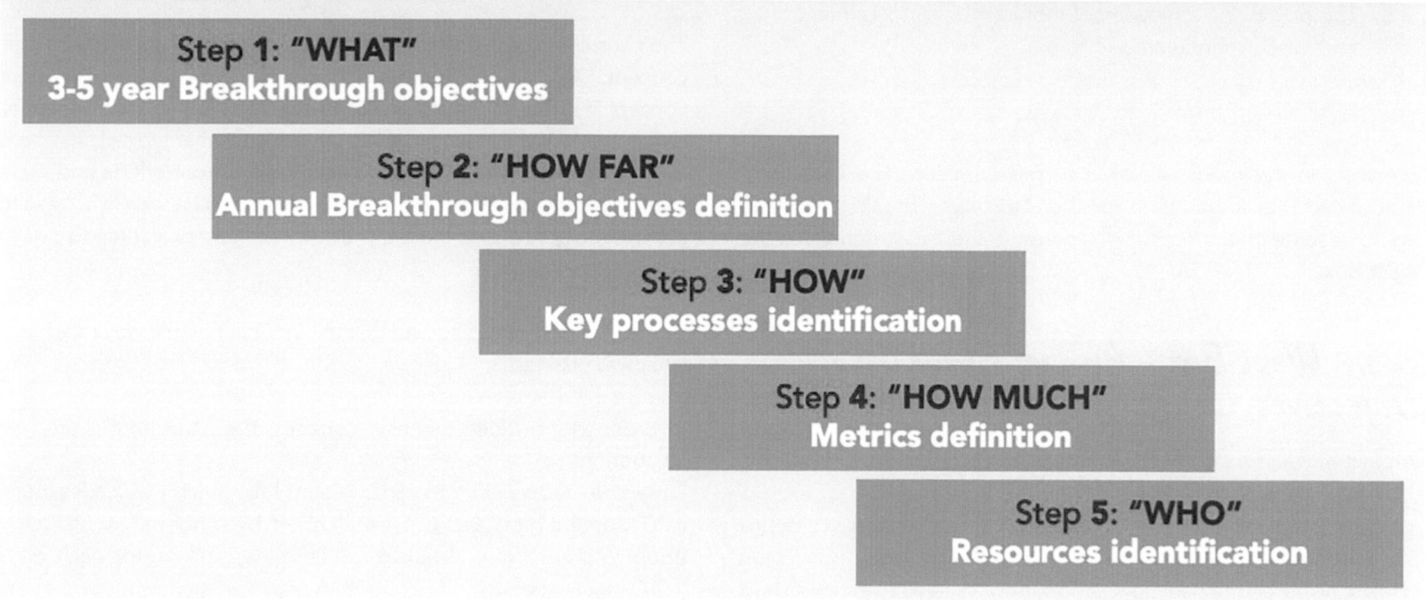

SOUTH BOX OF THE X MATRIX - CHECKPOINTS

To successfully complete step **1 of the Critical Thinking Process**, it is necessary to verify the effectiveness of the following points:

1. The 3-5-year objectives represent a significant change in customer perspective.
2. The organisation is a challenge in itself.
3. Objectives lead to a "breakthrough process" (organisation's new paradigm).
4. There is usually no standard or system for new breakthroughs (the solution is still unknown).
5. The objectives achievement requires the establishment of multidisciplinary teams.

Everyone in the room was able to raise a smile. The consultant announced that it was time for them to take a break. Then they would resume the discussion regarding the construction of the West Box.

3.3.2 West Box - Annual Breakthrough Objectives

When they returned to the room, the consultant began by introducing the next step in building the X Matrix. He explained that for each of the 3 to 5 years Breakthrough Objectives, it was essential to define how much of the goal should be achieved in the first year. - Having this in mind, he asked the participants: "So, now we need to establish how much of EBITDA we are going to achieve in the next year."

After a few seconds of silence in the room, the Financial Director replied:
"Since our current EBITDA is 2.3 million and that we want to reach 12 million in 3 years, then next year we must get at least 5.5 million euros."

"How do you think the Executive Committee will react to that? The consultant asked.

"I'd say they'll be pleased... Considering that we are expected to achieve an annual growth of 4% in sales and be able to achieve a 7.5% EBITDA in three years... so, if we deliver 5.5 million in the first year, this means reaching 6.6% EBITDA". The Financial Director replied, looking at the CEO.

The consultant wasn't satisfied with the answer and introduced a new concept: "OK, I think it's about time to explain another important concept in KAIZEN™, that we call **Front-End-Loading** which we use to define the West of the matrix. Let me ask you what typically happens in a 3-year project. We tend to back end load our efforts and quite often fail to hit our target. Do you think this could happen if we plan to achieve the goal only in the last year? How can we guarantee to deliver our stretched targets?

Everybody smiled and agreed that this wouldn't be the way to achieve what was planned.

In order to introduce this new concept, the consultant shared an illustration:
"Imagine that we want to climb Mount Kilimanjaro, which is almost 6000 meters high and can be climbed by a normal individual in about 6 days. What should this climber's goal be for each day? 1000 meters per day? It is clear that over the last few meters of the climb, we would not have the same performance we had on the

first day, when our energy levels were much higher. So, it doesn't make any sense to equally divide the goals by the several days of the journey. It is from the first day that we must challenge ourselves to give our maximum, because over the last few meters the air will be much thinner and the fatigue higher."

The Executive Committee remained very attentive while the consultant explained the metaphor.

"Now I ask you again, what is the challenging EBITDA value we want to get next year?" There was a short pause "The rule is to set goals to deliver 50% in the first year. Even if we can only reach 6 million in the first year, we need to realise that this figure is, in any case, much higher than the expectations of the Executive Directors." He concluded, "This approach is called Front-End-Loading".

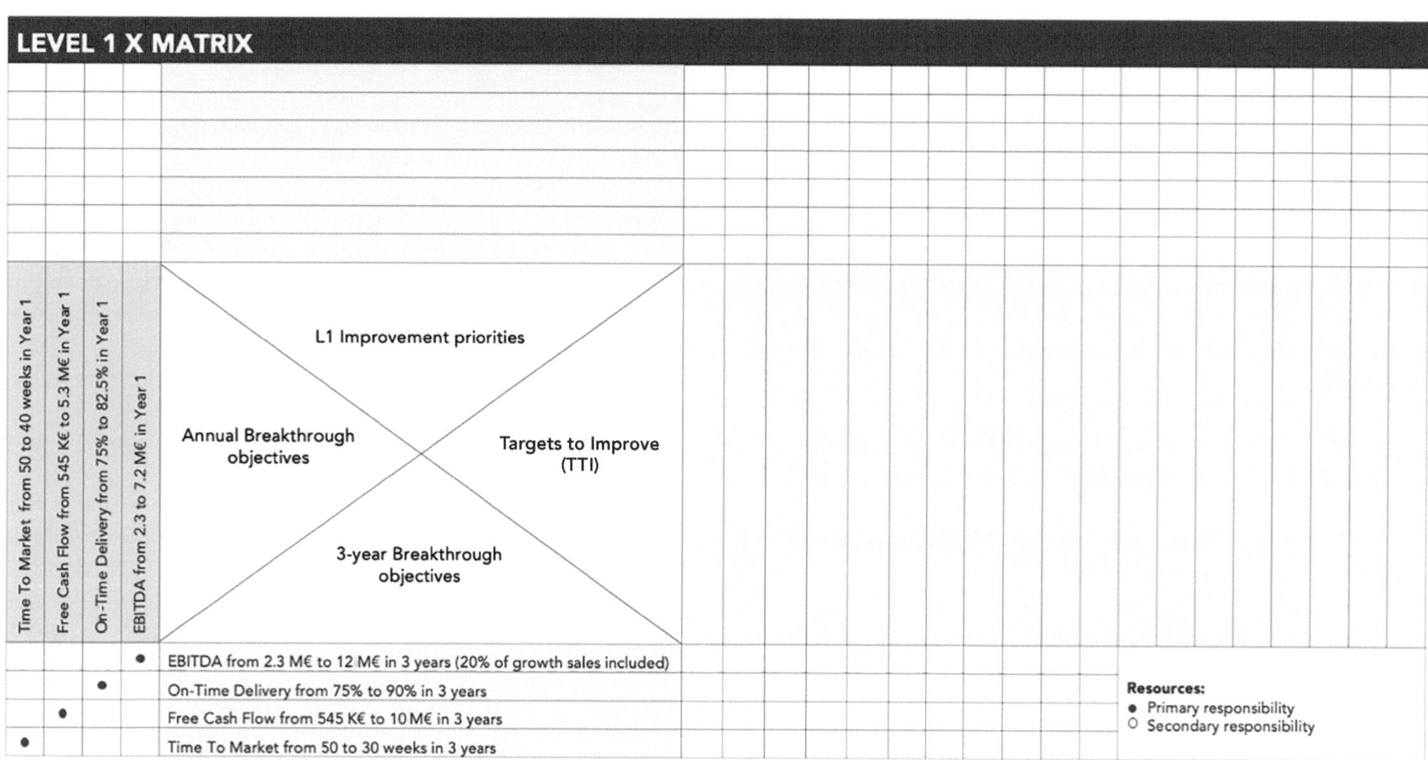

West box of the level 1 X Matrix, Year 1

The team calculated the Front-End-Loading for each objective in the South Box, according to their initial situation and considering the objectives set for the coming years. Even with all the Financial Director's restrictions, everyone agreed with the good practice proposed by KAIZEN™, to challenge themselves to reach 50% in the first year.

The team completed the Breakthrough Objectives for the following year. The consultant showed the team how they should link the 3-year Breakthrough Objectives by putting the Black Dot in their respective intersecting corners.

A few minutes later, when they had finished the West side, it was time for lunch. Everyone left the room while the CEO stayed a little longer with the consultant to share some ideas. "I hope we can ensure the alignment and commitment among the teams regarding the objectives we are setting. As far as I know, last year there was little alignment and no improvement in the results achieved"said the CEO while looking at the matrix partially filled in. "Shall we join the team?"

They both left the room commenting that the leaders seemed motivated.

WEST BOX OF THE X MATRIX - CHECKPOINTS

To successfully complete step **2 of the Critical Thinking Process**, it is necessary to check the following points:

1. The annual objectives are stretched.
2. When achieved, the annual objective brings benefits to the customer.
3. The objectives for the first year are significant, as they represent 50% of the objectives set for 3 to 5 years.
4. The outlined objectives exceed the budget.

3.3.3 North Box - Year 1 Improvement Priorities

After lunch they returned: "This afternoon we're going to define the X Matrix North Box, called the Improvement Priorities of the organisation. Whilst completing this, we need to consider several points." The consultant introduced: "First, let's look at the EBITDA; our main priority regarding the annual objectives is to think what process or processes must be implemented or improved to deliver 7.2 million euro in the next year."

The X Matrix North Box, as you would expect, has some fundamental rules for its completion:

- The North Box only describes processes, not projects, because creating or improving a process delivers benefits year after year. A process implies a standard, a definition of what is the best method today for completing the task. Whilst a project has a beginning and an end, it delivers the benefits once the team moves on. Projects rarely deliver processes that continue to benefit every year and to for this reason we talk about Process, not Projects.

- All improvement priorities should be written with an action verb attached to the process. Typically the verb "to implement" should be used when the process does not exist; the verb "to optimise or improve" applies when the process already exists; the verb "to speed up" is used when the process needs to drastically decrease the lead time.

At that moment, everyone started to discuss the impact with their teams and together they realised that there were several critical processes to generate an increase in EBITDA:

- **A process to increase productivity** - It was necessary to change ALFA's mindset, which had always considered investment in automation as the only way to increase productivity. However, without prior process simplification, automation generated more costs than results. Before automating, it was necessary to ensure waste elimination within a process, making it impossible to justify the full cost of automation. By allowing employees to differentiate Added Value from Non-Added value, it would be possible to work on productivity increases through the constant elimination of waste in processes.

- **A process to reduce costs** - In the past, cost reduction had been achieved through negotiation to obtain more competitive prices, with no regard to lower product quality or larger batch sizes purchased. The goal was to create a process to reduce cost in a structured and systematic way. A typical example of structured cost reduction is to clearly describe the functionalities and the utility that the customer was willing to pay for, through the KAIZEN™ tool called **Value Analysis** and **Value Engineering** (VA/VE).

- **A process to improve Quality** - Developing a process that will identify the causes of quality issues is crucial. This process would lead to building process that will not Receive, not Make and not Pass on defects at every step in the Value Stream. Any Quality improvement process must include structure problem solving at its core.

- **A process to improve Marketing and Sales** - ALFA would have to stop the randomised development of products looking for a market, and develop a process focussed on the Voice of the Customer as the highest factor for success. Instead of presenting the products and expecting to sell them, the company had to develop sales processes that added value, from the perspective of the customer (Value Selling). Rather than investing in promotions and advertising, ALFA had to implement processes for market segmentation and systematic listening the Voice of the Customer.

After defining the different processes with a direct impact on increasing profitability, it became clear to everyone that the word "process" was a must in the North Box. More important still, all improvement priorities must focus on processes.

The exercise continued for the remaining annual objectives:

- **A process to improve Customer Service** - In addition to implementing a strong OTD evaluation standard, it was necessary to adopt a demand-based pull planning process supported by Visual Management.

- **A process to reduce Working Capital** - 70% of the stock was raw materials and a process needed to be developed in order to be able to match the demand and the supplier's ability to deliver Just In Time. It would thus be possible to implement a simplified procurement process with deliveries based on demand ABC analysis.

- **A process for reducing lead time in new product introduction process** - Rather than developing products from a single idea, it was necessary to build a process that clearly described the different stages, from the initial idea up to the volume manufacturing. At each phase, the decision to move on would always be validated against agreed actions being completed, so that at every phase the risk was being assessed with no slippage to the final delivery date. At the same time, it was necessary to introduce a Lean Project Management methodology that would compress the critical path and manage the priority of resource allocation at each stage of the process.

Once the Improvement Priorities were identified, they were introduced into the North Box of the X Matrix and linked to their relevant annual Breakthrough Objectives by a solid black dot inserted at the intersection point in the upper left corner. The construction of the North Box of the Matrix was positive and informed because all the members of the Executive Committee had participated in the Enterprise Value Stream Analysis, giving them the common vision of the future state.

The North of X Matrix was complete.

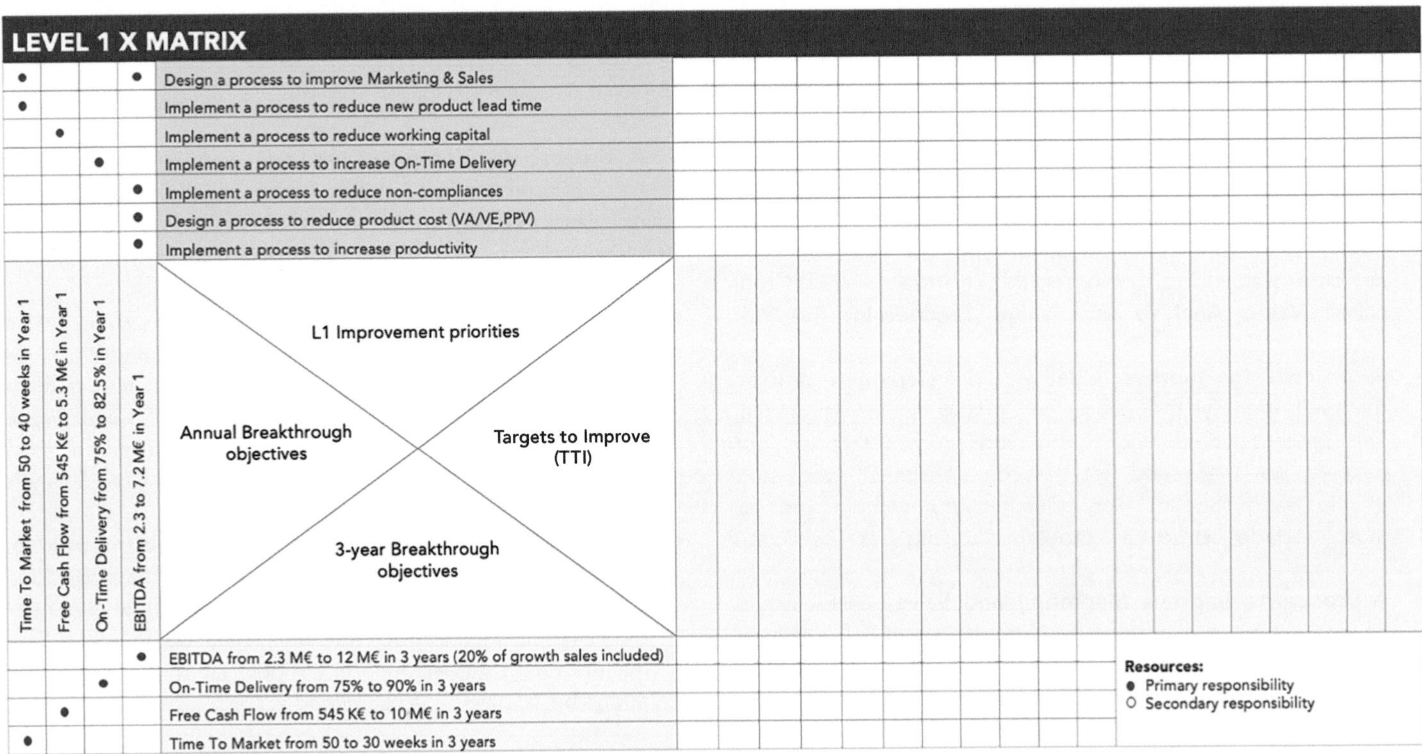

North box of the level 1 X Matrix, Year 1

NORTH BOX OF THE X MATRIX - CHECKPOINTS

To successfully complete **step 3 of the Critical Thinking Process**, it is necessary to check the following points:

1. The processes are sustainable.
2. Processes are result oriented.
3. The future needs of the customer are considered.
4. The processes are easy to understand.
5. Processes demonstrate flow.

3.3.4 East Box - Year 1 Targets to Improve

Most of the CEO's Matrix was already completed. The team felt comfortable in its construction and moments of tension were fewer and fewer, alignment was happening, and team spirit was becoming a reality. After a break, the consultant resumed the session to fill in the East Box of the Matrix.

"How shall we measure each of the Improvement Priorities in the North Box of our Matrix? We need KPIs that allow us to measure progress every month during the implementation of new processes."

"We already have almost every indicator required! More indicators will only generate entropy." The Operations Director protested.

"Let's look at the first improvement priority, the one mentioning a process to increase productivity. From my experience, each company measures productivity in its own way. How do you do it at ALFA's?" The consultant asked the whole team.

The Operations Director admitted that normally they didn't follow this parameter. After a brief discussion, they concluded that the best way to measure productivity at CEO level would be from sales per employee.

Before the team proceeded with the calculations, the consultant recalled:
"The rule for describing the objectives to achieve follows the same structure that we used in the writing of the Breakthrough Objectives. We must describe the indicator, followed by the initial value, the Target to Improve and the deadline to reach it."

In this context, the Financial Director obtained the sales figures per employee for the previous year, as well as the FTE[1] sales target for the following year. Applying the well-known concept of Front-End-Loading, they quickly reached the expected productivity value.

Sales per FTE **from 191 k€ to 200 k€** by Dec. Yr 1

Then the team repeated the exercise until they set all the KPIs needed to measure the Improvement Priorities listed in the North Box. During the discussion, they commented on the differences in relation to the objectives that were, at that time, followed in the company. Finally, they reached the last process in the North Box of the Matrix.

"How will we measure improvement in arketing and Sales?" The consultant asked.

The Sales Director replied: "This is an area where we have traditionally measured only sales indicators, but I think this could be an opportunity to build operational indicators related to Marketing and Sales activities."

1 Full Time Equivalent: it refers to a full-time employee.

"Do not forget that we will have the opportunity to deploy this Matrix. And each of you will need to define metrics that measure the operational improvement for each one of your processes. But in the level 1 matrix we must opt for indicators with the ability to measure the overall result." The consultant paused and looked directly at the CEO. "What do we intend to achieve by improving the Marketing and Sales processes?"

"We want to increase sales to current and new customers!" The CEO responded promptly looking at the Sales Director.

"So, what we have to measure is just that: A goal for total Sales and a goal for Sales to new customers." The consultant checked every indicator and questioned the team about any doubts they might have.

LEVEL 1 X MATRIX

Time To Market from 50 to 40 weeks in Year 1	Free Cash Flow from 545 K€ to 5.3 M€ in Year 1	On-Time Delivery from 75% to 82.5% in Year 1	EBITDA from 2.3 to 7.2 M€ in Year 1		Sales/ FTE from 191K€ to 200K€ by Dec/Year 1	FSE from 17.7% to 16.4% of sales (1M€) by Dec/Year 1	Planned waste from 8% to 7% (505K€) by Dec/Year 1	Purchase Part Variance (PPV) from 50.5M€ to 50M€ by Dec/Year 1	Non-Quality Costs from 2M€ to 1.52M€ by Dec/Year 1	# customer complaints from 84 to 42 by Dec/Year 1	On-Time Delivery from 75% to 82.5% by Dec/Year 1	Inventory from 12.9 M€ to 9.7 M€ (6.2 to 12.3 turns) by Dec/Year 1	Time To Market from 50 to 40 weeks by Dec/Year 1	Sales from 79.6 M€ to 87.6 M€ by Dec/Year 1	Vitality: new customer sales from 0 to 3M€ by Dec/Year 1
●			●	Design a process to improve Marketing & Sales										●	●
●				Implement a process to reduce new product lead time									●		
	●			Implement a process to reduce working capital								●			
		●		Implement a process to increase On-Time Delivery							●				
			●	Implement a process to reduce non-compliances					●	●					
			●	Design a process to reduce product cost (VA/VE,PPV)			●	●							
			●	Implement a process to increase productivity	●	●									
			●	EBITDA from 2.3 M€ to 12 M€ in 3 years (20% of growth sales included)											
		●		On-Time Delivery from 75% to 90% in 3 years											
	●			Free Cash Flow from 545 K€ to 10 M€ in 3 years											
●				Time To Market from 50 to 30 weeks in 3 years											

L1 Improvement priorities

Annual Breakthrough objectives

Targets to Improve (TTI)

3-year Breakthrough objectives

Resources:
- ● Primary responsibility
- ○ Secondary responsibility

East box of the level 1 X Matrix, Year 1

"The West Box is quite similar to the East Box, if you ask me..." Replied the HR Director, shrugging.

Smiling at the audience, the consultant explained that in the East Box they set the goals that must be met in order to achieve the Breakthrough Objectives designed in the West Box. The sum of the values obtained in the East Box must match the values on the West side. However, it was normal that some of the Breakthrough Objectives were described by metrics and hence were mirrored in the East Box of the matrix.

X MATRIX EAST BOX - CHECKPOINTS

To successfully complete **step 4 of the Critical Thinking Process**, it is necessary to check the following points:

1. Goals to be achieved materialise the annual objectives.
2. Goals to be achieved may be divided into monthly portions.
3. Goals to be achieved measure results but not performance.
4. Goals to be achieved are easy to calculate.
5. Goals to be achieved globally exceed the budget.

"Now we must appoint a person responsible for each Improvement Priority." The consultant looked directly at the CEO and went on. "These will be the people designated to deploy the Improvement Priorities into level 2 of the matrix. Afterwards, they will also have to define and implement the Action Plan within each of their teams."

Rules for Resource Allocation:

1. The CEO is the level 1 Matrix owner and usually has no allocated actions.
2. The allocation should be made when the matrix is already filled.
3. Each improvement priority can only be assigned to one primary responsible person who has the responsibility to submit any countermeasures in the event of a deviation.
4. Secondary responsibility should be assigned whenever another function is required to complete the improvement priority or specialised support is required.
5. The owner (CEO) of the matrix must demand and evaluate the effectiveness of the countermeasures when reviewing the monthly progress towards the Target to Improve.

The CEO assigned the primary and secondary responsibilities to the matrix among the members of his team.

Level 1 X Matrix was completed. It was then necessary to verify whether the impact of achieving the objectives in the East Box would be identical to the results presented in the West Box. The Financial Director performed this task, amending small differences.

At the end of the working session, the team seemed pleased with the results.

LEVEL 1 X MATRIX

Time To Market from 50 to 40 weeks in Year 1	Free Cash Flow from 545 K€ to 5.3 M€ in Year 1	On-Time Delivery from 75% to 82.5% in Year 1	EBITDA from 2.3 to 7.2 M€ in Year 1	L1 Improvement priorities / Annual Breakthrough objectives / 3-year Breakthrough objectives / Targets to Improve (TTI)	Sales/ FTE from 191 K€ to 200 K€ by Dec/Year 1	FSE from 17.7% to 16.4% of sales (1 M€) by Dec/Year 1	Planned waste from 8% to 7% (505 K€) by Dec/ Year 1	Purchase Part Variance (PPV) from 50.5 M€ to 50 M€ by Dec/Year 1	Non-Quality Costs from 2 M€ to 1.52 M€ by Dec/Year 1	# customer complaints from 84 to 42 by Dec/ Year 1	On-Time Delivery from 75% to 82.5% by Dec/ Year 1	Inventory from 12.9 M€ to 9.7 M€ (6.2 to 12.3 turns) by Dec/Year 1	Time To Market from 50 to 40 weeks by Dec/ Year 1	Sales from 79.6 M€ to 87.6 M€ by Dec/Year 1	Vitality: new customer sales from 0 to 3 M€ by Dec/Year 1	Operations Manager	Engineering Manager	Materials & Logistics Manager	Marketing & Sales Manager	Human Resources Manager	Purchasing Manager	Financial Manager	IT Manager
●			●	Design a process to improve Marketing & Sales										●	●				●				○
●				Implement a process to reduce new product lead-time									●			○	●						
	●			Implement a process to reduce working capital								●						●			○	○	
		●		Implement a process to increase On-Time Delivery							●					○		●	○				○
			●	Implement a process to reduce non-compliances					●	●						●							
			●	Design a process to reduce product cost (VA/VE,PPV)			●	●									●				○		
			●	Implement a process to increase productivity	●	●										●		○		○			○
			●	EBITDA from 2.3 M€ to 12 M€ in 3 years (20% of growth sales included)																			
		●		On-Time Delivery from 75% to 90% in 3 years																			
	●			Free Cash Flow from 545 K€ to 10 M€ in 3 years																			
●				Time To Market from 50 to 30 weeks in 3 years																			

Resources:
- ● Primary responsibility
- ○ Secondary responsibility

Level 1 X Matrix Owners, Year 1

ASSIGNMENT OF RESPONSILILITIES - CHECKPOINTS

To successfully complete **step 5 of the Critical Thinking Process**, it is necessary to check the following points:

1. Resources are able to achieve results.
2. Resources are at the point of impact (best resources are not always obvious).
3. The choice of the best resources is not conditioned by the organisation chart.
4. Multidisciplinary project teams are created.
5. Resources know and apply KAIZEN™ tools.

The CEO did not want to end the day without addressing his team: "Thanks for your participation, I think we did a great job! In fact, I did not know the Hoshin Planning methodology, but I am won over by its ability to make us focus on what is essential for our company! Look, we've been able to put ALFA's strategy on a single sheet! Something that seemed impossible, right? Now we have to concentrate all efforts on the deployment of your Matrices! Last but not least, I am grateful for the work of Kaizen Institute which has played a key role in enabling us to get here.

The CEO thanked all members of the Executive Committee after which they left the room as they discussed on each other's next steps.

On the way home, the CEO reflected on the process that had been taken and how challenging the times ahead would be. The fact that he had achieved an alignment between all the team members, reassured him.

3.4 X Matrix Level 2

It was 9 o'clock and the Operations team entered the room, under the curious glances of other teams watching them go by. The L1 Matrix was already affixed to the wall, printed in A0 format. Now, they needed to build the L2 Matrices. The first one was the operations matrix and the CEO wanted to be present.

3.4.1 The Concept of Catchball

Catchball is a negotiation technique where leaders "toss" ideas for objectives to the level of management below them. The managers then return the "ball" with their own input and ideas. The process is repeated until consensus is reached. Department heads then repeat the process with their team leaders, and so on, until the goals have been negotiated across the organisation. Everyone has clear objectives that they helped create. Despite not being complicated, it does take practice and a culture of commitment and valorisation. It is with this technique in mind that it is possible to build the L2 Matrix.

At that day's kick-off, the consultant explained once again the Hoshin Planning concept, since there were new collaborators in the room. He introduced the X Matrix and he summed up the connexion between L1 and L2, remembering that L1 defined the organisation's Breakthrough Objectives. Each main owner identified in the L1 Matrix would need to deploy the Improvement Priorities into the L2. That would be possible through the first Matrix rotation.

3.4.2 X Matrix rotation rules

1. A main owner is identified through a full black dot and this one will have to create an L2 Matrix.
2. A secondary owner is identified by an open dot, so they do not have to deploy an L2 Matrix, but to support the Improvement Priorities implementation.
3. The L1 Annual Breakthrough objectives are directly copied to the L2 Matrix.
4. The L1 Improvement Priorities associated with a main owner are transcribed to their L2 Matrix.
5. The milestones are not transcribed to the next level since most of the times they need to be deployed.

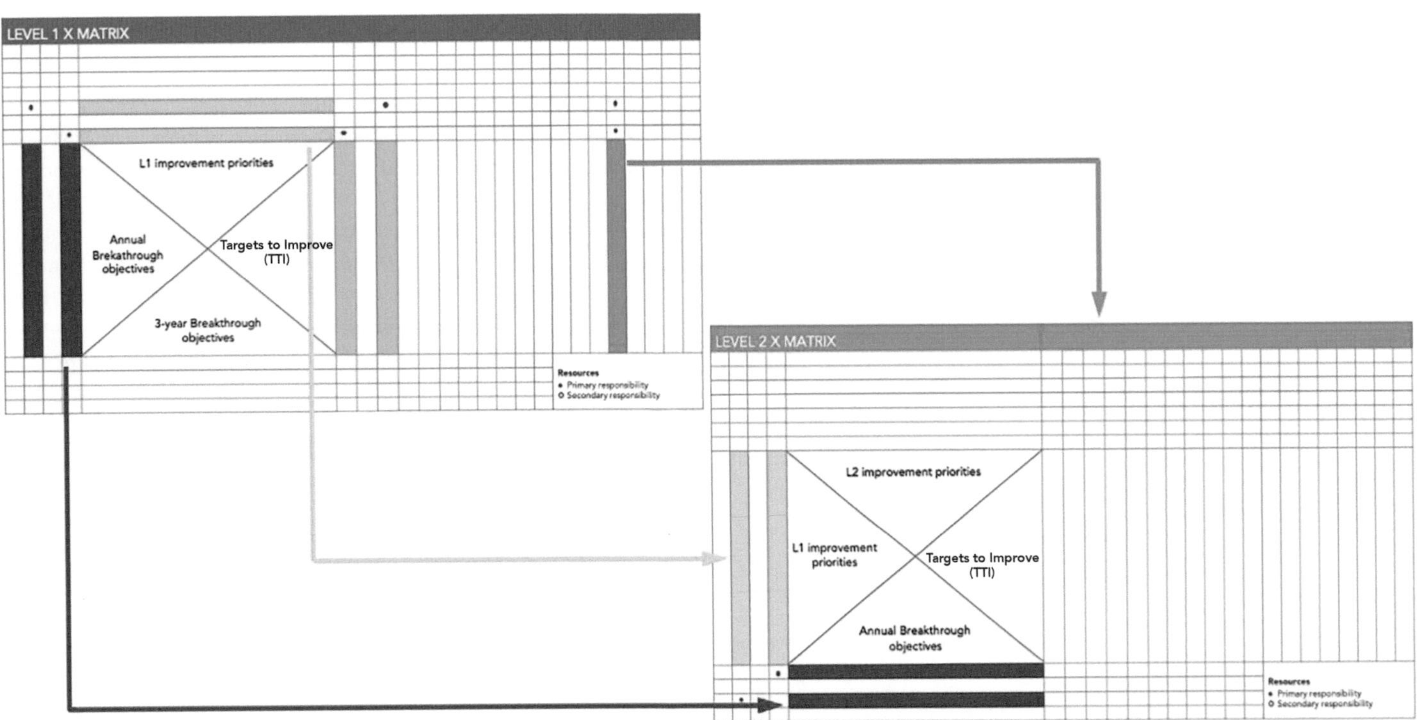

The consultant presented the agenda and explained to everyone how to fill in the new Matrix and Bowler chart, as well as define the Action Plan.

"This morning we shall put the Annual Breakthrough Objectives of the CEO's Matrix in our South Box, the Level 1 Improvement Priorities in our West Box, specifically define our Level 2 Improvement Priorities in our North Box and we'll finish with the Targets to Improve in our East Box." The Operations Director told his team.

The Operations Director was responsible for two Level 1 Improvement Priorities, as well as for their deployment to the teams of both industrial units. The first two quadrants of the Operations matrix were quickly filled in. Afterwards the team focused on the North side, following the same rules applied at Level 1. Even the new partucipants present at the KAIZEN™ Event were actively taking part in the discussion, seeming to fully understand the dynamics of the methodology.

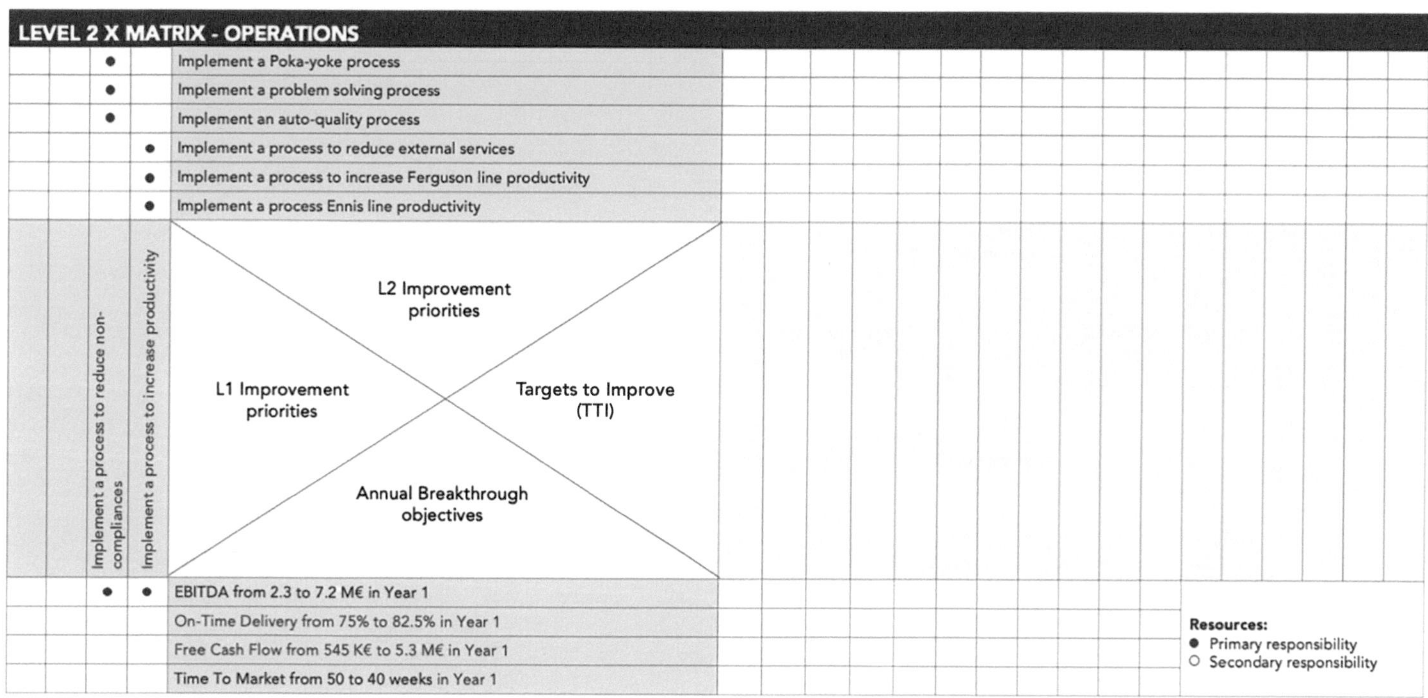

South, West and North of the level 2 X Matrix for Operations, Industrial Unit 1, Year 1

Having built the North Box the consultant continued: "We now need to move on to the East Box which, as you recall, will have the Targets to be met by Operations next year."

The Operations Director that had attended the building of the L1 Matrix started to proactively explain to the group that it should describe the Targets to be Improved in the form **FROM xxx TO yyy BY zzz.**

A few minutes later and upon the CEO's agreement, the Operations team had successfully completed the East Box.

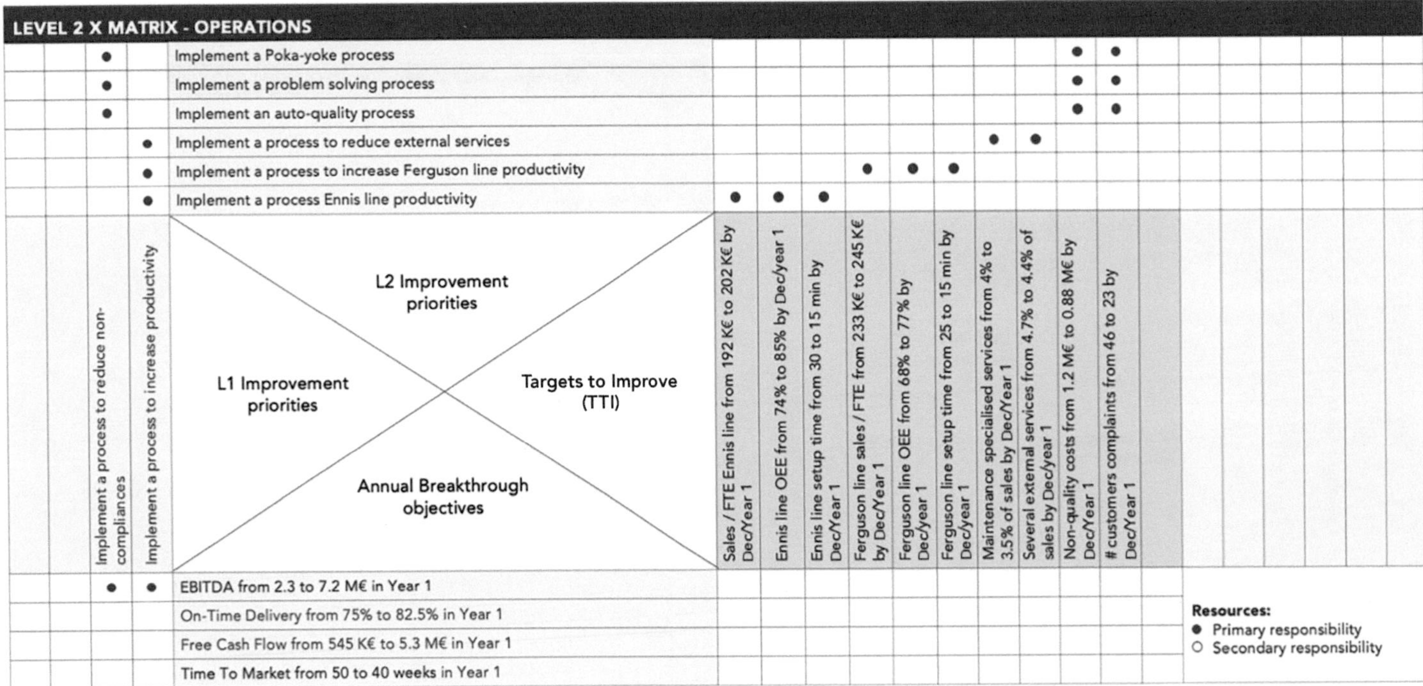

East of the level 2 X Matrix for Operations, Industrial Unit 1, Year 1

Both the CEO and the Operations Director seemed quite pleased with the results achieved so far. They both explained to the team that the next step would be to assign responsibility for each L2 Improvement Priority. In that sense, they questioned the leaders in the room, assessing who should take on what. The consultant intervened only to warn that this assignment was not necessarily to follow the organisational chart, but to select the best prepared employee to lead the implementation. The L2 Matrix was now completed.

"Well done! It is about time to stop for lunch. We will return to the room in due course so that each responsible person for the various initiatives can develop his or her Action Plan." The consultant concluded.

LEVEL 2 X MATRIX- OPERATIONS

		Implement a process to reduce Non-compliances	Implement a process to increase Productivity	L2 Improvement priorities / L1 Improvement priorities / Targets to Improve (TTI) / Annual Breakthrough objectives	Sales / FTE Ennis line from 192 K€ to 202 K€ by Dec/Year 1	Ennis Line OEE from 74% to 85% by Dec/Year 1	Ennis Line Setup Time from 30 to 15 min by Dec/Year 1	Ferguson Line Sales / FTE from 233 K€ to 245 K€ by Dec/Year 1	Ferguson Line OEE from 68% to 77% by Dec/Year 1	Ferguson Line Setup Time from 25 to 15 min by Dec/Year 1	Maintenance Specialised Services from 4% to 3.5% of sales by Dec/Year 1	Several External Services from 4.7% to 4.4% of sales by Dec/Year 1	Non-quality Costs from 1.2 M€ to 0.88 M€ by Dec/Year 1	# Customer Complaints from 46 to 23 by Dec/Year 1		Plant Manager	Production Manager	Purchasing Manager	Quality Engineer	Process Engineer	
		●		Implement a Poka-yoke process									●	●					○	●	
		●		Implement a Problem Solving process									●	●					●	○	
		●		Implement an Auto-quality process									●	●					●	○	
			●	Implement a process to reduce External Services							●	●				○		●			
			●	Implement a process to increase Ferguson Line Productivity				●	●	●							●				
			●	Implement a process to increase Ennis Line Productivity	●	●	●										●				
		●	●	EBITDA from 2.3 to 7.2 M€ in Year 1																	
				On-Time Delivery from 75% to 82.5% in Year 1																	
				Free Cash Flow from 545 K€ to 5.3 M€ in Year 1																	
				Time To Market from 50 to 40 weeks in Year 1																	

Resources:
● Primary responsibility
○ Secondary responsibility

Level 2 X Matrix Owners for Operations, Industrial Unit 1, Year 1

In parallel, the L2 Matrices were developed with the Engineering, Marketing and Sales and Logistics teams - shown below in that order.

LEVEL 2 X MATRIX - ENGINEERING

		Implement a process to reduce new products lead time	Design a process to reduce product cost (VA/VE,PPV)	L2 Improvement priorities / L1 Improvement priorities / Targets to Improve (TTI) / Annual Breakthrough objectives	Cost Reduction with VA/VE of 300 K€ until Dec/Year 1	Sales/ FTE from 191 K€ to 200 K€ by Dec./Year 1	Purchase Part Variance (PPV) from 50.5 M€ to 50 M€ by Dec/Year 1	FSE from 17.7% (5.1 M€) to 16.4% (4.7 M€) by Dec/Year 1	Capex expenses from 2.4 M€ maximum by Dec/ Year 1	New products lead-time from 50 to 40 weeks by Dec/Year 1	New products defect costs from 200 K€ to 100 K€ by Dec/Year 1					New Product Development Engineer	Process Engineer	Maintenance Engineer	Purchasing Manager	Quality Engineer	
		●		Implement a process to do a Stage Gate Review in new product development						●	●					●	○	○	○	○	
		●		Implement a process to accelerate new product development						●						●	○	○	○	○	
			●	Implement Lean Line Design in capex process					●								●	○			
			●	Implement a PPV process to services and materials supply			●	●											●		
			●	Implement a VA/VE process	●	●										●				○	
			●	EBITDA from 2.3 to 7.2 M€ in Year 1																	
				On-Time Delivery from 75% to 82.5% in Year 1																	
				Free Cash Flow from 545 K€ to 5.3 M€ in Year 1																	
		●		Time To Market from 50 to 40 weeks in Year 1																	

Resources:
- ● Primary responsibility
- ○ Secondary responsibility

Level 2 X Matrix for Engineering, Year 1

LEVEL 2 X MATRIX - MARKETING & SALES

L2 Improvement priorities

L1 Improvement priorities

Targets to Improve (TTI)

Annual Breakthrough objectives

Design a process to improve Marketing & Sales	L2 Improvement priorities	New segments for potential sales from 0 M€ to 15 M€ by Dec/Year 1	Sales from 79.6 M€ to 87.6 M€ by Dec/Year 1	Contribution margin from 9.5% to 15.2% by Dec/Year 1	Sales conversion rate from 19% to 30% by Dec/Year 1	Commercial visits productivity increase from 20% to Dec/Year 1	Vitality: new customers sales from 0 to 3 M€ by Dec/Year 1	New segments sales from 0 to 3 M€ by Dec/Year 1	New product sales from 0 to M€ by Dec/Year 1	Sales Manager	Marketing Manager	Engineering Manager	Operations Manager
●	Implement a process for Market Segmentation (MEKKO)	●									●		
●	Improve New Product launching							●	●		●	○	
●	Improve Marketing Planning process		●				●				●		
●	Implement a Sales Planning process					●				●			
●	Implement a Value Selling (VS) process			●	●					●			
●	Implement a Voice of the Customer (VOC) process	●	●								●	○	○

Design a process to improve Marketing & Sales	Annual Breakthrough objectives
●	EBITDA from 2.3 to 7.2 M€ in Year 1
	On-Time Delivery from 75% to 82.5% in Year 1
	Free Cash Flow from 545 K€ to 5.3 M€ in Year 1
●	Time To Market from 50 to 40 weeks in Year 1

Resources:
- ● Primary responsibility
- ○ Secondary responsibility

Level 2 X Matrix for Marketing and Sales, Year 1

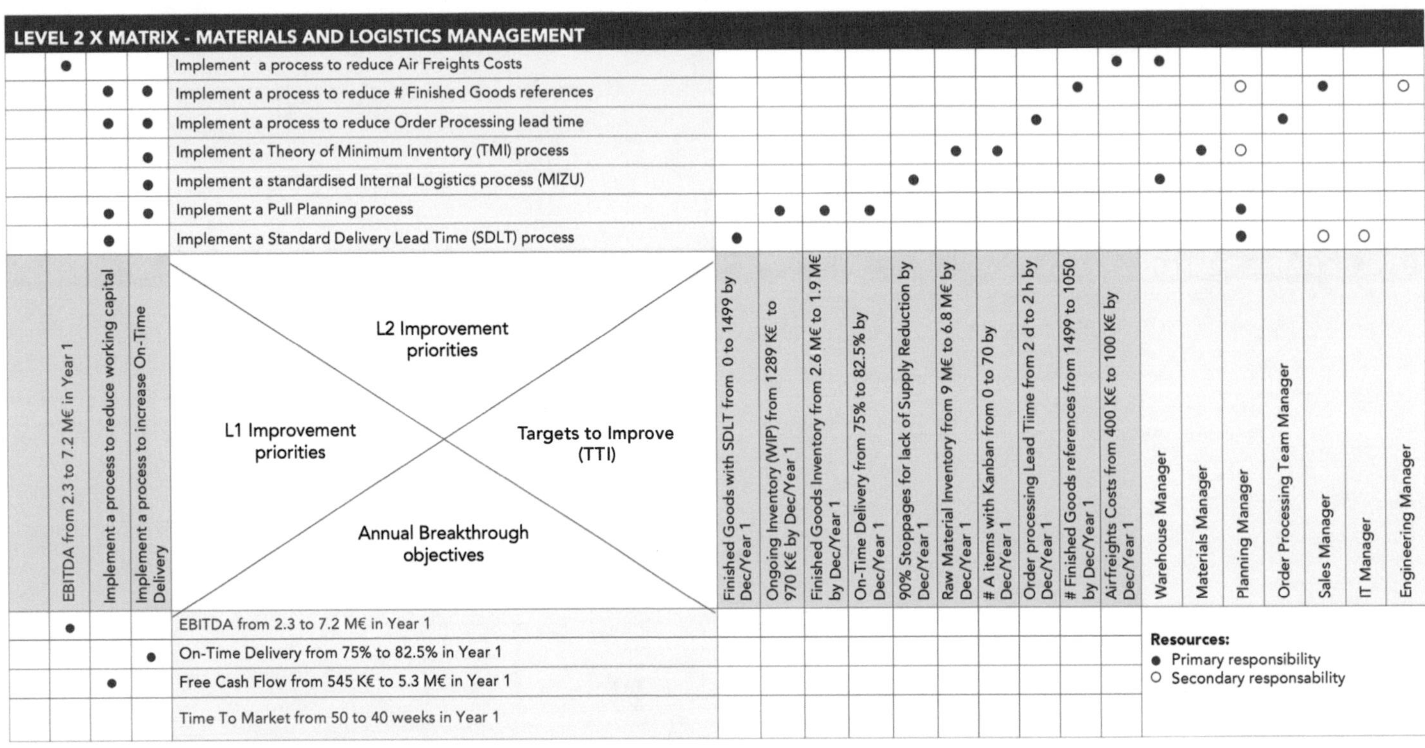

LEVEL 2 X MATRIX - MATERIALS AND LOGISTICS MANAGEMENT

	EBITDA from 2.3 to 7.2 M€ in Year 1	Implement a process to reduce working capital	Implement a process to increase On-Time Delivery	L2 Improvement priorities	Finished Goods with SDLT from 0 to 1499 by Dec/Year 1	Ongoing Inventory (WIP) from 1289 K€ to 970 K€ by Dec/Year 1	Finished Goods Inventory from 2.6 M€ to 1.9 M€ by Dec/Year 1	On-Time Delivery from 75% to 82.5% by Dec/Year 1	90% Stoppages for lack of Supply Reduction by Dec/Year 1	Raw Material Inventory from 9 M€ to 6.8 M€ by Dec/Year 1	# A items with Kanban from 0 to 70 by Dec/Year 1	Order processing Lead Tiime from 2 d to 2 h by Dec/Year 1	# Finished Goods references from 1499 to 1050 by Dec/Year 1	Airfreights Costs from 400 K€ to 100 K€ by Dec/Year 1	Warehouse Manager	Materials Manager	Planning Manager	Order Processing Team Manager	Sales Manager	IT Manager	Engineering Manager
	●			Implement a process to reduce Air Freights Costs										●	●						
		●	●	Implement a process to reduce # Finished Goods references									●				○		●		○
		●	●	Implement a process to reduce Order Processing lead time								●						●			
			●	Implement a Theory of Minimum Inventory (TMI) process						●	●					●	○				
			●	Implement a standardised Internal Logistics process (MIZU)					●						●						
		●	●	Implement a Pull Planning process		●	●	●									●				
		●		Implement a Standard Delivery Lead Time (SDLT) process	●												●		○	○	

	EBITDA from 2.3 to 7.2 M€ in Year 1	Implement a process to reduce working capital	Implement a process to increase On-Time Delivery	Annual Breakthrough objectives
	●			EBITDA from 2.3 to 7.2 M€ in Year 1
			●	On-Time Delivery from 75% to 82.5% in Year 1
		●		Free Cash Flow from 545 K€ to 5.3 M€ in Year 1
				Time To Market from 50 to 40 weeks in Year 1

Level 2 X Matrix for Materials Management and Logistics, Year 1

3.4.3 The Action Plan

The Matrix is useless if it does not trigger any action. Therefore, each Improvement Priority should generate an Action Plan, materialised in KAIZEN™ Events, acting directly at the point of impact. The consultant went on and designed the template to be applied. As he wandered about the room, he explained the fields that described it.

It is from the future state mapping that the KAIZEN™ Events are defined; each one of them has to implement a part of the Future Vision. To build the Action Plan, the following steps must be taken:

1. Discussion of the KAIZEN™ Events required and the scope of each one of them.
2. KAIZEN™ Event prioritisation, so events have to occur in sequence with others.

3. Identification of resources involved in each event.
4. KAIZEN™ Events agenda to avoid resources overlap.

The first Action Plan completed concerned the implementation of a process to increase productivity at the ENNIS line. Being responsible for this Improvement Priority, the Production Head at Industrial Unit 1 started filling in the document with the help of the consultant. The other team members remained attentive, while clarifying some issues and preparing themselves to complete their own Action Plans.

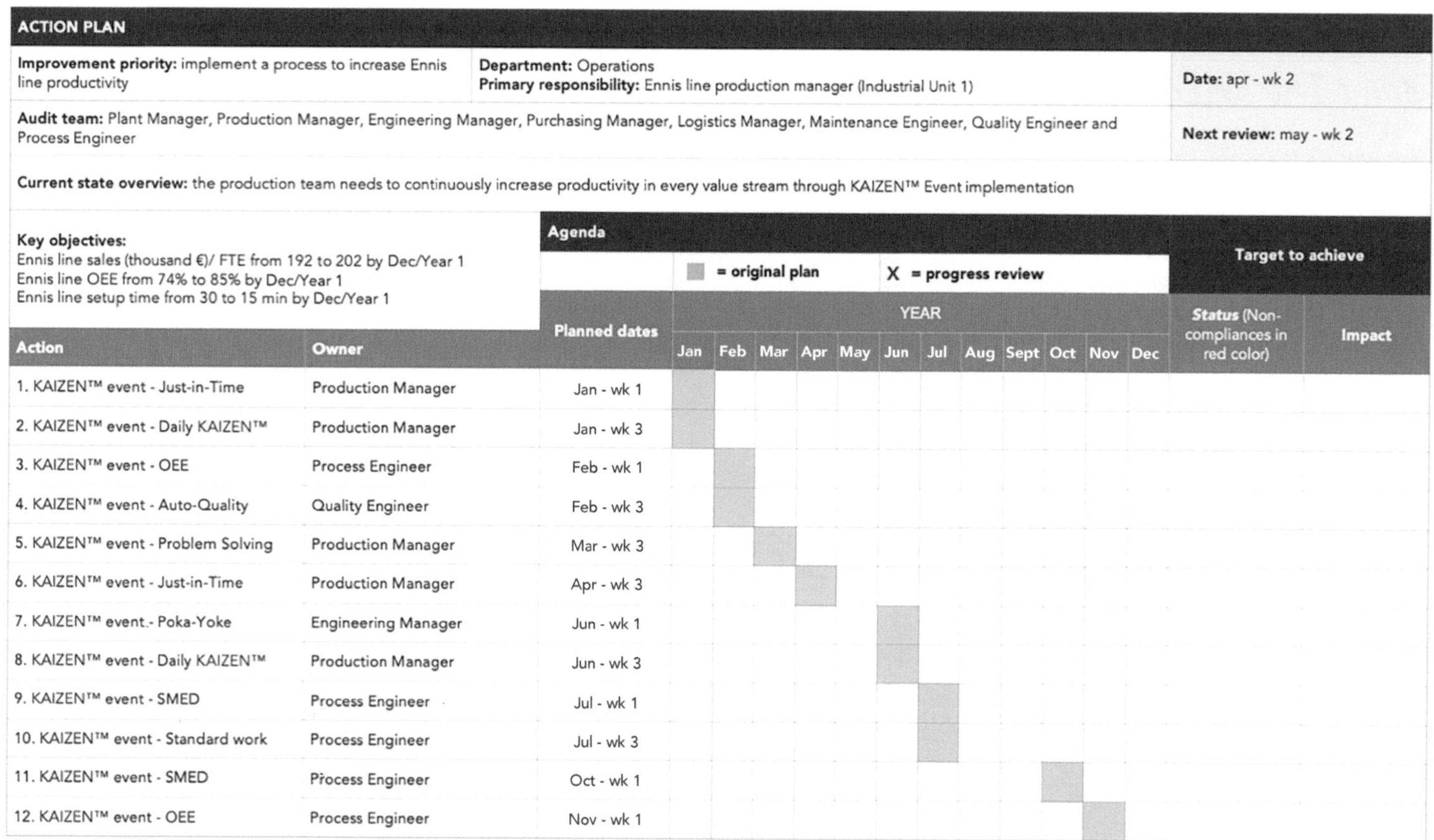

ACTION PLAN

Improvement priority: implement a process to increase Ennis line productivity

Department: Operations
Primary responsibility: Ennis line production manager (Industrial Unit 1)

Date: apr - wk 2

Audit team: Plant Manager, Production Manager, Engineering Manager, Purchasing Manager, Logistics Manager, Maintenance Engineer, Quality Engineer and Process Engineer

Next review: may - wk 2

Current state overview: the production team needs to continuously increase productivity in every value stream through KAIZEN™ Event implementation

Key objectives:
Ennis line sales (thousand €)/ FTE from 192 to 202 by Dec/Year 1
Ennis line OEE from 74% to 85% by Dec/Year 1
Ennis line setup time from 30 to 15 min by Dec/Year 1

Agenda — ■ = original plan; X = progress review

Target to achieve

Action	Owner	Planned dates	Jan	Feb	Mar	Apr	May	Jun	Jul	Aug	Sept	Oct	Nov	Dec	Status (Non-compliances in red color)	Impact
1. KAIZEN™ event - Just-in-Time	Production Manager	Jan - wk 1	■													
2. KAIZEN™ event - Daily KAIZEN™	Production Manager	Jan - wk 3	■													
3. KAIZEN™ event - OEE	Process Engineer	Feb - wk 1		■												
4. KAIZEN™ event - Auto-Quality	Quality Engineer	Feb - wk 3		■												
5. KAIZEN™ event - Problem Solving	Production Manager	Mar - wk 3			■											
6. KAIZEN™ event - Just-in-Time	Production Manager	Apr - wk 3				■										
7. KAIZEN™ event.- Poka-Yoke	Engineering Manager	Jun - wk 1						■								
8. KAIZEN™ event - Daily KAIZEN™	Production Manager	Jun - wk 3						■								
9. KAIZEN™ event - SMED	Process Engineer	Jul - wk 1							■							
10. KAIZEN™ event - Standard work	Process Engineer	Jul - wk 3							■							
11. KAIZEN™ event - SMED	Process Engineer	Oct - wk 1										■				
12. KAIZEN™ event - OEE	Process Engineer	Nov - wk 1											■			

A few hours later, the Operations team had already completed its Action Plans regarding their Improvement Priorities.

Before closing the work session, the Plant Manager said to his team: "Ok everyone, you have already realised how much commitment we have to these Action Plans. That's why it's not worth thinking about the difficulties we are going to face; it is best to concentrate all our energies in finding solutions to get things done!"

3.4.4 The KAIZEN™ Event

Focused on the organisation's need for improvement, a KAIZEN™ Event is an intensive workshop typically implemented over a week.

It is divided into 3 phases:

1. **Preparation** - data collection and provision of the equipment needed.
2. **Implementation** - solution design and testing.
3. **Follow-up** - monitoring results and correcting failures.

A KAIZEN™ Event necessarily delivers results because it implements a new and better working method in the shortest amount of time. The whole team is aligned and focused on the objective, following a structured methodology in order to achieve it. For example, in a JIT flow workshop the delivered results are typically:

1. Productivity gains of 30%.
2. Quality improvement by 50%.
3. Space reduction by 40%.
4. Stock reduction by 70%.

In order to achieve these results, it is important to follow the golden rules of a KAIZEN™ Event, namely:

- Work in a multidisciplinary team.
- Alignment and focus on a single theme.
- Quantified objectives.
- Well defined duration (intensive days).
- Preparation Work.
- GEMBA activities.
- Immediate implementation.
- Standard methodology (KAIZEN™ tools).
- Application of countermeasures for a quick correction of deviations.
- Results follow-up and financial impact calculation.

Many organisations are faced with a common dilemma: they plan change, but nothing happens. Why? Because their employees spend too much time thinking about what can stop them from improving, they look for the perfect solution and, without realising it, after six months there is no improvement.

The KAIZEN™ method leads the teams to stay focused on what they have to do in order to carry out the Action Plan as quickly as possible. This is the difference between planning and implementing.

When leaders participate in any KAIZEN™ Event and realise that it is truly possible to implement changes so fast, it becomes the only way to improve the organisation and deliver effective results.

There are several expressions that describe a KAIZEN™ Event, including:

- **Learn by doing:** This expression suggests that the team should test and do things on its own. The best way to learn is to start doing things independently.

- **Dirty hands, dirty boots:** This expression seeks to emphasise the importance of going to GEMBA, where value is added and where all opportunities for improvement can be identified. Getting one's hands and boots dirty is a metaphor for the team's total involvement in the accomplishment of actions.

- **MUDA eyes:** Indicates that the team must be focused on the identification of waste and on eliminating it.

- **Make all the changes in a week:** All changes must be designed, tested and implemented in the short time, including adjustments to be made, if necessary.

- **Intensive work sessions:** Describe KAIZEN™ days as intensive, focused and effective sessions.

- **Doing event, not a planning event:** The workshop should not be to plan actions, but rather to put them into practice. All preparation work must be done prior to the day of the KAIZEN™ Event.

Even if you consider you have already achieved the best level of performance, it is always a great opportunity to hold a KAIZEN™ event. Typically, the most productive work cells are essential for starting KAIZEN™ implementation. Why? Because they are already at the top of efficiency known so far. There follows a story that accurately describes the importance of this idea.

A consultant observed 48 fully balanced workstations of a value stream considered to be Best in Class in the air conditioning equipment industry used in transportation containers. However, a KAIZEN™ event took place to increase productivity. The Management was convinced that they had already "squeezed their skills up to the limit". However, after a 5 day workshop focused on online balancing, it was still possible to eliminate 7 workstations and increase productivity by 30%.

If waste elimination is a continuous task, after 6 iterations, it is possible to eliminate almost 90% of non-value-added steps. And then the team must start again. There is always potential for improvement.

Organisations that have never experienced the KAIZEN™ implementation and the effectiveness of KAIZEN™ Events, consider these results truly exceptional, when they are actually normal if the process is applied correctly. The consultant plays the facilitator role, helping with the application of the KAIZEN™ tools which will allow change implementation.

3.4.5 Year 1 Roadmap

By then, each Improvement Priority owner had already defined their L2 Matrix and their Action Plans. The Operations, Engineering, Procurement, Logistics and Marketing and Sales Managers were all on their way to a meeting where they would present their individual plans. The purpose of this session would be to aggregate all KAIZEN™ Events, resulting from several Action Plans, into a single Plan. This would provide the CEO and the Executive Committee with the visibility of all work to be done in that first year.

The consultant began by saying: "We already have our Action Plans and together with these, the number of KAIZEN™ Events to be performed. It is now necessary to convert all these into a single roadmap, so that we can follow the whole transformation. It would also be appropriate to take advantage of this day to decide which KAIZEN™ events should be attended by each member of the Executive Committee."

The team quickly consolidated the Action Plans. The constraints were solved through a joint effort to take advantage of similar activities. The roadmaps for the two industrial units were completed (a short description of each event can be found in appendix 5).

	Main responsibility	January (Year 1)				February				March				April				May				June				Total KE/ team
		s1	s2	s3	s4	s1	s2	s3	s4	s1	s2	s3	s4	s1	s2	s3	s4	s1	s2	s3	s4	s1	s2	s3	s4	
Semester 1	Operations	JIT		DK		OEE		AQ		JIT		PS		DK		JIT		PS		JIT		PY		DK		12
Semester 1	Purchasing & Engineering		VAVE				PPV				LLD				VAVE				PPV				LLD			6
Semester 1	Marketing & Sales				SEG				VOC				MPI				VS				SPI				SEG	6
Semester 1	Materials & Logistics Management		SDLT		PULL		WIP		PULL		SDLT		PULL		WIP		MIZU		SDLT		PULL		WIP		TMI	12

	Main responsibility	July				August				September				October				November				December				Total KE/ team
		s1	s2	s3	s4	s1	s2	s3	s4	s1	s2	s3	s4	s1	s2	s3	s4	s1	s2	s3	s4	s1	s2	s3	s4	
Semester 2	Operations	SMED		SW						SMED		OEE		SMED		DK		OEE		SMED		SW		OEE		10
Semester 2	Purchasing & Engineering		NPD								VAVE				NPD				NPD				NPD			5
Semester 2	Marketing & Sales				VOC								SPL				SOPM				VS				VS	5
Semester 2	Materials & Logistics Management		TMI		MIZU						TMI		PULL		WIP		MIZU		SDLT		PULL		WIP		PULL	10
																										66

Glossary:

PULL	Pull Planning
MIZU	Mizusumashi
SDLT	Standard Delivery Lead Time
WIP	WIP Inventory Supermarkets
TMI	Theory of Minimum Inventory
NPD	New Product Development
LLD	Lean Line Design
PPV	Purchase Parts Variance
VA/VE	Value Analysis/Value Engineering
JIT	Just-in-time
AQ	Auto Quality
PY	Poka-yoke
PS	Problem Solving
DK	Daily Kaizen
OEE	Overall Equipment Effectiveness
SMED	Single Minute Exchange of Die
SOPM	Sales Order Processing Mapping
SW	Standard Work
MPI	Marketing Plan Improvement
SPL	Sales Product Launch
SPI	Sales Planning Improvement
VS	Value Selling
SEG	Segmentation
VOC	Voice of the Customer

Roadmap for Industrial Unit 1, Year 1

After a final review, everyone was concerned about the scope of the task they were involved in.

"Do you think it is possible to carry out 66 events at industrial unit 1 and 63 at industrial unit 2 for a year?" The Financial Director asked.

At this stage of the process, it was essential for the Executive Committee to understand that other Best in Class companies had also experienced the same feeling: "this is an impossible mission".

The consultant started by presenting three case-studies of organisations from other sectors, which stood out for excellence in the practice of Continuous Improvement. In all these examples it was possible to recognise an implementation rate of more than 150 KAIZEN™ Events, year after year.

The CEO made several questions and acknowledged that the time and effort associated with the number of KAIZEN™ Events were essential to meet the commitments made.

"Right then! If others can do it, so can we! We must complete our Roadmap of 129 Events in both plants between January and December! We built this detailed plan, we all know what we must do, so we just have to get to work!" He stopped for a few seconds, then added "And this is not negotiable!" The team seemed surprised by this reaction.

The CEO had never taken such a strict approach, but he felt it was the only way not to make that meeting an opportunity for discussions that would lead nowhere. The commitment was assumed and nothing would change that.

"For the avoidance of doubt, I will set an example myself and commit to actively participate in 12 KAIZEN™ Events over the next year. And, of course, I hope all of you can, at least, match my number." The CEO challenged.

The remaining Executive Committee knew that there was no alternative and each one took on their responsibilities. It was decided: everyone wanted to take their seat on the bus.

Finally, the consultant reminded the team that these roadmaps were, in fact, two change management programs:

- **Breakthrough KAIZEN™** - to achieve Breakthrough results.
- **Daily KAIZEN™** - to support the new standards.

The consultant wound the meeting up by saying: "Do not forget today's Breakthroughs are tomorrow's standards, which can only be sustained with Daily KAIZEN™."

After the Hoshin Planning, ALFA was prepared to start the Hoshin Review, the next step of the **STRAT TO ACTION** process. This step includes the Roadmap implementation, as well as a monthly review of the Hoshin´s progress. The next chapter introduces the implementation of two KAIZEN™ Events.

Breakthrough KAIZEN™

Great Results require Great Changes

When implemented, Breakthrough KAIZEN™ leads to disruptive results by introducing improvements into the organisation's critical processes. This is a method that allows continuous improvement to deliver the organisation's improvement priorities, by breaking old paradigms and implementing new ones. This is achieved through the implementation of many KAIZEN™ Events cycles every month. At the end of each month their success will be evaluated, and the next cycle can be planned.

This chapter introduces Breakthrough KAIZEN™ as a 3-step model to change an organisation. In the following chapter we will explain the improvement priorities, including the necessary follow-ups to sustain results as well as two of the KAIZEN™ Events planned for the first year of the Hoshin implementation at ALFA's. The first event has to do with Operations and describes the implementation of the Just-in-Time methodology. The second event involves Logistics, implementing the Theory of Minimum Inventory.

4.1 Mission Control Room

The **Mission Control Room** (MCR) gathers, in the same space, all relevant information necessary to carry out a frequent follow-up of the Strat To Action progress. Since most people collect 80% of their information through their eyes, the MCR applies the principle of Visual Management as a way of gathering data and displaying the results achieved against the targets in order to improve.

After completing the Hoshin Planning phase, the consultant, together with two members from each plant, developed the respective MCRs. Project Management in both locations was essential, since the teams were different. Keeping the MCR close to the GEMBA was crucial because remote monitoring would not be as effective.

The MCR performs two key functions: (a) the Hoshin monthly review and (b) the ongoing weekly local management review of improvement priorities of the KAIZEN™ Breakthroughs.

The mission control rooms were now designated as the meeting place for the different improvement teams. This allowed all areas of improvement to be displayed and facilitated tracking the vital data not only for the evolution of ongoing improvement initiatives, but also for the analysis of the Hoshin Review process as a whole. To make this feasible, data was organised in 4 spaces, in accordance with the PDCA cycle or Deming cycle approach:

- **Plan:** Level 1 and Level 2 X Matrices.
- **Do:** Action Plans and A3 of the KAIZEN™ Events concluded.
- **Check:** Level 1 and Level 2 Bowling Charts.
- **Act:** Countermeasures and new standards followed.

Cetero accusamus ea vim, eibo autem doming ei vis. Libris omittam ea mei. Regione consequat eu has, recusabo eleifend conceptam per ut, ex duis brute ponderum his. Eu everti scripta ius, tantas oblique reformidans his te. Ei pri mentitum suscipiantur, vis aliquando similique ex, pri id illud interesset.
5
3
7
2
4
6

4.2 KAIZEN™ Just-in-Time Event

The consultant arrived at 7:30 am to set up the room, speak to the production manager and to meet the team. It was about 8 o'clock when the CEO entered the room, and noticed the team was a little anxious. He was wearing jeans and shirt, more relaxed than the usual suit and tie. He was excited about being involved with the production team and working directly with them. There were 9 members of the Operations team, including Operators, Supervisors, Maintenance staff and the Production Manager.

The Production Manager had already mentioned several times that he wouldn't be available for all the KAIZEN™ event, as almost all his team was participating.

"I understand your concern, but I will tell you what I have already told my colleagues in the Executive Committee: there is a bus about to leave and I have a place on it for you. So, you have two options: either you come with me or you can stop right now". The CEO said. Given this firm attitude, the issue did not even have a chance of forming.

Shortly after, the CEO opened the KAIZEN™ Event with a welcome to everyone present and said it was about time to "make change happen". He further emphasised that he would be there all week. He would only have to make occasional phone calls, which he would try to do during breaks, but he would be 100% dedicated to learning the KAIZEN™ Event methodology and he expected the same from all the participants.

"Our challenge for this week is to design and implement a solution that will improve Productivity by 30%, reduce space by at least 50% and permanently eliminate the quality issues that affect us daily. We are going to split the Ennis line into two parts and, in this workshop, we will focus only on the first part." The CEO was keen to motivate the whole team: "I'm not here as a CEO, but as one of you. We are all equal and we all have the same responsibility to give our utmost.

The consultant thanked the CEO for this introduction and briefly introduced himself. He anticipated a week of intense work with discovery and joint learning.

He started by explaining the concept of Just-in-Time and the creation of **Flow**:
"Let's turn the Ennis production line into a One-Piece Flow, typically called Just-in-Time. This will require deep changes in the current layout, moving equipment around and standardising workstations." Silence fell over the team members. "At the same time, we must evaluate the standard times for each operation and then balance the line so that it produces 1 piece at a time." The consultant went on: "The most important thing is to be focused on what we have to do to reach the goal and not spend our energy on finding reasons that prevent us from getting there. The next step is to identify all the small daily problems that prevent us from achieving excellent results. We must identify the problems and the root causes, because only then will we be able to implement actions that will eliminate them for good. Before starting our activities, I will introduce you to the **7 Muda** (refer to Appendix 3) and how, through a process of elimination, this will transform the line into a Just-in-Time One-Piece Flow. The next step is to visit the Gemba and observe the whole process, but with different eyes. We need to identify what is not considered

added value and what must be eliminated as waste. We will then return to the room to summarise all that we've been looking at and quantify it as much as possible. **"Talk with data"** is of the essence, remember that."

"What do you mean by "talk with data"?" One operator asked.

The consultant promptly replied, "It means that instead of just saying what we think or feel, let's look at what goes on in the Gemba and evaluate the facts. We can track times, count stock and movements, determine the number of stops and errors; everything we consider important to describe the current state of our process. Most of the waste will remain hidden until we all learn how to measure and quantify it."

At that point, the Production Manager concluded: "Yes, it is necessary to identify the difference: we all think we can see, but only a few actually stop to watch and understand."

The consultant spent the next 30 minutes presenting the main concepts associated with the Just-in-Time methodology.

After the presentation, the team was divided into small groups which would have to collect different data. For 2 hours waste was identified and categorised, all the operations mapped and their cycle times calculated. During the collection, mobile phones were used to photograph important content for more detailed examination.

By lunchtime, the first part of the workshop had been completed.

The consultant stated: "Well done, everyone. I see that the process flow diagram has already been correctly drawn up, the relevant cycle times gathered, the problems detected, and the waste identified. Good job!"

Time Registration Sheet — Ennis Line - Area 1

#	Description	Measurement point	Data (upper part – time readings, lower part – time differences – notes on the right side)										Time
1	Start saw / select blank Go to the station		06 6		39 5		16 8	Hanging tools	58 5		34 6		5
2	Remove part Insert + blank - start	Press "Start"	13 7		41 8		22 6		5'1" 9		41 7		7
3	Place part on the power drill - tighten	Hanging tool	22 9		54 7		29 7		15 8		50 9		7
4	Borehole	Press "stop"	34 12		2'5" 11		50 21	Damaged drill	24 9		7'0" 10		10
5	Remover parts	Drop tools	40 6		10 5		55 5		29 5		06 6		5
6	Place part on the power drill	Press "Start"	51 11		21 11		4'1" 12		42 13		17 11		11
7	Go to the Station. Turn the part over	Press "Start"	1'6" 15		37 16	Parts interruption	21 14		51 15		32 15		15
8	Go to the milling machine Remove parts	Drop tools	18 12		49 12		34 13		6'8" 11		44 12		12
9	Deburr part	Press "stop"	30 12		3'4" 15		48 14		22 14		59 15		14
10	Place part in the box	Press "Start" or "Saw"	34 4		08 4		53 5		28 6		8'4" 5		4
		Time per cycle:	94		94		105		95		96		90

4.2.1 Takt Time

"Now, we need to look at what the customer wants. In other words, the **Demand**." The consultant gave an example: "Let me ask you something: if our customers demand 500 units a day, what should the production pace be?"

After a few seconds, the supervisor answered: "To produce 250 products per shift, we must produce 33 units per hour."

"To produce 33 units per hour, what should the cycle time be?" The consultant asked.

After a few calculations, the same supervisor replied: "108 seconds. We must make a product every 108 seconds."

"Exactly! And it's this time period we call Takt Time. In KAIZEN™, we often say that Takt Time measures the heartbeat of the customer, i.e., how often he buys a product."

The consultant explained that this calculation should be the first step before any production line balancing. He then re-capped the calculation method on the flipchart so that everyone could understand this new concept.

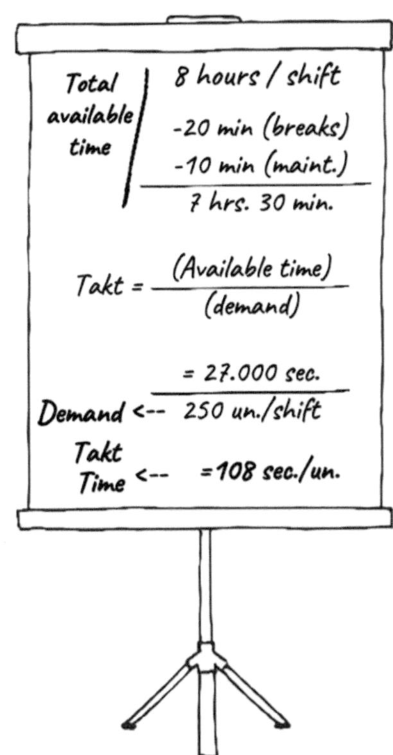

How to calculate Takt Time?

- **Define demand.**
- **Define available time for production, minus planned stops.**
- **Define available time for production by demand.**

After the Takt Time had been calculated, the next step was to balance the line. It was necessary to make visible the waste existing in the current balancing. The consultant asked one member of each group for the times collected while registering them on the flipchart. It did not take much time for everyone to realise that the cycle times corresponding to each of the operators were substantially different.

At that moment, the Process Engineer present in the room said: "Although it does not look like it, the ENNIS line is balanced to produce 36 units per hour, or 225 per shift. But we never got there..."

Once again, the consultant asked everyone in the room:
"All right... So, tell me, how much did we produce in this line yesterday?"

The answer came from the supervisor:
"We produced 155, during my shift."

The consultant did not seem surprised but asked:
"What happened?"

Quickly everyone began to speak at once, telling their own version of the difficulties they dealt with every day.

The Production Manager raised his voice and concluded the discussion: "The problem is that we have countless stops due to defects and failures from the suppliers, and, as if that were not enough, the poor line balance causes micro-stops that are not identified because they are hidden in the buffers and stockpiles we have on the line!"

"When we compare customer demand, i.e., Takt Time with our actual production capability, we realise that we must solve all these problems that have been identified, but they must be solved one by one, from their root cause." Everyone agreed.

First, a chart was drawn up for the initial state, which included 5 people on the production line, in which the balance loss of time between operators was evident. When the Takt Time value was marked on the Yamazumi chart, everyone realised that the line had too many operators, even through the initial impression had been that there weren't enough. Then they were shown how they could transfer operations from one employee to another until the best possible balance was attained. This sharing of work lead to the construction of a second chart that presented the line with five people, correctly balanced. The cycle time obtained in this case was 86 seconds, much faster than the Takt Time (Demand) required by the customer. A third line balancing was created with four people, obtaining a cycle time closer to Takt Time.

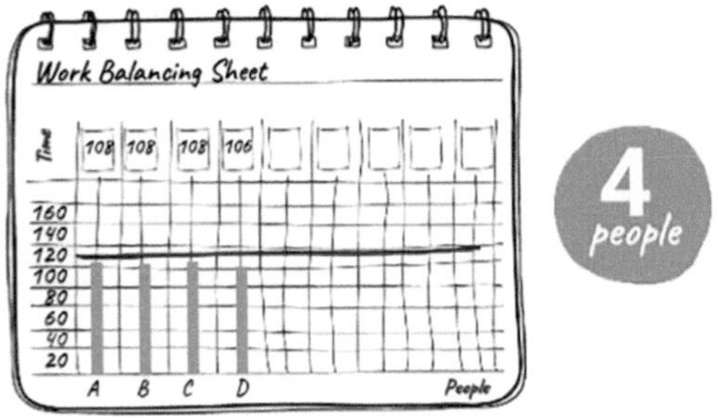

The consultant asked:
"Now that we have solved the line balance, let me ask you: What should you do with that overstaffing? Leave people on the line and not solve the problems? Or should we take them out right now?"

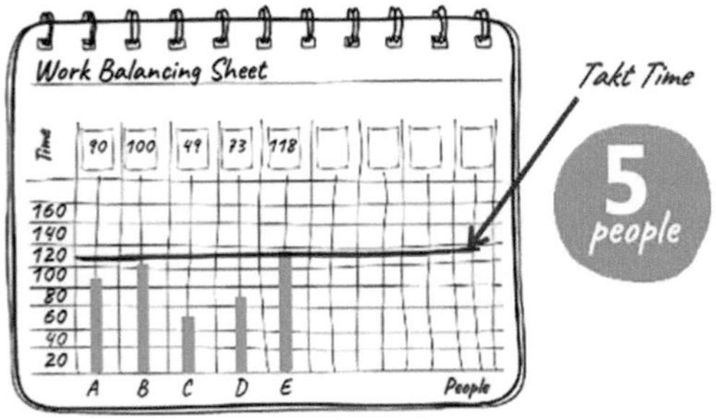

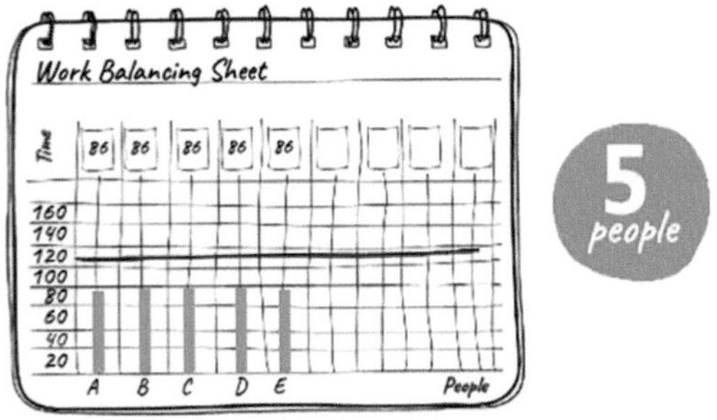

The team was caught in a trap: should they make a line with an efficient balance of 4 people, or leave more people to cover any problems? They were not used to taking decisions like this. The Production Manager with his team finally decided that the best solution would be to remove overstaffing and find and solve the root-causes of the issues.

The consultant took advantage of the situation to share another experience of his:
"Once, on a training course I had in Japan, my Sensei explained to me a very important rule for line balancing. Even if the workload is uniformly distributed and good flow is created, it takes only one person to have idle time to stop three other people from working effectively. So, next time an operator has idle time, remember that it can be multiplied by three."

The consultant summed up what had been done so far and indicated what the next step would be: "We have calculated Takt Time and balanced the line with the number of people needed to produce according to our customer demand. Now we need to design the best layout of machinery and equipment to avoid operators moving from one to another, as much as possible. We also need to check whether the machine time of each operation is not higher than the cycle time of each operator."

At that time, everyone went to the GEMBA and analysed the available equipment, deciding what would be incorporated into the new cell.

4.2.2 Standard Work Combination Sheet

The consultant presented a template for the Standard Work Combination Sheet that would be used to measure man/machine times for each operator. This would facilitate the identification of equipment delays and/or operator waiting time.

Shortly after, the room walls were full of layout proposals for the new cell. There was no lack of solutions and arguments about how each proposal would eliminate or reduce more MUDA than all the others. To avoid discussion based on "I think it's better to", a method was proposed to quantify the respective waste and added value for each suggestion.

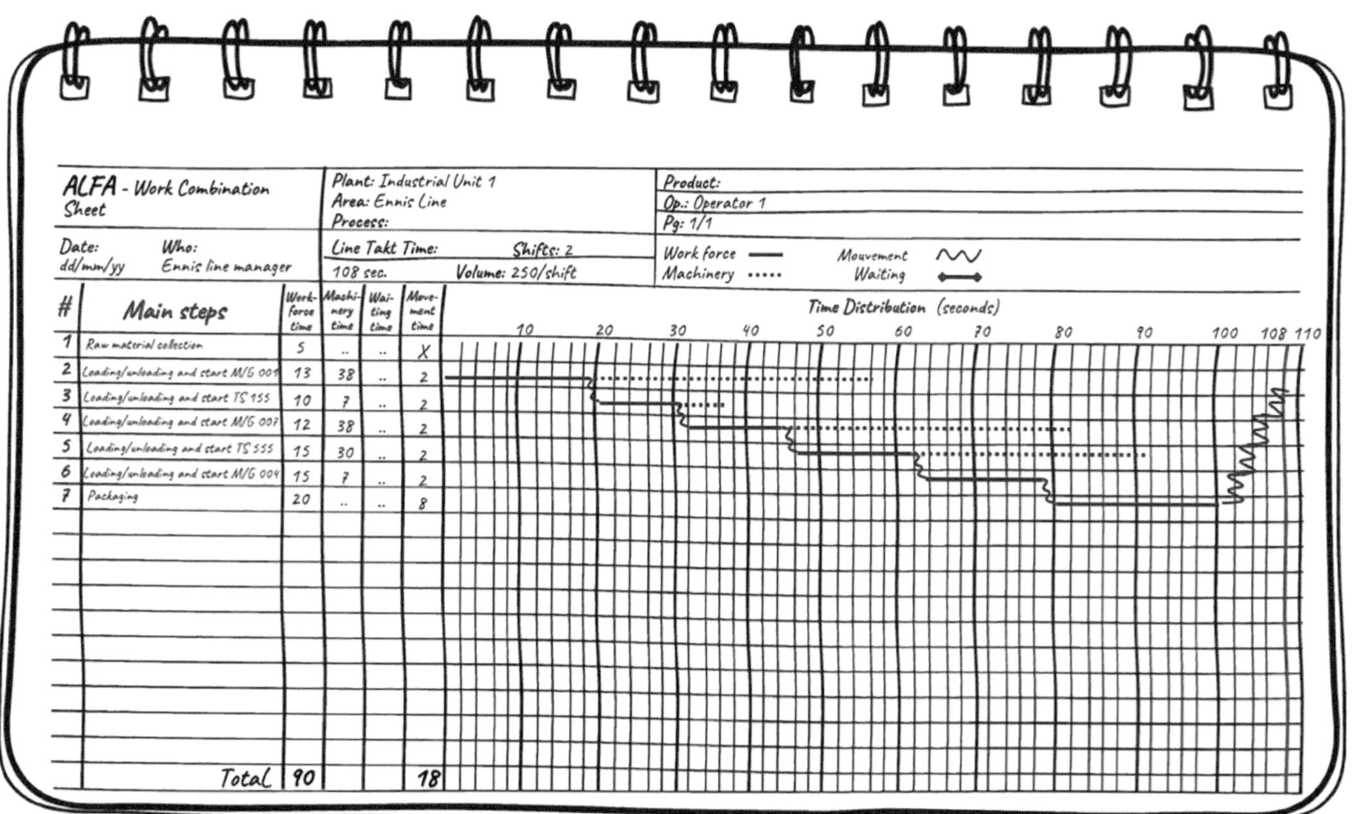

ALFA - Work Combination Sheet

Plant: Industrial Unit 1
Area: Ennis Line
Process:

Product:
Op.: Operator 1
Pg: 1/1

Date: dd/mm/yy
Who: Ennis line manager

Line Takt Time: 108 sec.
Shifts: 2
Volume: 250/shift

Work force ——
Machinery •••••
Mouvement ∿∿
Waiting ⟷

#	Main steps	Work-force time	Machinery time	Waiting time	Movement time
1	Raw material collection	5	..	..	X
2	Loading/unloading and start M/G 001	13	38	..	2
3	Loading/unloading and start TS 155	10	7	..	2
4	Loading/unloading and start M/G 007	12	38	..	2
5	Loading/unloading and start TS 555	15	30	..	2
6	Loading/unloading and start M/G 004	15	7	..	2
7	Packaging	20	..	..	8
	Total	90			18

After analysing some of the layout proposals, the consultant felt the need to challenge the teams to be more demanding with the solutions presented, and told them a short story:
"Look, what seems obvious is not always the only solution. We cannot just use math and forget about creativity. Let me give you an example that may help you. Some time ago, I worked in a vegetable production company for distribution to supermarkets and small retail stores. The owner wanted to increase productivity; he had measured the work and looked at the costs. He told me we needed to reallocate resources in a more effective way, as according to his calculations it should be possible to produce at least 30% more than what was then being produced. The first operation, considered the "bottleneck", consisted of washing the reusable containers used to transport the goods to customers. This washing was carried out in a long, narrow, automatic machine. Dirty containers were inserted by an operator at one end of the machine and, once they were cleaned, they were removed by another operator at the other end. He told me that he had calculated that only "half a person" was needed in order to load and "another half" to unload. In an attempt to make the best use of resources, he had already tried to place one single person performing both tasks, with repetitive going back and forth from the front to the back of the machine. But as daily output fell, once again he chose to have two people performing this task. In conclusion: ½ person + ½ person is not always equal to 1 person; in this case ½ + ½ = 2, a simple lesson." The consultant paused to let the team think.

"To solve this problem, a thought beyond the obvious was required. Why not build a return conveyor for the clean containers from the back to the loading station? The goal was not to install an expensive automated transport, rather a solution called Karakuri. A simple device which uses the laws of gravity to produce automatic movements. In this case, a gravity roller conveyor. Thus, whenever a clean container came out, it was automatically returned to the loading station, allowing the same operator to carry out the loading and unloading operations as alternate tasks with no toing and froing. Consequently, a resource was saved as well as some space. The lesson learned was that math alone cannot eliminate waste. We must use our heads." He concluded.

4.2.3 Standard Operation Procedure

At that moment, it was necessary to create a document, a summary of the new work standard, called the Standard Operation Procedure. This would be used as a visual instruction for the activities assigned to each operator. The consultant explained the preparation method, highlighting the importance of the quality and safety checks.

Different Standard Operation Procedures were developed, depending on the demand required (for the staffing variation of 1 to 4 people).

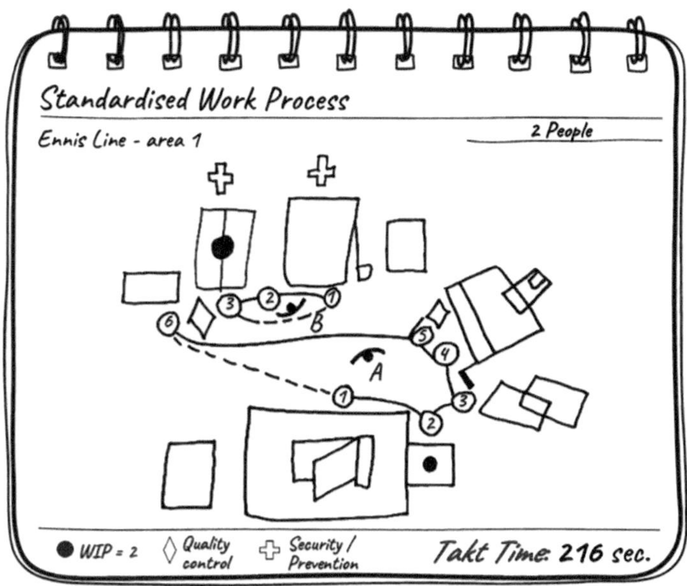

- *Assigned people by letters*
- *Numbers representing a sequence*
- *Solid lines representing movements*
- *Dashed lines representing movements to the starting point*

The team was then in a position to build the new line according to the approved layout. They all went to the GEMBA and got to work, as they had to build and test the line and be ready for production the following day. Respecting all safety standards, each machine was carefully placed in its new position. During the new cell installation, the CEO himself helped to determine the position of the support equipment.

While watching the changes taking place on that line, some employees, who were not engaged in the KAIZEN™ Event, seemed interested. One of them was the Maintenance Responsible who promptly took a measuring tape from his pocket and started to measure the distance between machines. With a serious expression, he approached the Production Manager and asked him to stop the work since the machines would be too close to one another, making it impossible to carry out maintenance.

The CEO was not directly involved in the discussion but was interested to see what would happen. The Production Manager explained the situation to the consultant and asked what they could do. The consultant approached the machines and asked the Maintenance Responsible:
"When were these machines last opened?"

The Maintenance Responsible was reluctant to answer: "Normally, we don't need to open these doors, but if the machine breaks down, we may have to do so."

"Are you saying that it is better for each operator to walk another metre every minute, because perhaps it will be necessary to open these doors? We cannot do that; we must change the paradigm! I suggest we analyse each of these machines and, depending on their specifications, we apply one of two solutions: either we remove the door or we create a door with vertical opening." The consultant said.

The Maintenance Responsible quickly understood the new paradigm and he was the first to come up with new ideas. The CEO was pleased with his attitude, asked him if he would like to join the team, since there would be many other issues related to equipment safety and maintenance, where his help would be fundamental.

4.2.4 Results Presentation

On the last day of the KAIZEN™ Event, the consultant brought the team together early in the morning to plan the TO DO list. It was essential to complete the Standard Work Procedures for each product family, analyse the difficulties arisen and prepare the results presentation for the Executive Committee. The consultant informed everyone that they would have to participate in the presentation, assigning each team member a different process step to present. Considering that, for most people involved, this would be the first time that they would be making a presentation to the management team, a schedule of 45 min for presentations and 15 min for questions was established.

Two days after the new production cell kick-off, the results were as follows:

- **Productivity** improve by 31%.
- **Lead time** reduced by 73%.
- **Inventory in the line** (WIP) reduced by 94%.
- Zero **quality problems**, which prevents complaints recurrence.
- **Space reduction** by 47%.

After thanking all the team, the CEO concluded: "During this week I have been able to prove that KAIZEN™ Events are the fastest and most effective way to implement improvement priorities. In five days, we were able to implement what would normally take us 5 months!"

In the weeks that followed, the project team met three more times to review follow up results and action plans. Now that the process was consolidated with all operators fully trained as per the new standards, it was possible to sustain a productivity increased by 38%.

4.3 Theory of Minimum Inventory

World Class Corporations have developed ways of maximising their free cash flow through a steady reduction in working capital. In a medium size business this usually means focusing on reducing inventory with the added benefit of improving service levels. The Theory of Minimum Inventory, also called TMI, is a fundamental methodology to achieve the reduction of working capital and the OTD improvement.

A very strong component of this theory is based on Little's Law, introduced by John D C Little. This law relates the average waiting time of items in a given stable system to the average number of items (inventory) and the average arrival rate of these items. In other words, it is possible to associate lead time to inventory for a given customer client demand:

Lead time = Inventory (units) / Customer Demand (units per time period)

By analysing this, it is easy to conclude that inventory reduction causes a lead time reduction and the possibility of serving the customer faster, leading to the OTD improvement.

This conclusion was proven by a study carried out in 251 companies, comparing the inventory turn over of each company and its respective OTD. It was found that no business could have high OTD to its customers with low inventory turns.

1 Work in progress (WIP): it refers to the on going inventory, goods partially finished and that are waiting for the processing to be completed.

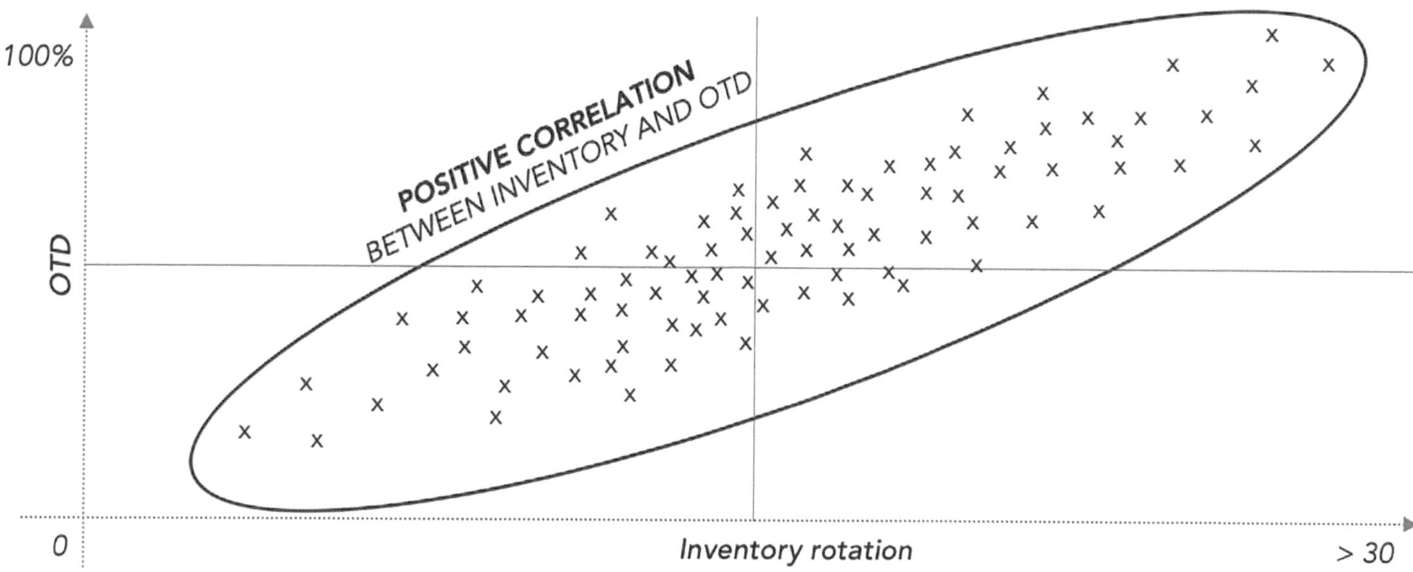

The chart above shows a positive relationship between these two indicators: an increase in inventory turnover leads to an increase in OTD.

FISH AND CHIPS AND INVENTORY

This is a true story that describes how inventory turnover is directly proportional to OTD. A common mistake is in not understanding that using large batches leads to high levels of inventory (low inventory turns) and a reduced customer service level.

Recently, a consultant who carried out a KAIZEN™ Event in a big company in the United Kingdom experienced a situation that describes this concept. It was Friday and in England this means fish and chips for lunch. The consultant walked to the canteen where there was a long queue to the front door and the Managing Director commented: "If you don't want fish and chips for lunch, we can go to the front of the line." As he looked at the queue, the consultant gave up on having fish and chips and settled down to the idea of having a salad.

When they were both seated, the consultant commented: "This endless queue is the perfect opportunity to implement KAIZEN™!"

The Managing Director was curious.

Every Friday the canteen prepared huge quantities of fish and chips for lunch, using large baskets in anticipation of the increased demand, but this made the whole process slower. Why? When the large baskets filled with potatoes were put into the frying oil, they made the temperature drop dramatically, which took a long time to reheat and to cook the contents. This process resulted in long waiting times and an already cold fish lunch was often handed over. This got worse, as more chips were fried, the greater the demand.

Many people in the line through that solution to this problem would be to get a larger fryer. But the truth is that the solution was exactly the opposite. When the consultant suggested using smaller baskets, most people thought he was being silly. In fact, there was a paradox. After some discussion, the large baskets were replaced with 6 smaller ones which, together, would take up the same space in the fryer. With this solution, whenever a small basket of potatoes needed to be fried and was placed into the fryer, it no longer caused a drastic drop in oil temperature. This way, small batches were produced, ensuring a constant production flow and guaranteeing hot chips whenever necessary.

On the following Friday everyone that had participated in the discussion couldn't wait for lunch time to check the results. For many, it was surprising to realise that the queue no longer existed, and a better piping hot meal was delivered. The moral of this story is the right change may seem like the wrong choice.

4.3.1 The TMI Framework

Sometime later, the consultant met with the Logistics Director to plan the TMI KAIZEN™ Event. The meeting was comprised of 4 team leaders from the Logistics and Materials Division from both industrial units. The consultant began by explaining that it would be necessary to prepare an ABC analysis of the raw materials inventory by value, as this would be critical for identifying opportunities to reduce inventory with the greatest financial impact and lowest effort for implementation.

"Usually, raw materials represent a large share of the total inventory value. Therefore, it is important to master a concept that, in KAIZEN™, we call 3PL (PPPL)." The consultant explained.

"Third Party Logistics?" The Materials Manager asked.

"No, I am referring to the variables Price, Pack size, Payment terms and Lead time," The consultant responded quickly before continuing. "From the KAIZEN™ perspective, I will explain the relevance of each of these terms to you."

1. **PRICE** - is the most obvious way of decreasing or increasing the inventory value.

2. **PACK SIZE** - is the most common way for suppliers to increase the volume of customers' inventory. The supplier always wants to provide the largest possible SKU (Stock Keeping Unit), they like to supply in whole units, namely one pallet, one box, etc.

3. **PAYMENT TERMS** - an easy way to create free cash flow is to extend payment terms. When you analyse payment terms it can be surprising to see that many suppliers have very beneficial payment terms compared to the industry

average. If there is no regular review of the supply chain, the terms and conditions can be in favour of the supplier.

4. **LEAD TIME** - represents the supplier's preferred delivery period and can have a drastic effect on the raw materials inventory. For example, if a company buys products from China, it is normal to have inventory values greater than 24 weeks.

"Now we need to prepare the 3PL profile for the main suppliers. And from here, you can be sure that we will find many opportunities to reduce our stock and create free cash flow." The consultant said.

The KAIZEN™ consultant then presented another fundamental concept in the implementation of the TMI, the Kanban system. This comes from the simplest visual management system for inventory restocking - the "empty box / full box" system. It was originally developed in the UK in Spitfire factories and became known as the "two box system". This concept was later applied in Toyota, when the company started to implement supermarkets for control and restocking of components inventory.

Kanban is a Japanese word that means card or sign, a term that has been used by Toyota to control production and transportation flows. Today, there are many ways to use this tool, but each Kanban typically identifies a batch that, when consumed, should lead to its replacement (pull system). The use of physical cards or digital replicas makes it easier to manage flows, and the visual control of inventory. Kanban always replenishes according to current demand. The signal, either physical or digital, indicates to the supplier that a new batch needs to be produced. These signals are monitored daily using visual management to show suppliers are delivering on time.

The TMI insures that Kanbans are applied to manage the supply of high value/high volume raw materials.

The next task was data collection and visual management that would support TMI implementation at ALFA's and the necessary documents were filled out with data.

1. **Inventory Value**
   The consultant explained that in this GEMBA a chart would be used to compare the current inventory level of ALFA's with the Hoshin objectives and the budget for each month.

2. **Pareto Chart of 'A' Items**
   This chart would present the high value items and the number of items on Kanban by suppliers.

3. **Inventory Bowling chart**
   Inventory value versus Budget versus Hoshin Objectives and current value in each month.

4. **Gross Inventory Value**
   This is used to register the monthly inventory value of raw materials, WIP and finished goods.

5. **Surplus and Obsolete Inventory**
   Classifying as surplus the inventory not used but ordered over the last 12 months, and as obsolete the inventory not used but ordered in the last 24 months, the relevant actual values relating to each month, compared with the estimated values are placed in this field.

6. **ABC Analysis of the raw materials SKUs**[2]
   The importance of the ABC analysis in TMI is to identify which SKU (normally 20% of the SKUs stand for 80% of the raw material inventory value) and separate them into class A, B and C items. With 'A becoming prime

targets for Kanbans. Also, the goals for batch size and replenishment lead time (delivery time forecast).

7. **Kanban Data**
   This is a primary cause of inventory reduction and will identify the number of SKUs where Kanban management has already been implemented, including smaller batch sizes and shorter replacement lead times (estimated delivery term). This calculator allows you to predict the minimum inventory levels based on reducing lead times. If suppliers deliver more often, we reduce the amount of inventory in the warehouse.

8. **Minimum inventory calculator**
   This field allows you to simulate the minimum inventory levels based on lead time reduction. It makes it clear that, if suppliers deliver more often, the quantity of inventory in storage is reduced, leaving you to calculate the optimum theoretical inventory and set improved supplier targets.

9. **Countermeasures**
   It is essential that root causes and their countermeasures for deviations in monthly inventory reduction objectives are immediately put into action should a deviation be spotted, and a physical countermeasure presented.

10. **Action plan**
    The purpose is to describe improvement initiatives for inventory reduction. Once again, the ABC value analysis is vital to identify the number of 'A' Class suppliers of raw materials. By using TMI we target suppliers to reduce lead times, with the application of Kanban and long-term supply contracts.

2 Stock-keeping unit (SKU): it refers to a specific stock item that is associated to a specific product reference.

After explaining the framework to be used in the TMI event, the consultant commented: "The important thing is to ensure that today all data is prepared for the intensive KAIZEN™ Event." He went on. "We also need to understand why in May we are close to reaching 1.7 million euros in Excesses and Obsoletes. It would be very useful to the Pareto to know what the main causes of the growth in E&O are."

Then, the consultant explained the new methodology to be followed, in order to reduce excess and obsolete inventory. This control would now become a basic part of the monthly meetings for the new product introduction. The purpose of this meeting was to integrate the Development Engineering, Value Engineering and Inventory Management team Managers to follow a process of controlling and reducing the number of SKUs in ALFA's inventory.

In conclusion, and after selecting the team, the consultant addressed his speech to the Logistics Director:
"We need to share with your teams, before starting the KAIZEN™ Event, that ALFA has a serious problem of excess inventory. This will lead to radical changes in the purchasing and procurement processes, and this will need to happen very quickly."

After the preparation session, everyone had some tasks that would necessarily have to be completed in preparation for the workshop the following week.

4.3.2 The TMI Event

"This is an event that requires you to focus on a very specific theme: The reduction of inventory at ALFA! In the coming days we will define the Action Plan that will allow us to eliminate the adverse deviation of 1.4 million euros against our goal in Hoshin." The Director of Logistics explained, in a lively way. "Over the next few days, which will be intense, we will need to implement a set of actions which turns the elimination of this gap over the next 3 months into a reality."

The consultant began the workshop with a presentation of the methodology that underpins the TMI and quickly shared the Templates, already populated with current data and inventory values from the two industrial units. He asked one of the Materials Managers to explain in detail the concept of the document, and its contents. In the room there were the key people from both ALFA Logistics and Materials teams, as well as some members of the Executive Committee who were keen to participate in this KAIZEN™ Event.

TMI FRAMEWORK

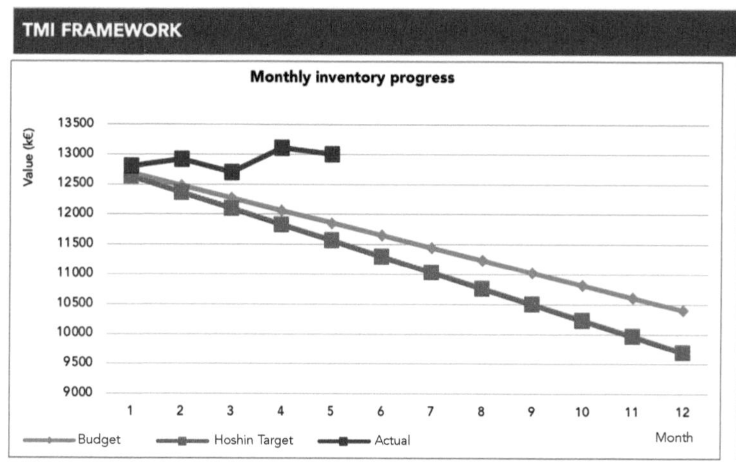

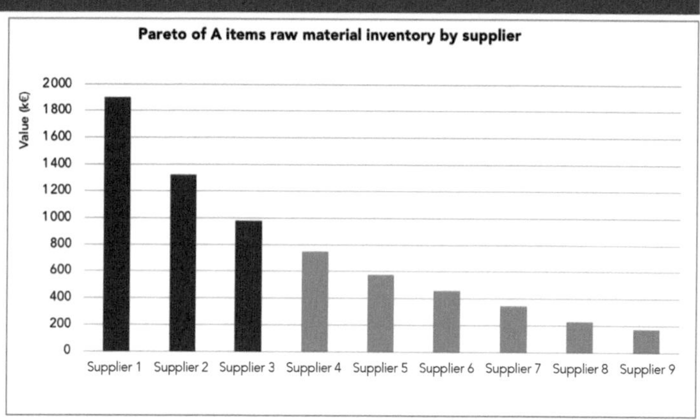

TMI framework (1st part)

Total inventory k€	End of the year	Jan	Feb	Mar	Apr	May	Jun	Jul	Aug	Sep	Oct	Nov	Dec
Budget	12 895	12 692	12 483	12 275	12 067	11 858	11 650	11 442	11 233	11 025	11 025	11 025	11 025
Hoshin target		12 633	12 367	12 100	11 833	11 567	11 300	11 033	10 767	10 500	10 500	10 500	10 500
Actual	12 895	12 809	12 920	12 700	13 112	13 000							
Variation vs. Hoshin		176	554	600	1 279	1 434							
Raw material	9 026	8 966	9 044	8 890	9 178	9 100							
WIP	1 289	1 281	1 292	1 270	1 311	1 300							
Finished Goods	2 579	2 562	2 584	2 540	2 622	2 600							
E & O - financial provision	960	80	80	80	80	80	80	80	80	80	80	80	80
E & O - actual	1 436	1 569	1 578	1 588	1 679	1 680							
E & O - variation vs. provision	476	529	458	388	399	320							

Labour days/year 240

Raw material	Total # SKU	# Kanban SKU	# SKU w/ target leat time	# SKU w/ target batch sice	Annual consump-tion (k€)	Value of current inventory	Ideal value (k€)	Difference ideal vs. actual (k€)	Current inventory turns	Inventory turnover target	Current inventory days	Lead time supply target	Difference target vs. actual	Average consumpti-on/day (k€)
A Items	117	13	2	1	32 226	6 734	3 357	3 377	4.8	9.6	50	25	25.2	134
B Items	141	0	0	0	6 042	1 729	881	848	3.5	6.9	46	35	33.7	25
C Items	226	0	0	0	2 014	637	319	318	3.2	6.3	41	38	37.9	8
Total	484	13	2	1	40 283	9 100	4 557	4 543	4.4	8.8	54		54.2	168
	% total	3%	0%	0%										

TMI framework (2nd part)

The presented data referred to the months between January and May of Year 1 and the main outputs identified were:

- Raw material value = € 9.1 million euros.
- Surplus and Obsoletes value = € 1.7 million euros (€800k + €900k, respectively).
- 'A' class items = € 6.7 million euros (117 SKUs).
- 'A' class raw materials items with Kanban system = 13 SKUs.
- 'A' class raw material items on standard lead time = 2 SKUs.
- 'A' class raw materials items on standard batch size = 1 SKU.

There was already an atmosphere of discomfort and surprise in the room. The Materials Manager said: "With this Kaizen Institute approach, it is clear how important it is to properly manage our suppliers. All together, we will have to decide, using the TMI methodology, what actions to take in order to reach our goal of releasing 1.4 million euros of inventory."

The Materials Manager continued the explanation, while pointing out the projected values:

"At present, we have 6.7 million euros of inventory only in items 'A' of raw materials, i.e., 117 SKUs. Which means, we have to concentrate on these references. Notice what happens if we reduce the lead time from 50 to 25 days."

Raw material	Total # SKU	Annual Consumption (k€)	Value of Current inventory
A Items	117	32 226	6 734
B Items	141	6 042	1 729
C Items	226	2 014	637
Total	484	40 283	9 100

After changing this data in the inventory calculator, he said. "Look: we released 3.4 million euros! This totally convinces me of the importance that lead time can have on the supply chain. What we need to determine is our lead time 'TARGETS'."

Raw material	Difference actual vs. ideal (k€)	Current inventory turns	Inventory turnover target	Days of current inventory turns	Lead time supply target	Difference target vs. actual	Average consumption/day (k€)
A Items	3 377	4.8	9.6	50	25	25.2	134
B Items	848	3.5	6.9	69	35	33.7	25
C Items	318	3.2	6.3	76	38	37.9	8
Total	4 543	4.4	8.8	54		54.2	168

The team simulated several lead time scenarios in order to figure out the changes that this would make in the total inventory value. After a few adjustments, they easily identified what would be the target lead time to achieve a 1.4 million euro reduction. Gradually, they were all getting excited and testing the simulator with ever shorter lead times.

The consultant intervened:
"Now that we have seen how small changes in the supply time results in large impacts in inventory, we must realise how this will affect our suppliers. The next task is to find the easiest and quickest way to reach our goal." He paused to let the team think about the possible alternatives.

The team promptly concluded that there were two options considered valid:

- **Option 1:** to reduce small-scale lead times with all 'A' class suppliers.
- **Option 2:** to reduce lead time on a large scale in some of the 'A' class suppliers.

The next step was to scrutinise the result of calculating the annual purchase value of 'A' item raw materials, for each of the suppliers. Everyone quickly realised that the top three suppliers represented 50% of the annual purchase values, made in 73 out of 117 'A' class SKUs. After some calculation, it was verified that if these 3 suppliers reduced the average delivery lead time by half, i.e., from 50 to 25 days, it would be possible to reduce inventory by more than 2.1 million euros. These conclusions made everyone feel more confident.

4.3.3 TMI Action Plan

They continued with the Action Plan definition in the Kanban system implementation for the 3 main suppliers. Actions were defined to negotiate new contracts with those suppliers, to perform replenishment according standard batch dimensions and delivery times of each Kanban. The goal was to conclude the plan by the end of the following month.

ACTION PLAN

Breakthrough activities: implement a Kanban system in the A items top 3 suppliers.

Top suppliers out of the Lead Time target

	Supplier	# SKUs			Annual Consumption A items (k€)	Current Lead Time			Actions	Impact (k€)	Who	When
		A	B	C		A	B	C				
1	Supplier 1	33	25	-	9 089	49	-	-	Define the contract model with Kanban; validate plan to place 33 SKU with Kanban and a 25-day Lead Time supply.	953	Purcha-sing	jul
2	Supplier 2	23	11	-	6 335	52	-	-	Define the contract model with Kanban; validate plan to place 23 SKU with Kanban and a 25-day Lead Time supply.	664	Purcha-sing	aug
3	Supplier 3	17	35	-	4 682	55	-	-	Define the contract model with Kanban; validate plan to place 17 SKU with Kanban and a 25-day Lead Time supply.	491	Purcha-sing	sep
4	Supplier 4	13	25	-	3 581	39	-	-				
5	Supplier 5	10	18	-	2 754	55	-	-				
6	Supplier 6	8	10	-	2 203	51	-	-				
7	Supplier 7	6	8	-	1 653	44	-	-				
8	Supplier 8	4	7	-	1 102	45	-	-				
9	Supplier 9	3	2	-	826	57	-	-				
		117	**141**		**32 226**					**2 107**		

4.3.4 Year 1 TMI Results

The results of the TMI application were clear at the end of Year 1. It was possible to achieve a reduction of over € 2.1 million in raw material inventories and to reach the Hoshin's target for December. In view of these results, it became clear that in the following years, ALFA should extend the implementation of the Kanban system to the remaining 'A' class suppliers, continuing to reduce lead times, thereby contributing to the achievement of free cash flow objectives. These are just two of the KAIZEN™ Events held at ALFA's throughout the first year of Hoshin implementation. Their description intends not only to present in detail the implementation of methodologies relevant to the improvement of the company's performance, but also to describe the dynamics of the workshops as intensive, integrative and highly focused work sessions.

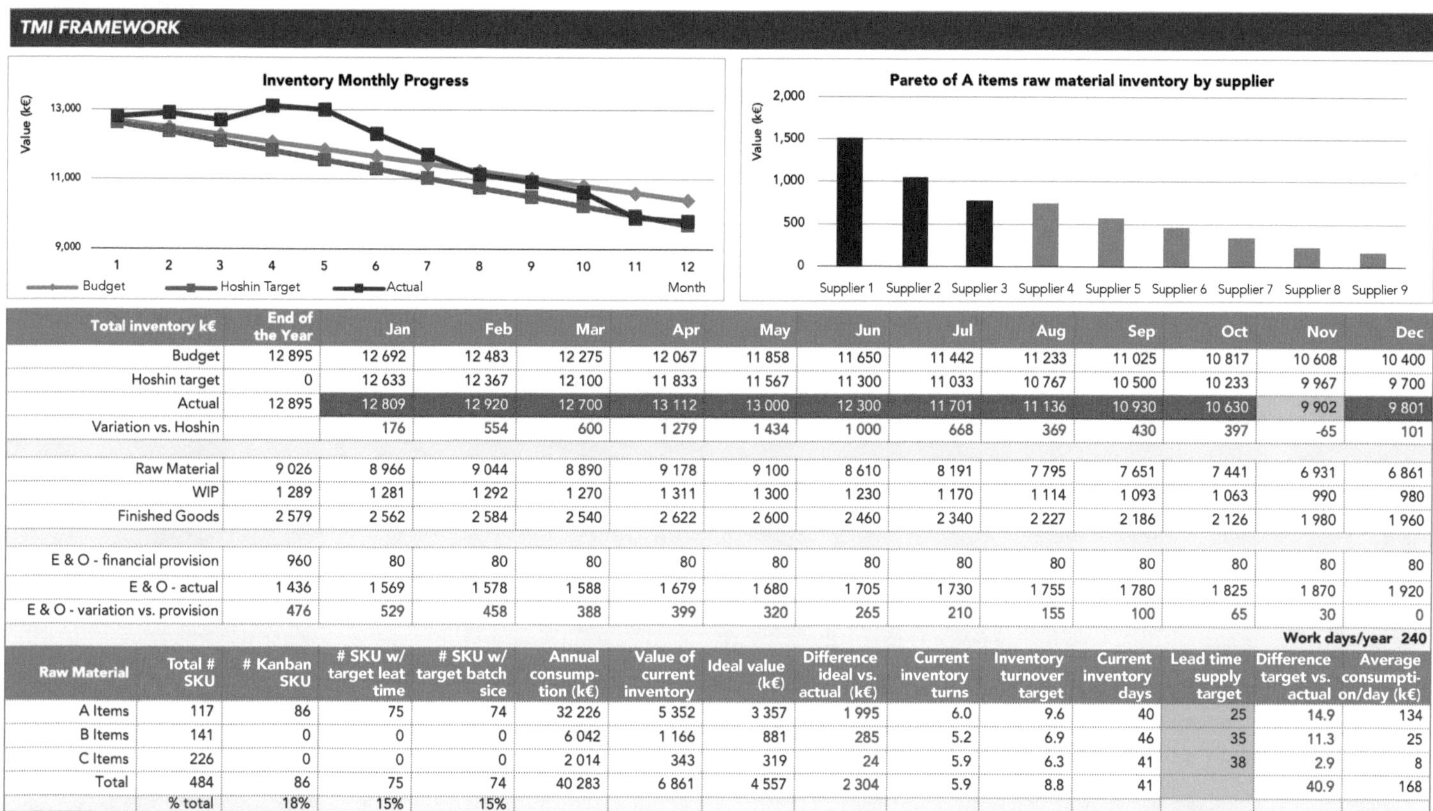

Total inventory k€	End of the Year	Jan	Feb	Mar	Apr	May	Jun	Jul	Aug	Sep	Oct	Nov	Dec
Budget	12 895	12 692	12 483	12 275	12 067	11 858	11 650	11 442	11 233	11 025	10 817	10 608	10 400
Hoshin target	0	12 633	12 367	12 100	11 833	11 567	11 300	11 033	10 767	10 500	10 233	9 967	9 700
Actual	12 895	12 809	12 920	12 700	13 112	13 000	12 300	11 701	11 136	10 930	10 630	9 902	9 801
Variation vs. Hoshin		176	554	600	1 279	1 434	1 000	668	369	430	397	-65	101
Raw Material	9 026	8 966	9 044	8 890	9 178	9 100	8 610	8 191	7 795	7 651	7 441	6 931	6 861
WIP	1 289	1 281	1 292	1 270	1 311	1 300	1 230	1 170	1 114	1 093	1 063	990	980
Finished Goods	2 579	2 562	2 584	2 540	2 622	2 600	2 460	2 340	2 227	2 186	2 126	1 980	1 960
E & O - financial provision	960	80	80	80	80	80	80	80	80	80	80	80	80
E & O - actual	1 436	1 569	1 578	1 588	1 679	1 680	1 705	1 730	1 755	1 780	1 825	1 870	1 920
E & O - variation vs. provision	476	529	458	388	399	320	265	210	155	100	65	30	0

Work days/year 240

Raw Material	Total # SKU	# Kanban SKU	# SKU w/ target leat time	# SKU w/ target batch sice	Annual consump-tion (k€)	Value of current inventory	Ideal value (k€)	Difference ideal vs. actual (k€)	Current inventory turns	Inventory turnover target	Current inventory days	Lead time supply target	Difference target vs. actual	Average consumpti-on/day (k€)
A Items	117	86	75	74	32 226	5 352	3 357	1 995	6.0	9.6	40	25	14.9	134
B Items	141	0	0	0	6 042	1 166	881	285	5.2	6.9	46	35	11.3	25
C Items	226	0	0	0	2 014	343	319	24	5.9	6.3	41	38	2.9	8
Total	484	86	75	74	40 283	6 861	4 557	2 304	5.9	8.8	41		40.9	168
	% total	18%	15%	15%										

Chapter 5

The relationship between Daily KAIZEN™ and Breakthrough KAIZEN™ is symbiotic in that Breakthrough KAIZEN™ needs Daily KAIZEN™ to turn breakthroughs into today's best standard, which sustains breakthrough thinking. Furthermore, an organisation that only applies Daily KAIZEN™ will eliminate incremental variability but will not deliver large double-digit results because it does not act on the larger value stream.

This chapter aims to present Daily KAIZEN™ as a crucial program to the successful implementation and sustainability of the breakthrough actions in an organisation.

5.1 The Importance of the Daily KAIZEN™ in the Hoshin

There was a feeling of great anticipation at ALFA's first implementation session of Daily KAIZEN™. Before work began, the conversation was that, despite the good results of the JIT KAIZEN™ Event, there were still opportunities to reduce variability.

The consultant began by exploring the first point on the agenda, which aimed at identifying and clarifying the role of the Daily KAIZEN™:
"Daily KAIZEN™ is an improvement tool used within a natural team to implement continuous improvement in their own areas or departments. This training enables teams to daily maintain and improve their processes. Through a structured implementation of Daily KAIZEN™ you will be able to understand and act on the causes of variation that occur in daily work. This Daily Management is essential for Hoshin Planning in that **today's Breakthrough** must become **tomorrow's Standards**; without this mechanism the breakthroughs cannot be sustained."

The consultant went on explaining the implementation method: "Daily KAIZEN™ follows a bottom up approach and aims to develop leaders' skills to teach, guide and motivate their teams to continuously improve. This program consists of 4 levels which will be implemented in about 12 months, as can be seen in the roadmap." The team observed the projected roadmap, while the consultant continued to speak. "Now, let's briefly go through the approach for each of these levels, and after that we will start implementing level 1 with an ENNIS line pilot team."

"Sounds great! Let's do it!" the Operations Director said, who had come to participate on the first day of the event, and was trying to encourage his team.

5.2 Daily KAIZEN™ Steps

The 4-implementation levels of this model deliver, in a structured way, the development of people and the sustainability of the improvement of the organisation. At each level the teams are required to have a higher capability to reduce variation by applying Continuous Improvement.

5.2.1 Level 1: Daily Management

How should Daily Management be practiced in an organisation? According to the KAIZEN™ vision, management requires the establishment of routines to follow-up progress, work planning, and communication. The Daily KAIZEN™ Level 1 key tool consists of frequent meetings (possibly on a daily basis) between leaders and their teams. Standardised information , displayed in a visual or digital form, is then analysed regarding performance, organisation and improvement actions. The daily team meeting objectives are work plan delivery, analysis of deviations and implementing countermeasures. This is the backbone of a Daily KAIZEN™.

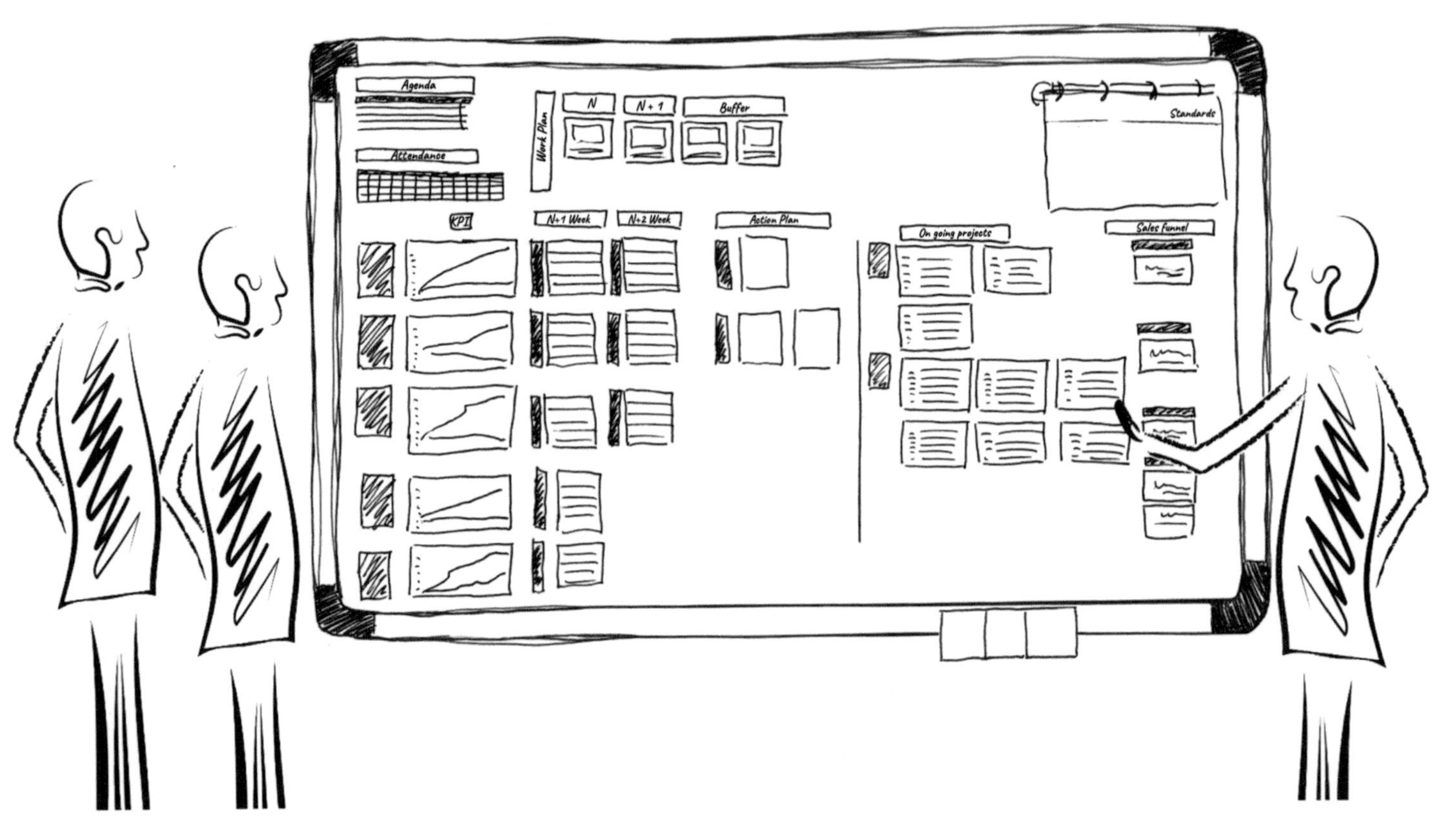

Each work team has a set of behaviours that determine overall performance. For example, the execution of an operational procedure when changing one reference to another on a certain machine should be 30 minutes, this being an operational procedure intended to be kept for a certain operational team of workers. When this happens, the setup will be analysed and root causes identified. With the team leader taking responsibility for countermeasures implementation.

The Daily KAIZEN™ Level 1 aims to identify a team's key behaviours, in order to support and improve performance incrementally by defining metrics that show progress and follow-up measures.

The importance of this follow-up can easily be understood through a real-life example. Imagine that there is a boat trip planned to an island in 4 days. There is a captain (leader), the crew (team members) and navigation instruments as well as provisions.

If the captain only checked the position on the last day, he would realise that the boat is not going to reach the island and a large course correction would be necessary. By then the captain would not be able to identify the cause of the deviation; strong winds, tides or bad planning.

However if the captain checks the boat's position more often, the deviation will be less, and it will be easier to identify the cause and act accordingly. Ideally, the captain should check position regularly and implement countermeasures to correct possible deviations from the planned course.

For that reason, the captain must have the right navigation instruments (visual information) and a standard way to communicate with the team. Thus, the successful arrival of the boat to the intended destination becomes a certainty.

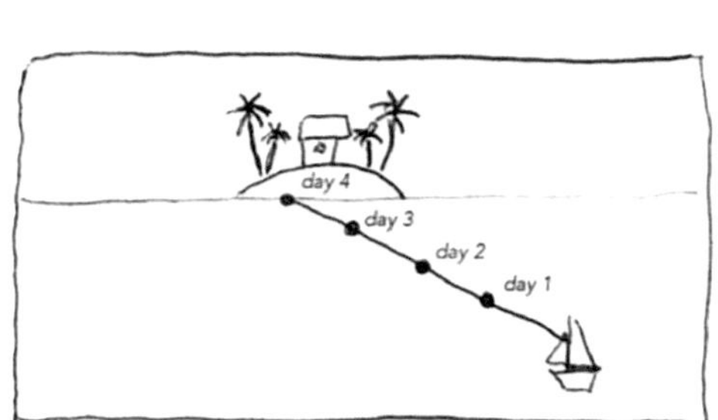

A SHIP TRIP USUALLY TAKES 4 DAYS

The captain checks the course **after 4 days**

Trip duration: 7 DAYS

The captain checks the course **everyday**

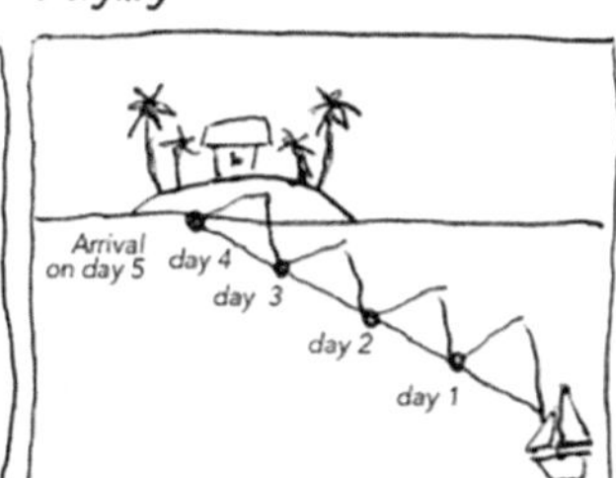

Trip duration: 5 DAYS

The captain checks the course **every hour**

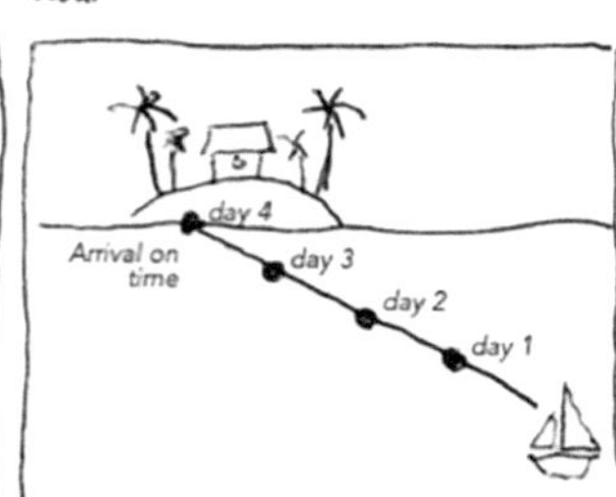

Trip duration: 4 DAYS

5.2.2 Level 2: Digital and Physical Spaces Organisation

Take the example of an individual who decides to have lunch at a freeway Service Station. Before his meal, he goes to the bathroom to wash his hands. However, when he pulls the paper towel to dry them, dozens of other towels fall to the ground. In this situation, if the floor is visible dirty and already has other paper towels on it, most people would ignore them and leave, taking no action. But if the same person goes for lunch in a good hotel the next day and, by unfortunate coincidence, the episode repeats itself, but at that time the bathroom floor is found clean, what would his behaviour be? The truth is that, under these circumstances, about 90% of people would pick up the paper and look for the appropriate container to deposit it, even if they were alone.

So, what motivates the same individual to adopt a different behaviour in similar situations? Why is it that the same person, faced with the same problem, has a different behaviour? The answer is simple: the environment where individuals are inserted conditions their behaviour.

Daily KAIZEN™ Level 2 aims to begin by positively conditioning individuals' behaviour. Changing physical or digital workspaces makes easier, in the first instance, changing people's behaviour and allowing the elimination of time spent on searching for materials or information, improving information management and reducing costs through better use of materials and equipment. This tool is called 5S.

Those who know the japanese business world also know that managers give special importance to 5S.

At first, this seems hard to understand. Typically, japanese people explain the importance of the tool through a very practical example: when a man wakes up every morning and he notices that he has developed a fever, what does he conclude? That he is sick, of course. When transposing the same situation to the business world, the japanese ask themselves how they can quickly understand if the "organisation is sick".

Assuming that respect for "cleaning and organisation" standards is the easiest task to be abandoned by employees, this can be a rapid way to identify whether the standards (quality, security, productivity) are being followed. The 5S is a fundamental tool for managers to understand if their organisation is "feverish", if there is the discipline needed to maintain standards that ensure the expected results.

5S is a working organisational method performed in 5 steps, in which every step begins with an "S" in the original Japanese language of its creation. It can be applied to physical or digital spaces:

1. ***SEIRI*** (Sort): separate the necessary from the unnecessary.
2. ***SEITON*** (Organise): put essential things in order so that they can be accessed easily.
3. ***SEISO*** (Clean): clean everything - tools and workplaces - removing stains, spots and debris and eradicating sources of dirt.
4. ***SEIKETSU*** (Standardise): make cleaning and checking routine.
5. ***SHITSUKE*** (Discipline): standardise the preceding four steps to make the process one that never ends and can be improved further.

5.2.3 Level 3: Standardisation

Standardisation is an undervalued concept, perhaps due to its simplicity. Many people are not able to define the most efficient method for performing a given task. They assume that all people, once "trained", will be able to perform their work in the best possible way.

A typical example used when describing this concept is when a KAIZEN™ consultant was speaking to the person in charge of a team of precision steel components, who was being constantly interrupted with questions from the machine operator who wanted to ask him questions about the correct tolerance and the quality of the finish to be applied to each component.

In face of constant interruptions, the consultant decided to challenge him: "As far as I can see, you are irreplaceable. If you miss one day, your production line won't fabricate anything and the factory will come to a stop!

The area leader added at once: "Exactly! I cannot miss a day. And for your information, I have never missed a single day in the past 20 years."

"Yes, but you can never be promoted either. By being irreplaceable, you have remained and will always remain in the same position for the next 20 years. A person can only be promoted when he teaches others how to do their work and becomes available to do more challenging tasks"- the consultant commented regarding the responsible person thoughtful posture.

A week later, when the consultant returned to meet this team leader, he was surprised with the reaction: "I want to know when I will get a promotion! I am already replaceable. I taught my team how to do my job and now I am ready to move on."

The team leader had placed a standard on all machines in his working area, allowing every operator to set up all the matchining tolerances and finishes to fabricate Quality Assured components on their own. It had taken him 20 years to understand that good standardisation made it possible to release team leaders from doing operational tasks, enabling them to focus in more added value functions.

Daily KAIZEN™ Level 3 aims to introduce study and work standardisation routines that must be implemented in each team to continuously eliminate waste, variability and overload; all concepts that in KAIZEN™ are respectively called **MUDA, MURA** and **MURI**.

This level focuses on improving existing methods, creating or updating standards, and training employees. Standards also serve as a reference to identify deviations, feeding problem solving. On most occasions, teams solve their problems based on a trial and error approach, also called the "sticking plaster" approach, where they only act partially on effects using containment measures. In order to solve the problem completely, a structured problem-solving approach should be adopted, which seeks to identify and solve the root causes, avoiding their recurrence. The simplest tool to be used is the so-called 3C (originally **Case, Cause** and **Countermeasure**). It consists of 4 steps: problem definition, root causes analysis, countermeasures identification and verification of solutions.

Some managers advocate that one of the differentiating factors of their organisation is people's creativity. Ask yourself this question then: should an organisation have two people doing the same task differently? Is this the result of the creativity we are seeking? The answer is NO. If there are two people performing the same task, however differently, at least one of them is not performing it more efficiently or more safely. In this context, the organisation has scope for improvement, if it trains people to perform the task according to the best practices known so far. At the end of the process, teams have a higher level of autonomy, versatility and efficiency.

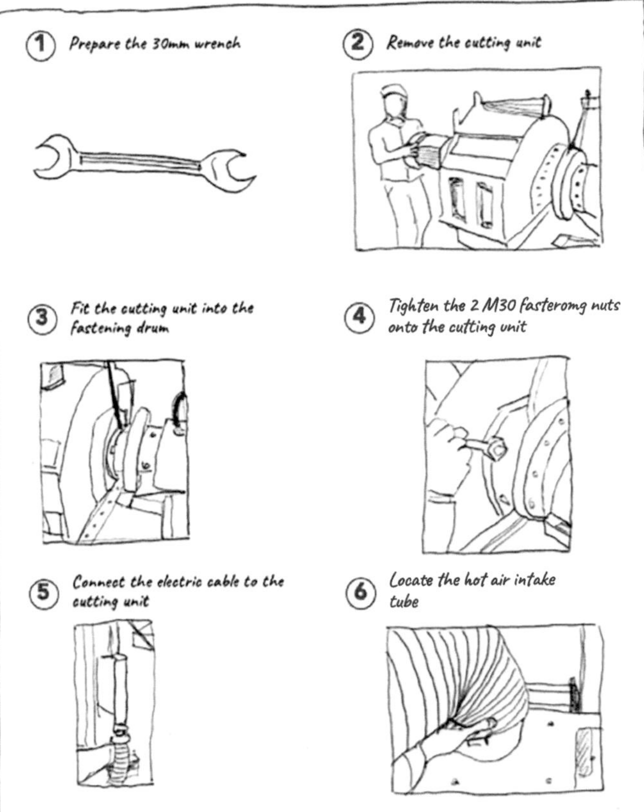

5.2.4 Level 4: Process Improvement

In order to increase the efficiency of a bottle filling line in a given industrial unit, a KAIZEN™ Event was carried out in the presence of a multidisciplinary team composed of Quality, Process, and Production Engineering members, including the filling line operator, close to retiring, who also performed general line maintenance tasks.

Using a Pareto diagram, the causes of micro stoppages (stoppages of less than 5 minutes) were identified as the main cause of the low OEE on the line. The bottle height variation was identified as the root cause since, although every bottle went through an electronic and visual control, they often failed. If a bottle went to the filling unit the machine had to be stopped for manual removal, which stopped the line for a few minutes. The Engineering team defended the need for a technological solution, with the introduction of a laser sensor fitted onto a pneumatic auto ejector which, if an irregular height were identified, would automatically remove the bottle. This would reduce the machine stoppages from a few minutes to just a few seconds. Meanwhile, the line operator and maintenance technician had come up with another idea that, in their opinion, would solve the problem. Finally, the consultant asked everyone to listen to the alternative proposal: to simply put a tight fishing line across the filling line at a height slightly higher than the required height of the bottle. So that, whenever a taller bottle touched the line, it would be knocked over and would be removed by the existing reject ramp already built into the machine whenever a bottle fell over. Despite the initial scepticism of the rest of the team, the solution was promptly implemented, and its success proven. Over the following week there were no micro stoppages recorded on that line. Its implementation proved to be quick and investment-free. And while everyone was convinced that this would be a temporary alternative, the truth is that it continued to be applied to the same machine for another 4 years until it was dismantled.

Level 4 has as its main goal, the setting up of improvement and problem-preventing routines within natural teams, thus ensuring the ultimate purpose of Daily KAIZEN™: to make teams capable of sustaining and improving their processes, on a daily basis. This is developed in two phases. Firstly, teams work on the identification and development of autonomous quality means to make processes "bulletproof" and, secondly, they are trained in the method of approaching more complex problems: Improvement Kata[1].

Autonomous automatic quality inspection procedures, Poka-yoke[2] and Jidoka[3] concepts, and Statistical Process Control are developed to address the major failure modes identified by teams. The goal is not to receive, create or pass defects along to the next process in the value chain.

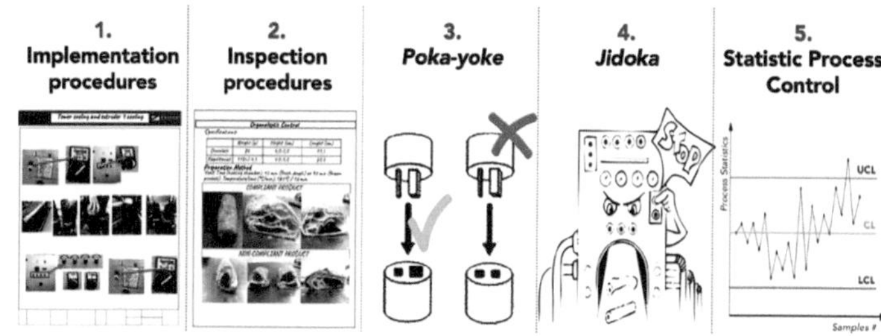

1 Kata means standard of behaviour and, within KAIZEN™, refers to Improvement Kata and Coaching Kata. The first is a 4-step routine by which an organisation improves and adapts, and the second is the routine by which team leaders and managers guide the process of improvement.

2 Jidoka: also called autonomation, this system immediately stops the process when a problem first occurs, leveraging improvements.

3 *Poka-yoke:* low cost, error-proof device designed to avoid the occurrence of defects in a process.

With Improvement Kata, the focus for improvement is directed toward a target state, deployed from a challenge (ideally by Hoshin). Teams work on the elimination of obstacles, incorporating the lessons learned from the previous step in an interactive way. This improvement process is supported by coaching sessions led by the top management: Coaching Kata.

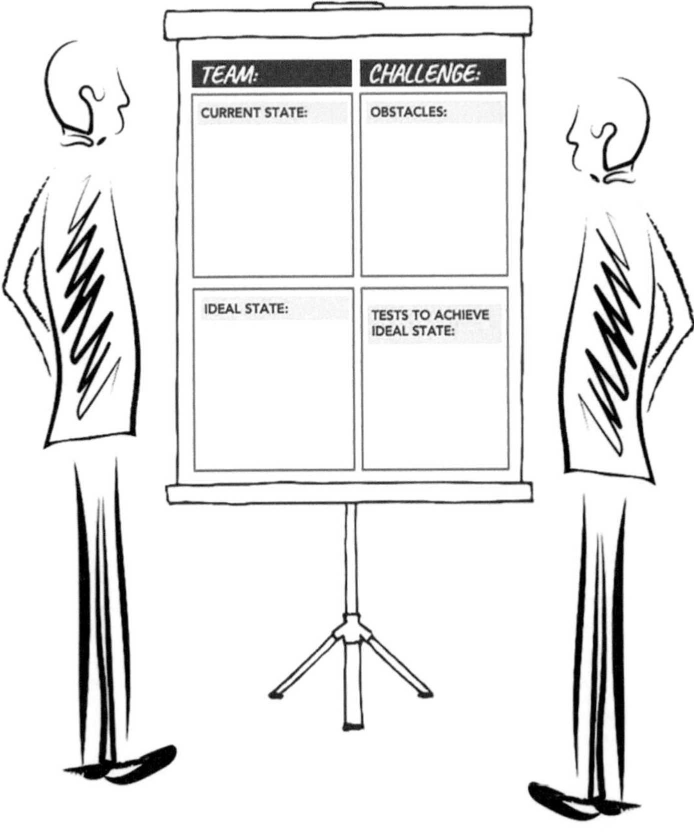

5.3 Daily KAIZEN™ Implementation Kick-Off

After a brief explanation of the different levels of Daily KAIZEN™, the consultant informed everyone that they would start implementing the first level in a pilot team. It would thus be necessary to form working groups focused on the different elements of the team that they would build.

The exercise was carried out by applying the four-corner method, where each group would take some time to draw their proposal on a flipchart arranged in one of the four corners of the room. At the signal of the consultant, the groups would run to the next corner to verify and complement the previous group's proposal. The first interaction of each group was the one where they had the most time available to discuss and put ideas on paper.

The consultant explained: "We need a group that thinks about team standards and sets the agenda for the meeting; another group to define QCD indicators (Quality, Cost and Delivery Service); yet another group that builds the team work plan; and finally, another group to be focused on the improvement cycle and already presenting some suggestions of actions that can be implemented by the pilot team."

Everyone quickly prepared the room so that all groups had at least one member of the pilot team who could contribute to more specific issues in their daily routines. By the end of the exercise, and after a 360 degree rotation, each group presented the final proposal represented on their flipchart.

After all the elements of the Visual Management Board had been discussed, the team members, with the aid of laptops and a printer, stationary, laminating machines and coloured adhesive tape, began to assemble the final version of the Daily Visual Management.

"When it's finished, will we take it to our workplace?" The pilot team leader asked. The consultant agreed and informed them that, prior to the end of the workshop, it would be fundamental to simulate the first team meeting.

"Yes, I agree! So, the consultant will be able to share important tips with us during the meeting, and the remaining team leaders will be able to take notes which can help with their own implementation." the Plant Manager intervened, enthusiastically.

The day after, the board was finished and appropriately placed. Then, with everyone present, the first meeting of the pilot team was held. There were some difficulties in filling the indicators and in achieving the agenda - constraints that the consultant knew to be normal in the first iterations.

The Operations Director and the CEO, invited to attend the first team meeting of this new model, were pleased with what they saw and exchanged comments with each other:

"They are all participating and enthusiastic about the goals they set for the indicators. And they continue to give suggestions for improvement." the CEO commented, visibly pleased. "Honestly, this is the first time I have seen this level of involvement in my operational teams. Look! They are even looking at the numbers and discussing them! Usually, only the Team Leader was concerned about results."

The consultant, who had heard the comments, took the opportunity to conclude:
"This program will allow not only better communication and alignment between teams, but also an efficient distribution of the workload, a faster reaction to performance deviations and an increase in leadership skills. And this will be deployed to the whole organisation."

The importance of Daily KAIZEN™ in Hoshin's implementation and support was, by then, clear to every single participant in the workshop. The coming months would serve to implement the remaining levels of this improvement program.

Daily KAIZEN™ is therefore a structured process which, through the application of simple tools, can support improvements implemented in the organisation, ensuring the maintenance of good results. Teams become more autonomous in their daily control of performance indicators, correction of deviations and problem solving.

The next chapter presents the importance of and the way of acting quickly on identified deviations.

Countermeasure Culture

Building a Countermeasure Culture - The Hoshin Impact

This chapter will give you insights on how to coach your team for them to take the initiative, to be proactive and confident in delivering the Stretched Goals. This will be leadership-intensive and you will have to take every opportunity to coach your team in every meeting, Gemba walk or general review.

Regarding the creation of a Culture of Countermeasures, the leader must be seen as the promoter and coach of how to define "Exceptional Countermeasures". The leader is not required to do the work, but to help the team to detect complex situations in order to make clear what has to be done. Leaders need to be deeply aware of the Countermeasures process and this will only be possible by leading the team and "learning by doing".

We will go step by step into what makes a good countermeasure, and this will become your template for the future. As a first insight you should always review the countermeasure process and not the results, the best coaching opportunities are when there is an error or misunderstanding in using the process, this is your opportunity to share your experience with the team letting them know that you have also tripped up in some similar situation.

1 GEMBA Walk: standard observation practice in GEMBA, for process confirmation and verification of behaviors to be improved.

6.1 The Origins of a Countermeasure Culture

The greatness of Toyota and the "Toyota Production System" has been built on the leadership driving the organisation through a strong countermeasure culture.

Some experts have suggested that the "Toyota Production System" was in itself a Countermeasure to Japan's needs in the post war period. When Taichi Ohno with Eiji Toyoda wanted to build a successful production model at Toyota, they took American industry as an example, and set the goal of matching its levels of productivity and profitability. However, their main constraint was that they didn't have the same volumes of demand. Ohno's countermeasure was to create an efficient manufacturing model with more flexibility and less dependency on volume. Today, this countermeasure, developed in the 1950's, is known as TPS - "Toyota Production System".

Ohno tells how there was great resistance to the two fundamental pillars of TPS "Just in Time" and "Jidoka "and since its introduction much of the KAIZEN™ Events done at Toyota's can be seen as countermeasures against threats and situations that it faces every day. In essence, Countermeasures and Continuous Improvement have the same aim, i.e. to attain perfection.

The question you are most probably asking right now is "are countermeasures just problem solving but with another name"? No, countermeasure and problem-solving may use many of the same tools to gather data, organise facts and create action plans, but there are also some fundamental and yet subtle differences.

Problem Solving, in any of its forms, is intended to identify the root causes of a problem to eliminate them, and thereby reducing their negative impact on the process, product, or service. Classical Problem-Solving tools, such as the 5 Whys, Cause and Effect Diagram, Analytical Trouble Shooting, A3 Problem Solving, and increasingly digital interactive solutions, all share this goal. However, the application of Countermeasures presents a slight difference.

Countermeasures have a subtle difference. Ohno realised that it was often hard to be able to get to the root cause. In fact, it was a difficult exercise almost every time. He was aware that there were too many different variables running in a normal business and to find one or all the root causes in order to develop the perfect fix would be time consuming. His approach was to continuously look for improvement, developing the "Best Method of Today", another way of saying that a countermeasure needs to correct the trend or poor performance quickly, even when the preventive action may not be immediately clear because all the root causes are buried deep.

Problem Solving Approach vs Countermeasures

Problem solving is a way of thinking that considers the permanent resolution of problems and Countermeasures are a flexible view of the "Best Method of Today". In the Toyota Production System most Actions, KAIZEN™ Events, Services Improvements and Process Improvement can be considered to be countermeasures rather than permanent fixes. This has been built around Deming's teachings of Plan, Do, Check, Act, which drives Continuous Improvement and promotes the Kaizen ideal of change Every day, Everyone, Everywhere. Problem Solving, on the other hand, can be seen as a ridged project sort of activity that has a beginning and an end, and that can be data intensive and long winded, looking for the perfect solution.

So now we find ourselves facing a dilemma: you could read into this that countermeasures only focus on Effect and not Cause; countermeasures are the course corrections necessary to keep us on the right track. Where the Problem Solving philosophy drives us to examine the effect to find the root causes and to eliminate them, we must remember the complexity and variability of both internal and external factors that are constantly changing and which can cause the re-emergence of the problem.

The pragmatic approach is to "make the best process for today's standard" and to continuously look for improvement. This gives us greater flexibility to react quickly whenever needed, and we can always return and continue to make improvements.

This Countermeasure Culture promotes a wide range of learning opportunities within teams rather than just remedying the problem and moving forward. The application of a Countermeasure seeks to implement improvements in a quick way, without having to wait for the perfect solution, which may take an indefinite time. In this way, gains have already been achieved before repeating another improvement cycle that always seeks to go deeper.

The reasons why Ohno adopted this approach can be directly attributed to his "teachers" - Deming and Juran.

William Edwards Deming - *was an American engineer, who in 1947 went to Japan as part of the US occupation at the behest of General Douglas MacArthur who grew frustrated at being unable to complete so much as a phone call without the line going dead due to Japan's shattered post-war economy. While in Japan, Deming's expertise in quality-control techniques earned him an invitation from the Japanese Union of Scientists and Engineers. Deming's message to JUSE and Japan's chief executives was that improving quality would reduce costs, while increasing productivity and market share. A number of Japanese manufacturers applied his PDCA techniques widely and experienced unheard-of levels of quality and productivity improvements. The improved quality combined with the lowered costs created a new international demand for Japanese products.*

The Deming Wheel or PDCA cycle was an adaption of the Shewhart Cycle developed in the 1920's that, over time, eventually evolved into Plan-Do-Study-Act (PDSA) cycle. It is generally accepted that Deming taught the Japanese in the 1950's how to use and apply "The PDCA Continuous Improvement Cycle" illustrated below.

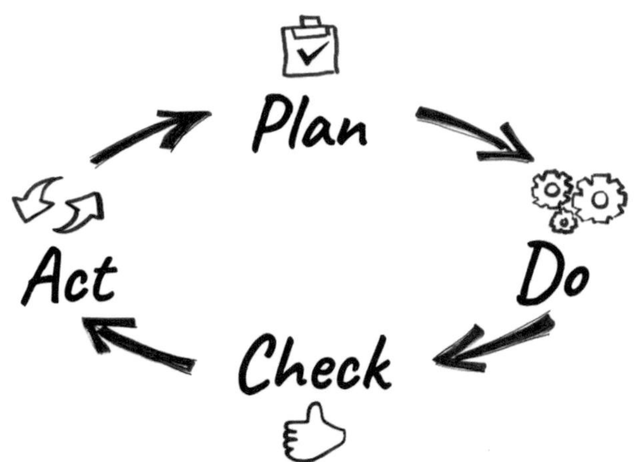

Joseph Moses Juran - *was a Romanian-born American engineer and management consultant. He was an evangelist for quality and quality management. At end of World War II, Japan had to change its focus from becoming a military power to becoming an economic one. Despite Japan's ability to compete on price, its consumer goods manufacturers suffered from a long-established reputation for poor quality. Juran's Quality Control Handbook, in 1951, attracted the attention of the Japanese Union of Scientists and Engineers, which invited him to Japan in 1952. When he finally arrived in Japan in 1954, Juran met with many executives from manufacturing companies.*

Juran focused on managing for quality and started courses (1954) in quality management. The training began with top and middle management and it would take some 20 years for the training to pay off. In the 1970s, Japanese products began to be seen as the leaders in quality.

Both Juran and Deming shaped Japan's ability to rise from a shattered economy to being seen in the 1980's as leaders in Products and Processes such as Toyota and The Toyota Production System.

6.2 Countermeasure Definition

The literal meaning of a countermeasure is to take action against an event or occurrence to counteract the effects of that event, and, in most cases, it can be seen as a defensive response. Typically, there are two main types of countermeasures: Passive and Active. **(1) Passive** is a countermeasure already taken "just in case", an extreme example would be a soldier or policeman wearing Kevlar body protection. **(2) Active** is when an event or an action occurs which requires a "just in time" countermeasure, such as a ship adjusting or making a course correction because of drift, tides or winds.

As already described, the Hoshin Planning process begins by deciding critical Breakthroughs and identifying Improvement Priorities that will allow achieving a superior performance. This thought is represented in the X Matrix Level 1. In the next step, Breakthrough Objectives unfold to their point of impact, with the participation of the whole team in the preparation of Action Plans. These include as many KAIZEN™ Events as necessary to achieve the outlined objectives. Throughout the implementation, in order to correct any deviations, periodic reviews are made that evaluate the current performance against the partial objectives.

The reality is that we will not always hit the targets exactly and we will fall short, this is not different in Toyota or in your business. Without countermeasures you will continue to miss the mark and the process will collapse. The real power of Strat to Action is the strength of the organisation to quickly correct and reverse trends and its ability to apply countermeasures to negative situations or events.

The Hoshin planning process determines what the breakthroughs are, but it is through our ability to keep moving towards our targets by constantly creating countermesures against the effect of external and internal events that will deliver our goal. Communicating this across the whole organisation and empowering everyone to be part of the solution will start to create the countermeasure culture. There will be a new way to engage all areas. Use expressions such as "show me your countermeasures" and "how can I help for you to deliver better performance" will encourage your teams to continue to deliver stretched goals.

All Countermeasures should be a structured automatic response. The rule is quite simple: a Countermeasure should be adopted when a Target to Improve on the Bowler chart is red (below the monthly objective) and it is necessary to take corrective action to bring the KPIs back into the green. No permission is required to carry it out, as it is the "obligation" of the person responsible for Improvement Priority to present the Countermeasure at the Hoshin monthly review meeting. Deploying this behaviour in the organisation and enabling everyone to be part of the solution will begin to create a Culture of Countermeasures.

6.3 The Leader's Role

If you cannot make a difference when your team is getting "stuck in the mud," cannot get traction and the results just are not coming, when "winning is difficult", then quite frankly you are wasting your time trying to implement Hoshin. Remember Kaizen and Hoshin are leadership Intensive.

As leaders you will need to become a coach in generating effective counter measures and must be able to give the team insights that help them to prioritise what needs to be done now and take the corrective action needed to get the team back on track. After this you can discuss the preventive action to stop this from happening again, which will take longer. You have to coach your team to separate what the threat is and what is the immediate action needed to reverse the threat right now.

Some fundamentals that are needed for Problem Solving and Counter measure generation are "Good Data = Good Kaizen". Over the next paragraphs we will discuss the essential data collection tools you would expect to see in any countermeasures.

The Pareto principle (also known as the 80/20 Rule) was suggested by Juran and he named it after the Italian economist Vilfredo Pareto, who in 1896 noted the 80/20 connection. While at University of Lausanne, Pareto showed that approximately 80% of the land in Italy was owned by 20% of the population.

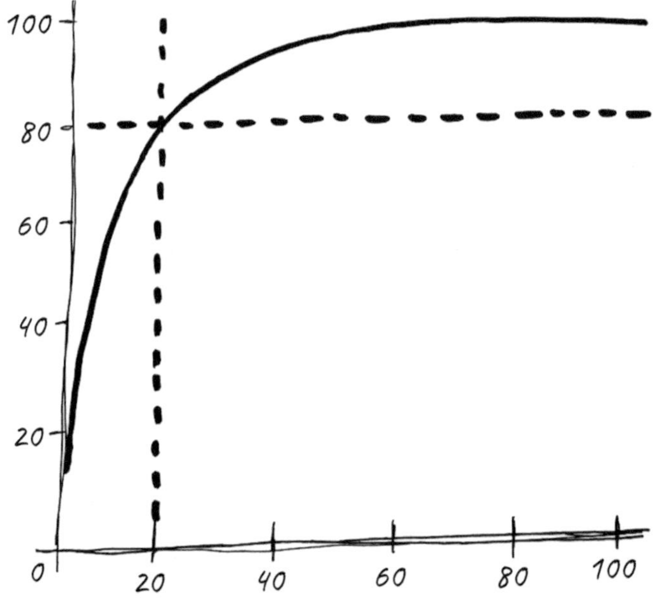

This is particularly useful in business where there is a lot to be done with limited resources and we are unsure of where to start. In other words, if we want to do a sales campaign, "80% of sales come from 20% of clients." Or improve quality, "80% of our rejects come from 20% of our product". This simple law allows us to marshal our efforts and energy into the 20% as illustrated in the graph above. This is essential in setting priorities for countermeasures. There will always be many more actions than you have resources so making a smart choice using Pareto can be very effective.

Knowing that 80% of the earnings will come from 20% of the total effort allows us to clarify what the priorities of the organisation should be. Juran taught that "the focus must be on the FEW and not on the MANY."

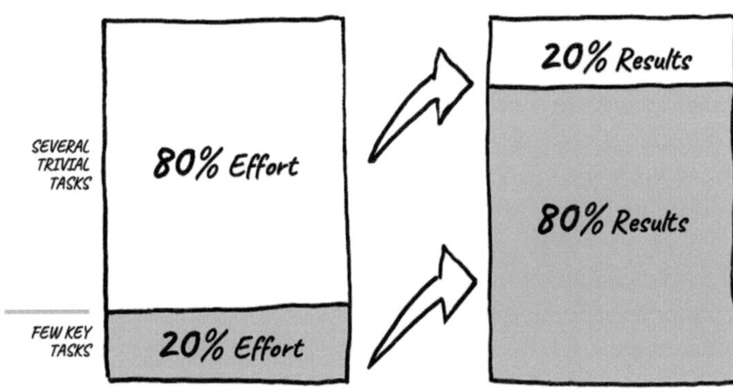

As confidence builds so "We Don't Wait"; Hoshin has empowered the organisation to take action. There is no need to "wait for the next meeting" as it can be done at once. As soon as the Bowler starts to go RED, take the necessary countermeasures to fix and reverse the trends. You can go to the next meeting and talk about the countermeasure that pulled the team back into line, rather than looking at the monthly reports, trying to find the mythical goose that lays the golden egg.

Another powerful tool used in the definition of Coutermeasures an that can easily be applied in assessing process quality is the Ishikawa Diagram, also known as the Cause and Effect Diagram.

Kaoru Ishikawa - *A Japanese engineer who joined JUSE in 1949. He learned the principles of statistical control and quality management with Deming and Juran and became known for expanding them into the Japanese system. With the Cause and Effect Diagram, this management leader has made significant strides in improving quality. Ishikawa Diagrams are useful as systematic tools for finding, classifying and documenting the causes of a problem, and organising the relationships between them. According to Ishikawa, quality improvement is an ongoing process, and can always be improved.*

Ishikawa sustained that the resolution of about 95% of an organisation's problems can be achieved through the use of 7 simple tools, namely:

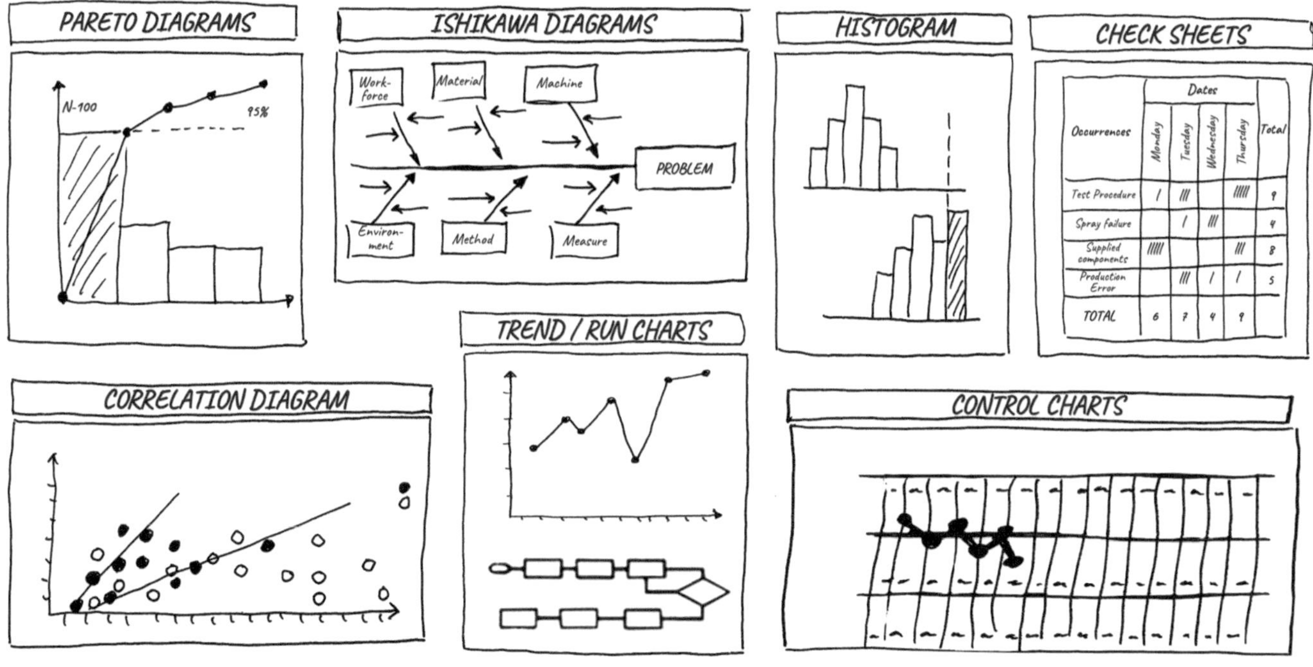

1. **Pareto diagrams** - column chart that classifies the frequency of occurrences, from highest to lowest, allowing problem prioritisation.
2. **Ishikawa or Fishbone Diagrams** - are a cause and effect diagrams and are a problem-solving tool showing all the potential causes that can emerge from a single effect.

3. **Histograms** - are useful for showing both attributes and variable data and can show the distribution of the values.

4. **Check sheets** - used to structure data in a table format, the benefit being that they can be easy to understand and can identify the frequency and type of problems present.

5. **Correlation diagrams** - are useful in looking for correlations between two variables and can show a direct relationship as: (1) Positive Correlation, (2) Negative Correlation, (3) No Correlation.

6. **Trend Charts or Run Charts** - a simple chart that shows the ongoing trend; when linked to action this can show the effectiveness of the action taken.

7. **Control charts** - developed by Walter. A. Shewhart in the 1920's, this is a Run chart that shows the variation in the process over time and can be said to be in control or out of control which occurs when special causes are present, useful in determining the presence of special causes which will result in defects.

It is obvious that a leader is not required to be an expert in problem-solving tools, but rather to master the ability to assess the quality of Countermeasures.

This way, leadership takes a new approach in the organisation, and expressions such as "How did you come to these Countermeasures?" or "Which data supported this decision?" should become usual in the management daily vocabulary.

A good Countermeasure has the following characteristics:

- Based on facts, all assumptions and changes must be supported by data. Always ask "Can you show me the data?".
- Specifically associated with the X Matrix target to be improved, exactly quantifying the difference compared to it.
- Clearly identifies the person responsible for the action and the date of completion.
- Uses problem-solving tools to determine the corrective actions to be taken.

The measurement frequency (data collection) can be increased to obtain more suitable information for analysis.

6.4 Countermeasures in Hoshin Review

The purpose of the Monthly review can be separated into making sure **Action Plans** are on track and that any slippages in the month are being **Countermeasured.**

Every month, usually in the second week, you will review progress towards delivering your Year 1 Breakthrough Objectives, but before we start the deep dive, we need to understand that we are now thinking about Managing Performance vs Being a Victim of Poor Performance. The differences are noteworthy:

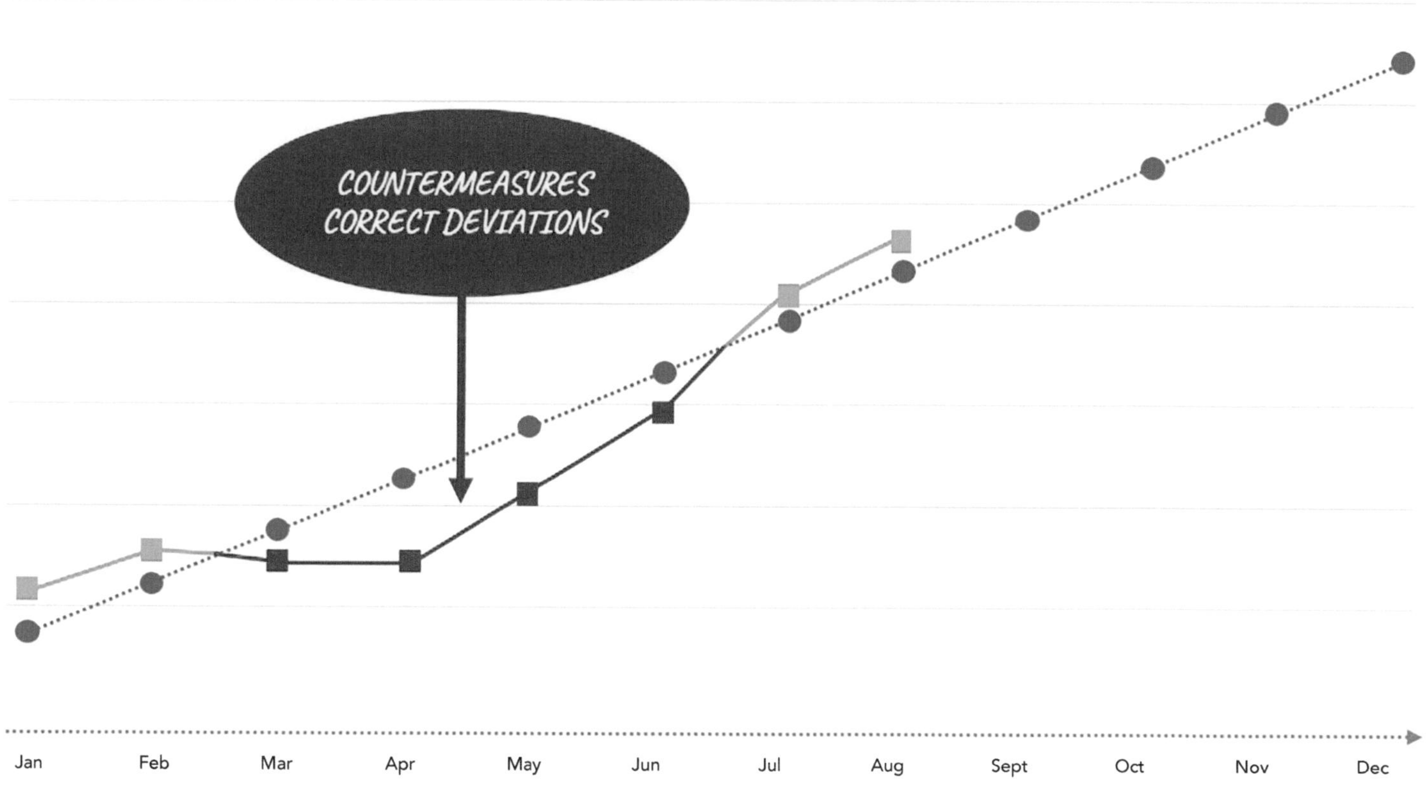

At the monthly Review we can no longer sit around the table waiting to be asked what has happened, we have to be prepared to lead the meeting using countermeasures to explain when it is our turn to speak and when we finish, having completed a successful countermeasure, we celebrate our victories for 15 seconds and move onto the next.

To do a monthly review means reviewing in detail the targets that are in red. This automatically means there is a countermeasure in place and its purpose is to take corrective action that will bring the target back before the next review, usually within 30 days. You need to question each countermeasure as you would a large overspend in the profit and loss to satisfy yourself that you will not see the same performance next month. Whilst the result is the trigger and not the focus of the review, it should be the application of the countermeasure process that will deliver the corrective action, do not focus on the result, focus on the quality of the countermeasure.

Here is a story that demonstrates the need for leaders to engage in countermeasure validation.

Selling hot dogs as I enter my local football ground, the hot dog seller was always asking the customers queue on the other side of the window against the natural flow of people coming into the ground. This was really causing him some aggravation and lost sales, so he decided to reorganise all of his internal tools, hot plate, hot drinks dispenser in the other direction. I've known Pete, the hotdog vendor, since school, so I suggested he turned his hotdog stand around and put it on the other side of the path. This took 5 minutes as the stall was on a trailer and achieved the same result. Sometimes we need to step back to find the easiest, simplest, most cost-effective solution.

Go to Gemba to verify the action, this type of activity has to be done at the point of impact with the people who have made the change, you should verify what the countermeasure is telling you with your own eyes, and it's a good opportunity for you to go see and stretch your legs, get out of the stuffy meeting room.

Good results do not appear by chance. It is not enough for leaders to validate the quality of Countermeasures, since countermeasures must be implemented at the point of impact. It is always necessary to go to the GEMBA to check with your own eyes that change is happening. This is also a good opportunity for management to get out of the stuffy meeting room and stretch their legs and exercise a bit. To sustain results, and to emphasise the sense of urgency in the application of Countermeasures, there should be a GEMBA Walk routine.

A good practice at Toyota is applied when the leader is satisfied with the implementation of a given countermeasure by simply writing "well done" in the Action Plan along with their signature. This regular behaviour, rather than demonstrating the leaders' commitment to the improvement process, allows us to certify the compliance of the applied countermeasures.

The absolute minimum points to check on any countermeasure:

1. Absolute Tie Back to the Hoshin Matrix, so you know which Improvement priority is being actioned. This will lead you back to the Hoshin Action Plan and you can make sure that all the planned KAIZEN™ Events have taken place.

2. The target to improve must be at the point of impact. The best way to test this is to ask who owns this countermeasure and if that is the right person. Be careful that managers do not steal your time, rather talk to the operators who are affected in the Gemba. The best reviews are done in Gemba, at the place where the action is taken.

3. The missed Improvement Priority is clear, the run chart will use the Bowler data to match the Plan data to the Actual data.

4. Pareto - this is the drill down point to check whether we have good data and a good understanding of the missed target. You should see more than one level of Pareto supported by other data so you can clearly picture WHY this miss occurred. Check that the Pareto focuses on the WHY and not the WHERE it happened.

5. Cause or causes must quantify the total amount of the miss otherwise we are searching in the wrong area.

6. The Countermeasure Actions, Focus on the FEW not the MANY; you may have longer term preventive actions but these should not stop the team correcting the miss. I have seen many examples where a machine has a noisy bearing which isn't effecting the performance but needs to be replaced; so do you do it now, or at the next preventive maintenance schedule? Doing it now would not improve the machines performance.

7. Clearly describe the owner of the Action and when it will be completed and always follow up on your next Gemba walk make sure the change has been implemented. A Toyota QA tip is when you have checked and satisfied yourself, write a simple "Well done" or "Good job" with your initials on the countermeasure action plan. This will go a long way and your team will appreciate it. Do not go over the top, this is the normal behaviour you want to see across the whole company.

8. Measure if the impact of the change has closed the gap. Congratulate the team and share their sense of achievement.

Another way to assess the quality of countermeasures is to reflect on "What went well?"; "What went wrong?"; "What helped?" and "What made it difficult?". This reflection will help to build a stronger countermeasure process.

It is recognised that the Japanese have some attributes that enable them to be very competent in the application of Countermeasures, but currently there are already many Western organisations with this competence, which proves that this is not a unique characteristic of Japanese culture. In fact, developing a Culture of Countermeasures is an attitude that all organisations should target.

In an ever-changing society, organisations with a strong Countermeasure Culture stand out for the above average speed of knowledge acquisition and innovation. This kind of culture encourages and supports a continuous learning of all employees, taking risks with new ideas, allowing mistakes and valuing individual contributions.

With Hoshin, the organisation's learning capabilities are tested by stressing goals, and using KAIZEN™ to promote change and "learning by doing." This kind of organisation, known as a "Learning Organisation" offers society a superior performance.

Hoshin Review

Not even the best Action Plan is free from deviations

In the second week of each month, the Executive Committee meets to review the evolution in delivering the Breakthrough Objectives.

This chapter describes some review meetings held at ALFA's to illustrate the dynamics of these work sessions and to reinforce the most relevant points of the Hoshin Review method.

7.1 The Visual Impact of the Bowling Chart

One of the foundations of KAIZEN™ is to make waste visible. During Hoshin's development, its creators felt the need to identify a visual method to present progress towards the targets to be improved. After several adaptations, they decided to use the same score cards used in 10-pin bowling, since they realised that the accumulated score after each period could easily be adopted to analyse the progress of results. So, they modified the Bowling Chart turning it into a performance measurement tool and called it "The Bowler".

The Bowler allows a quick analysis of results and reduces the time spent on emails, reports, meetings and presentations. The results are either in green or red, depending on whether the Hoshin goals have been met or not. Although it seems contradictory, teams should view the results in red as good because they indicate an opportunity for improvement for the organisation.

This tool is an essential element to monthly reviews.

TAERGET TO ACHIEVE	Starting point	Annual target	Un.		Jan	Feb	Mar	Apr	May	Jun	Jul	Aug	Sept	Oct	Nov	Dec
Ennis Line Sales/FTE from 192 K€ to 202 K€ by Dec/Year 1	192	202	thousand €	**Hoshin**	192.8	193.7	194.5	195.3	196.2	197.0	197.8	198.7	199.5	200.3	201.2	202.0
				Actual	194.0											
Ennis Line OEE from 74% to 85% by Dec/Year 1	74%	85%	%	**Hoshin**	75%	76%	77%	78%	79%	80%	80%	81%	82%	83%	84%	85%
				Actual	74%											
Ennis Line Setup Time from 30 to 15 min by Dec/Year 1	30	15	min	**Hoshin**	29	28	26	25	24	23	21	20	19	18	16	15
				Actual	30											
Ferguson Line Sales/FTE from 233 K€ to 245 K€ by Dec/Year 1	233	245	thousand €	**Hoshin**	234	235	236	237	238	239	240	241	242	243	244	245
				Actual	233											
Ferguson Line OEE from 68% to 77% by Dec/Year 1	68%	77%	%	**Hoshin**	69%	70%	70%	71%	72%	73%	73%	74%	75%	76%	76%	77%
				Actual	68%											
Ferguson Line Setup Time from 25 to 15 min by Dec/Year 1	25	15	min	**Hoshin**	24	23	23	22	21	20	19	18	18	17	16	15
				Actual	25											
Maintenance Specialised Services from 4% to 3.5% of sales by Dec/Year 1	4.0%	3.5%	%	**Hoshin**	4.0%	3.9%	3.9%	3.8%	3.8%	3.8%	3.7%	3.7%	3.6%	3.6%	3.5%	3.5%
				Actual	4.0%											
Other Services from 4.7% to 4.4% of sales by Dec/Year 1	4.7%	4.4%	%	**Hoshin**	4.7%	4.7%	4.6%	4.6%	4.6%	4.6%	4.5%	4.5%	4.5%	4.5%	4.4%	4.4%
				Actual	4.8%											
Non-quality Costs from 1.2 M€ to 0.88 M€ by Dec/Year 1	0	880	thousand €	**Hoshin**	73	147	220	293	367	440	513	587	660	733	807	880
				Actual	77											
Nr. Customer Complaints from 46 to 23 by Dec/Year 1	0	23	#	**Hoshin**	2	4	6	8	10	12	13	15	17	19	21	23
				Actual	3											

Level 2 Bowling chart example for Operations, month 1, Year 1

7.2 The First Month of the Hoshin Review

It was the second week of February. The CEO entered the MCR of Industrial Unit 1, knowing that several KAIZEN™ events had already been performed since the start of the Hoshin implementation. Although optimistic, he showed a natural feeling of uncertainty about the results. All of his executive team was present, as were the leaders of the improvement events already implemented in the unit. Each leader had been invited to briefly present the A3 of his workshop and the results obtained. The CEO had planned to carry out, after the meeting, a GEMBA Walk with his team, for everyone to observe the changes.

Most of those responsible for Level 1 and Level 2 Matrix Improvement Priorities had worked to ensure that the MCR had the necessary information posted, with duly updated Bowler Charts. They had spent a few hours with the KAIZEN™ consultant, who helped them in the preparation of the review process. Unlike the typical management meetings, the purpose was to introduce a completely new concept. They should focus only on those deviations that required countermeasures.

The consultant began the session by saying: "We are here to begin the Hoshin Review process with the CEO. Although this is our first session, from now on we will make an effort to follow the standard agenda. Obviously today we will have a lot of reds in the Bowler, as we are still in the first month of the implementation."

The CEO stood in front of the MCR's boards. No one was sure yet of what to say, until the CEO asked the Marketing and Sales Director to start.

The Director of Marketing and Sales began by sharing the good news from the market and his optimism about its positive sales growth potential. While he was still speaking, the CEO looked at the Sales and Marketing Bowler and promptly asked: "But why is your Bowler not up to date?"

In an attempt to get around the question, the Marketing and Sales Director explained that he had been totally absorbed with a new customer, who would potentially bring in a lot of sales. With all the interest the news had caused, the question about the Bowler updating had been overlooked.

A few minutes later, the CEO went to the board and looked at the Engineering X Matrix. Feeling a little more confident to see that everything seemed up to date, he focused on the Action Plan reading the contents out loud.

The Engineering Director smiled proudly at all his colleagues. The CEO thought the review was going well, until the consultant interrupted the meeting, visibly annoyed: "I'm sorry, but I must interrupt." The consultant could not let the meeting go on without alerting the CEO and the rest of the team to the mistakes they were making. "The agenda says that we have to analyse the Bowler's, the targets to be improved that are in red in order of importance of their Improvement Priorities, and to define the Countermeasures. That is, in fact, not what we are doing."

The standard of any Hoshin Review meeting is to review the Improvement Priorities in the order of importance defined in the Level 1 X Matrix; those that are closer to the centre have the highest priority. All Improvement Priorities are linked to the Bowler, and only those with a deviation (marked in red) should be analysed in detail to create the necessary countermeasures.

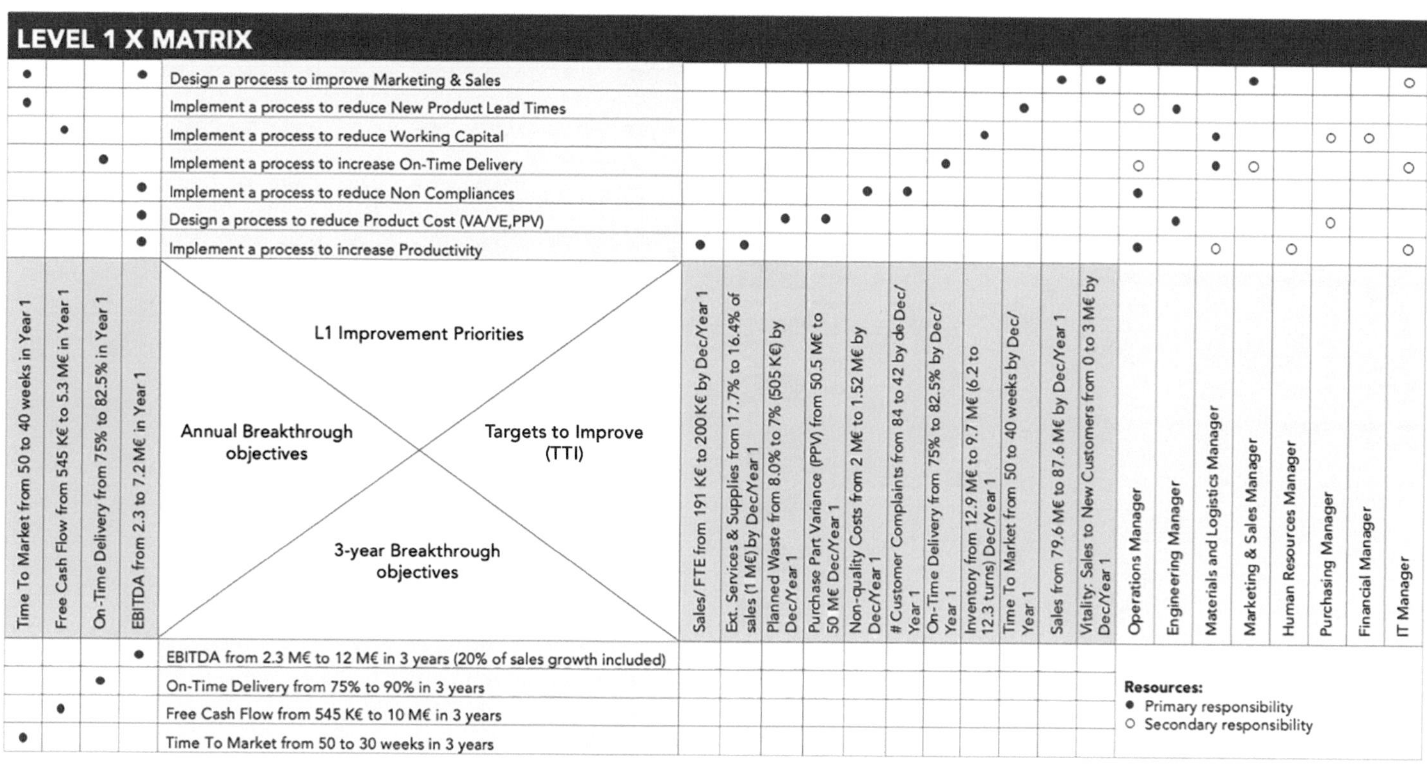

Level 1 X Matrix, Year 1

"We've heard the Marketing and Sales Director tell us about potential new clients and we're all patting each other's backs. The truth is that we don't have an updated Bowler and we also do not have any Action Plan. May I remind you: no Action Plan, no Hoshin!" Said the consultant, taking a tougher attitude than usual.

The CEO quickly understood the purpose of the intervention and seized the opportunity to regain control of the meeting. Looking at his Bowler, he found that the January target had not been achieved in any of the Improvement Priorities and so he decided that time would be equally allocated for each of the seven priorities. From that moment onwards, the meeting went in according to plan and with the CEO fully aligned with the method. The consultant stepped back, knowing that the mistakes made at the beginning of the session would not be repeated.

TARGET TO ACHIEVE	Starting point	Annual target	Un.		Jan	Feb	Mar	Apr	May	Jun	Jul	Aug	Sept	Oct	Nov	Dec
Sales/FTE from 191 K€ to 200 K€ by Dec/Year 1	191.0	200.0	thousand €	**Hoshin**	191.8	192.5	193.3	194.0	194.8	195.5	196.3	197.0	197.8	198.5	199.3	200.0
				Actual	191.0											
External Services & Supplies from 17.7% to 16.4% of sales (1 M€) by Dec/Year 1	17.7%	16.4%	%	**Hoshin**	17.6%	17.5%	17.4%	17.3%	17.2%	17.1%	16.9%	16.8%	16.7%	16.6%	16.5%	16.4%
				Actual	17.7%											
	0.0	1 035	thousand €	**Hoshin**	7.2	28.7	64.7	115.0	179.7	258.7	352.2	460.0	582.2	718.7	869.7	1 035.0
				Actual	0.0											
Planned Waste from 8.0% to 7.0% (505 K€) by Dec/Year 1	8.0%	7.0%	%	**Hoshin**	7.9%	7.8%	7.8%	7.7%	7.6%	7.5%	7.4%	7.3%	7.3%	7.2%	7.1%	7.0%
				Actual	8.1%											
	0	505	thousand €	**Hoshin**	42	84	126	168	210	253	295	337	379	421	463	505
				Actual	45											
Purchase Part Variance (PPV) from 50.5 M€ to 50 M€ by Dec/Year 1	0	500	thousand €	**Hoshin**	41.7	83.3	125.0	166.7	208.3	250.0	291.7	333.3	375.0	416.7	458.3	500.0
				Actual	0.0											
Non-quality Costs from 2 M€ to 1.52 M€ by Dec/Year 1	0	1.52	million €	**Hoshin**	0.13	0.25	0.38	0.51	0.63	0.76	0.89	1.01	1.14	1.27	1.39	1.52
				Actual	0.15											
# Customer Complaints from 84 to 42 by Dec/Year 1	0	42	#	**Hoshin**	4	7	11	14	18	21	25	28	32	35	39	42
				Actual	7											
On-Time Delivery from 75% to 82.5% by Dec/Year 1	75.0%	82.5%	%	**Hoshin**	75.6%	76.3%	76.9%	77.5%	78.1%	78.8%	79.4%	80.0%	80.6%	81.3%	81.9%	82.5%
				Actual	70.0%											
Inventory from 12.9 M€ to 9.7 M€ (6.2 to 12.3 turns) by Dec/Year 1	12.9	9.7	million €	**Hoshin**	12.6	12.4	12.1	11.8	11.6	11.3	11.0	10.8	10.5	10.2	10.0	9.7
				Actual	12.8											
Time To Market from 50 to 40 weeks until Dec/Year 1	50	40	wk	**Hoshin**	49	48	48	47	46	45	44	43	43	42	41	40
				Actual	50											
Sales from 79.6 M€ to 87.6 M€ by Dec/Year 1	0	87 575	thousand €	**Hoshin**	7 298	14 596	21 894	29 192	36 490	43 788	51 085	58 383	65 681	72 979	80 277	87 575
				Actual	6 897											
Vitality: New Customer Sales from 0 to 3 M€ by Dec/Year 1	0	3 000	thousand €	**Hoshin**	250	500	750	1 000	1 250	1 500	1 750	2 000	2 250	2 500	2 750	3 000
				Actual	203											

Level 1 Bowling chart, month 1, Year 1

Addressing the group, the CEO asked "Before we decide any countermeasures, I would like to know whether we have completed all the planned KAIZEN™ Events.

The team checked the Kaizen roadmap and concluded that everything was running as planned. Three events had been held in Operations, one VA/VE - (Value Analysis / Value Engineering) event with the Engineering team, and three events with the Marketing and Sales team.

After the presentation of each A3 (summary of the events), the CEO went to his team and told them that he was impressed with the results, but even so, he questioned each director about the ongoing actions. His objective was to ensure that nothing would prevent them from achieving results in the coming months. He also made a mental note to ensure that he would visit the GEMBA in the following weeks. With this, he intended to demonstrate to his teams the importance of commitment by them all regarding ALFA's improvement process.

He reminded those present the rules of the Hoshin Review calendar: The reviews of level 2 matrices were to be held in the first week of each month, so that countermeasures could be ready for the level 1 review, which was to take place in the second week of each month. The CEO wanted to follow the Level 2 meetings so that he would personally check whether the teams were succeeding with the Hoshin Review process. This was particularly relevant during the first 4 months of the implementation.

When the meeting ended, the CEO pointed out: "Before closing, I would just like to remind you all that the direction we wish to give ALFA is a path of no return. Today we had a first demonstration that obtaining very quick results is indeed feasible, and that the transformation we are seeking can actually happen. I know it will not be easy, we will need the effort and commitment of everyone, but we are together in this endeavour and my door is always open to support continuous improvement.

LESSONS LEARNED IN THE MONTH 1 REVIEW:

- Everyone agrees with the agenda, but no one follows it.
- Indicators often do not measure exactly what is required.
- Lack of data means no countermeasure.

7.3 The 3rd Month of Hoshin Reviews

Three months had elapsed since the start of the Hoshin implementation and the CEO decided to participate in the Operations Level 2 Review at Industrial Unit 1, in order to learn more about its development in delivering the Breakthrough Objectives. The Operations were involved with the highest commitment assigned to contribute € 3.5 million directly to EBITDA. The CEO was pleased with the feedback received from the KAIZEN™ Events but wanted to be sure that they were doing all that was needed to ensure the annual objective was being met.

LEVEL 2 X MATRIX- OPERATIONS

L2 Improvement priorities

L1 Improvement priorities

Targets to Improve (TTI)

Annual Breakthrough objectives

		Implement a process to reduce Non-compliances	Implement a process to increase Productivity	L2 Improvement priorities	Sales / FTE Ennis line from 192 K€ to 202 K€ by Dec/Year 1	Ennis Line OEE from 74% to 85% by Dec/Year 1	Ennis Line Setup Time from 30 to 15 min by Dec/Year 1	Ferguson Line Sales / FTE from 233 K€ to 245K€ by Dec/Year 1	Ferguson Line OEE from 68% to 77% by Dec/Year 1	Ferguson Line Setup Time from 25 to 15 min by Dec/Year 1	Maintenance Specialised Services from 4% to 3.5% of sales by Dec/Year 1	Several External Services from 4.7% to 4.4% of sales by de Dec/Year 1	Non-quality Costs from 1.2 M€ to 0.88 M€ by Dec/Year 1	# Customers Complaints from 46 to 23 by Dec/Year 1		Plant Manager	Production Manager	Purchasing Manager	Quality Engineer	Process Engineer	
		●		Implement a Poka-yoke process									●	●					○	●	
		●		Implement a Problem Solving process									●	●					●	○	
		●		Implement an Auto-quality process									●	●					●	○	
			●	Implement a process to reduce External Services							●	●				○		●			
			●	Implement a process to increase Ferguson Line Productivity				●	●	●							●				
			●	Implement a process Ennis Line Productivity	●	●	●										●				

		Implement a process to reduce Non-compliances	Implement a process to increase Productivity	Annual Breakthrough objectives
		●	●	EBITDA from 2.3 to 7.2 M€ in Year 1
				On-Time Delivery from 75% to 82.5% in Year 1
				Free Cash Flow from 545 K€ to 5.3 M€ in Year 1
				Time To Market from 50 to 40 weeks in Year 1

Resources:
- ● Primary responsibility
- ○ Secondary responsibility

Level 2 X Matrix for Operations, Industrial Unit 1, Year 1

TARGET TO ACHIEVE	Starting point	Annual target	Un.		Jan	Feb	Mar	Apr	May	Jun	Jul	Aug	Sept	Oct	Nov	Dec
Ennis Line Sales/FTE from 192 K€ to 202 K€ by Dec/Year 1	192	202	thousand €	**Hoshin**	192.8	193.7	194.5	195.3	196.2	197.0	197.8	198.7	199.5	200.3	201.2	202.0
				Actual	194.0	196.0	197.5									
Ennis Line OEE from 74% to 85% by Dec/Year 1	74%	85%	%	**Hoshin**	75%	76%	77%	78%	79%	80%	80%	81%	82%	83%	84%	85%
				Actual	74%	73%	74%									
Ennis Line Setup Time from 30 to 15 min by Dec/Year 1	30	15	min	**Hoshin**	29	28	26	25	24	23	21	20	19	18	16	15
				Actual	30	35	29									
Ferguson Line Sales/FTE from 233 K€ to 245 K€ by Dec/Year 1	233	245	thousand €	**Hoshin**	234	235	236	237	238	239	240	241	242	243	244	245
				Actual	233	234	237									
Ferguson Line OEE from 68% to 77% by Dec/Year 1	68%	77%	%	**Hoshin**	69%	70%	70%	71%	72%	73%	73%	74%	75%	76%	76%	77%
				Actual	68%	69%	67%									
Ferguson Line Setup Time from 25 to 15 min by Dec/Year 1	25	15	min	**Hoshin**	24	23	23	22	21	20	19	18	18	17	16	15
				Actual	25	24	26									
Maintenance Specialised Services from 4% to 3.5% of sales by Dec/Year 1	4.0%	3.5%	%	**Hoshin**	4.0%	3.9%	3.9%	3.8%	3.8%	3.8%	3.7%	3.7%	3.6%	3.6%	3.5%	3.5%
				Actual	4.0%	4.1%	4.0%									
Other Services from 4.7% to 4.4% of sales by Dec/Year 1	4.7%	4.4%	%	**Hoshin**	4.7%	4.7%	4.6%	4.6%	4.6%	4.6%	4.5%	4.5%	4.5%	4.5%	4.4%	4.4%
				Actual	4.8%	4.9%	4.8%									
Non-quality Costs from 1.2 M€ to 0.88 M€ by Dec/Year 1	0	880	thousand €	**Hoshin**	73	147	220	293	367	440	513	587	660	733	807	880
				Actual	77	163	249									
Nr. Customer Complaints from 46 to 23 by Dec/Year 1	0	23	#	**Hoshin**	2	4	6	8	10	12	13	15	17	19	21	23
				Actual	3	6	9									

Bowling chart for Operations, Industrial Unit 1, first trimester, Year 1

The Operations Director took over leadership of the meeting, beginning with Bowler and explained how the KAIZEN™ Events would achieve the improvements over the next two months. The activities further developed productivity and quality levels of the Ennis and Ferguson lines. The director was pleased with the results in productivity, and actually thrilled about the improvements regarding quality.

It was within this framework that he led the team through the Action Plans update, and also analysed the countermeasures to be applied.

ACTION PLAN		
Improvement priority: implement a process to increase Ennis line productivity	**Department:** Operations **Primary responsibility:** Ennis line production manager (Industrial Unit 1)	**Date:** Apr - wk 2
Audit team: Plant Manager, Production Manager, Engineering Manager, Purchasing Manager, Logistics Manager, Maintenance Engineer, Quality Engineer and Process Engineer		**Next review:** May - wk 2
Current state overview: the production team needs to continuously increase productivity in every value stream through KAIZEN™ Event implementation		

Key objectives:
Ennis line sales (thousand €)/ FTE from 192 to 202 by Dec/Year 1
Ennis line OEE from 74% to 85% by Dec/Year 1
Ennis line setup time from 30 to 15 min by Dec/Year 1

Agenda — ■ = original plan; X = progress review

Target to achieve

Action	Owner	Planned dates	Jan	Feb	Mar	Apr	May	Jun	Jul	Aug	Sept	Oct	Nov	Dec	Status (Non-compliances in red color)	Impact
			YEAR													
1. KAIZEN™ event - Just-in-Time	Production Manager	Jan - wk 1	x													92 thousand €
2. KAIZEN™ event - Daily KAIZEN™	Production Manager	Jan - wk 3	x													-
3. KAIZEN™ event - OEE	Process Engineer	Feb - wk 1		x												-
4. KAIZEN™ event - Auto-Quality	Quality Engineer	Feb - wk 3			x											42 thousand €
5. KAIZEN™ event - Problem Solving	Production Manager	Mar - wk 3			x											-
6. KAIZEN™ event - Just-in-Time	Production Manager	Apr - wk 3														
7. KAIZEN™ event - Poka-Yoke	Engineering Manager	Jun - wk 1														
8. KAIZEN™ event - Daily KAIZEN™	Production Manager	Jun - wk 3														
9. KAIZEN™ event - SMED	Process Engineer	Jul - wk 1														
10. KAIZEN™ event - Standard work	Process Engineer	Jul - wk 3														
11. KAIZEN™ event - SMED	Process Engineer	Oct - wk 1														
12. KAIZEN™ event - OEE	Process Engineer	Nov - wk 1														

The CEO was impressed that the Operations team recognised their quality issues and proactively started to act on their resolution.

COUNTERMEASURES

Improvement priority:	Non-quality costs (Industrial Unit 1)
Target to achieve:	From 1.2 million € to 0.88 million € by Dec/Year 1

Problem definition:

40% of 249 thousand € refers to technical problems by ensuring dimensional tolerances
30% of 249 thousand € refers to operational scrap

Countermeasures

What	Who	When	How much (impact)
Technician: component redesign for a better fit	Engineering Manager	March 20	18 thousand €
Technician: thickness tests with alternative materials	New Product Development Engineer	March 22	25 thousand €
Technician: inspection process improvements through light sensors	Process Engineer	March 22	-
Operations: cutting variation reduction through fixed stops inclusion in press bottom piston	Process Engineer	March 18	20 thousand €
Operations: control inspections frequency increase until the problem no longer exists	Quality Engineer	March 18	-
Operations: team and training define the new production process	Production Manager	March 18	-
		Total:	**63 thousand €**

Review date: Apr - wk 2	**Primary responsibility:** Engineering Manager

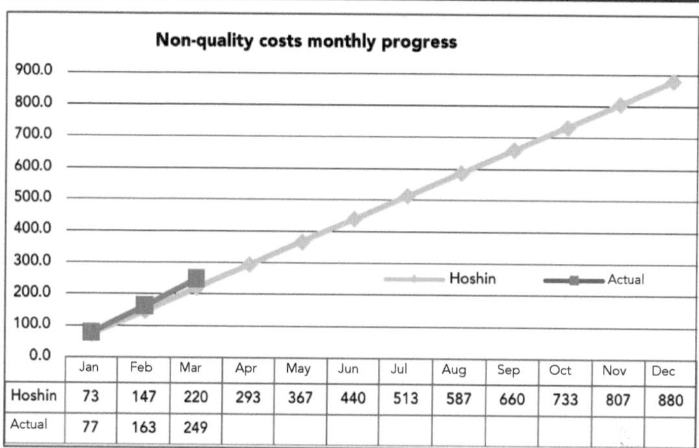

	Jan	Feb	Mar	Apr	May	Jun	Jul	Aug	Sep	Oct	Nov	Dec
Hoshin	73	147	220	293	367	440	513	587	660	733	807	880
Actual	77	163	249									

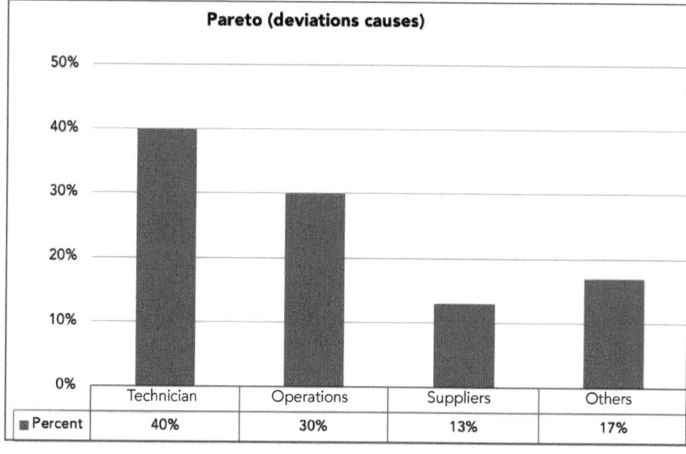

	Technician	Operations	Suppliers	Others
Percent	40%	30%	13%	17%

Quality and Process Engineering explained the countermeasures to reduce non-quality costs. The first one to speak was the Process Engineer who was rather nervous since it was the first time he had spoken in front of the CEO. He explained how he outlined the countermeasures using the KAIZEN™ process in which they had been trained. He concluded that there were two main causes why they were failing in their objectives, namely:

1. 40% of the problems were technical. Improvements were suggested in the inspection process and in component redesigns.
2. 30% of problems were caused by variability in the process. A new process control would be implemented and some tools redesigned.

After the different managers had presented the countermeasures to be applied, the CEO and the whole team went to the GEMBA to check some of the actions that had already begun to be implemented. As they walked, the CEO felt even more confident in thinking about the advantages of having process owners implementing their own countermeasures.

At the end, the CEO shook hands with everyone and said, "I am very pleased with your work and how you have systematically reached at countermeasures. I am convinced that we will achieve the objectives. Congratulations!"

Back in the MCR, the team discussed follow-up actions and potential impacts.

The following week, the CEO conducted the Level 1 review and took the chance to share with the Executive Committee the good work performed by the Operations.

LESSONS LEARNED IN THE MONTH 3 REVIEW:

- Consolidated data hide the source of problems. Raw data directly collected is better to identify causes. Indicators should measure at the point of impact.
- The team has to go to the GEMBA to observe changes and check on results.

7.4 The 6th Month of Hoshin review

In the biannual review, the CEO concluded that productivity and quality already showed a trend aligned with the end-of-year target. However, he was concerned about the lack of movement in reducing inventory and therefore decided that further countermeasures should be applied in this area. After realising that the KAIZEN™ TMI Implementation Event (already described in Chapter 4 - Breakthrough KAIZEN™) had been postponed several times, he announced that he would participate in this event and immediately set new dates for it to be carried out.

With the same effort, the remaining reds of the Bowler were duly analysed. The team was increasingly efficient in presenting countermeasures at these meetings.

TARGET TO ACHIEVE	Starting point	Annual target	Un.		Jan	Feb	Mar	Apr	May	Jun	Jul	Aug	Sept	Oct	Nov	Dec
Sales/FTE from 191 K€ to 200 K€ by Dec/Year 1	191	200	thousand €	**Hoshin**	191.8	192.5	193.3	194.0	194.8	195.5	196.3	197.0	197.8	198.5	199.3	200.0
				Actual	191.0	193.0	194.5	195.0	195.0	194.0						
External Services & Supplies from 17.7% to 16.4% of Sales (1 M€) by Dec/Year 1	17.7%	16.4%	%	**Hoshin**	17.6%	17.5%	17.4%	17.3%	17.2%	17.1%	16.9%	16.8%	16.7%	16.6%	16.5%	16.4%
				Actual	17.7%	17.5%	17.5%	17.4%	16.9%	16.9%						
	0	1 035	thousand €	**Hoshin**	7.2	28.7	64.7	115.0	179.7	258.7	352.2	460.0	582.2	718.7	869.7	1 035.0
				Actual	0.0	26.5	39.8	79.6	265.4	318.5						
Planned Waste from 8% to 7% (505 K€) by Dec/Year 1	8%	7%	%	**Hoshin**	7.9%	7.8%	7.8%	7.7%	7.6%	7.5%	7.4%	7.3%	7.3%	7.2%	7.1%	7.0%
				Actual	8.1%	7.9%	9.0%	7.8%	7.7%	7.4%						
	0	505	thousand €	**Hoshin**	42	84	126	168	210	253	295	337	379	421	463	505
				Actual	45	81	122	165	208	256						
Purchase Part Variance (PPV) from 50.5 M€ to 50 M€ by Dec/Year 1	0	500	thousand €	**Hoshin**	41.7	83.3	125.0	166.7	208.3	250.0	291.7	333.3	375.0	416.7	458.3	500.0
				Actual	0.0	0.0	55.2	110.1	184.5	294.6						
Non-Quality Costs from 2 M€ to 1.52 M€ by Dec/Year 1	0	1.52	million €	**Hoshin**	0.13	0.25	0.38	0.51	0.63	0.76	0.89	1.01	1.14	1.27	1.39	1.52
				Actual	0.15	0.29	0.43	0.50	0.57	0.64						
# Customer Complaints from 84 to 42 by Dec/Year 1	0	42	#	**Hoshin**	4	7	11	14	18	21	25	28	32	35	39	42
				Actual	7	12	14	15	17	19						
On-Time Delivery from 75% to 82.5% by Dec/Year 1	75.0%	82.5%	%	**Hoshin**	75.6%	76.3%	76.9%	77.5%	78.1%	78.8%	79.4%	80.0%	80.6%	81.3%	81.9%	82.5%
				Actual	70.0%	71.0%	72.7%	73.0%	74.6%	75.0%						
Inventory from 12.9 M€ to 97 M€ (6.2 to 12.3 turns) by Dec/Year 1	12.9	9.7	million €	**Hoshin**	12.6	12.4	12.1	11.8	11.6	11.3	11.0	10.8	10.5	10.2	10.0	9.7
				Actual	12.8	12.9	12.7	13.1	13.0	12.3						
Time-To-Market from 50 to 40 weeks by Dec/Year 1	50	40	wk	**Hoshin**	49	48	48	47	46	45	44	43	43	42	41	40
				Actual	50	49	49	45	49	46						
Sales from 79.6 M€ to 87.6 M€ by Dec/Year 1	0	87 575	thousand €	**Hoshin**	7 298	14 596	21 894	29 192	36 490	43 788	51 085	58 383	65 681	72 979	80 277	87 575
				Actual	6 897	13 766	20 636	27 505	34 375	41 244						
Vitality: New Customer Sales from 0 to 3 M€ by Dec/Year 1	0	3 000	thousand €	**Hoshin**	250	500	750	1 000	1 250	1 500	1 750	2 000	2 250	2 500	2 750	3 000
				Actual	203	380	525	607	871	1 016						

Level 1 Bowling chart, first semester, Year 1

LESSONS LEARNED IN THE MONTH 6 REVIEW:

- Countermeasures are urgent and should correct the trend in 30 days.
- The CEO must act by providing additional resources to facilitate countermeasures when a Bowler has two or more consecutive "red" months.
- A countermeasure can only be applied to a part of the process, so the indicator has to be focused on the area causing deviation.
- Several actions may be required to completely eliminate a deviation, as it is essential to separate each action to be discussed and its respective impact.

7.5 The 9th Month of Hoshin Review

In the September review, the CEO highlighted the progress in improving quality. The results on the number of complaints showed a substantial reduction following the application of the countermeasures set out in the May review, but there was still room to improve. The team was reminded that there was a lot of work to be done in order to achieve the annual objective of reducing costs of non-quality in Industrial Unit 1 by 320 thousand euros.

COUNTERMEASURES

Improvement priority:	Implement a Problem Solving process
Target to achieve:	# Customer Complaints from 46 to 23 by Dec/Year 1

Problem definition:

Defective prints represent 76% of customer complaints, of which 50% are for stains issues, 20% for print out of the printing area and 20% for errors in color specifications

Countermeasures

What	Who	When	How much (impact)
Technician: oven temperature control to better cure the paint	Maintenance Engineer	May 18	4 complaints
Technician: rail material change and characteristics adjustment	Process Engineer	May 22	2 complaints
Technician: color standardisation for control rules implementation regarding final printouts variations	Quality Engineer	May 22	2 complaints
		Total:	8

Date review: Sep - wk 2	**Primary responsibility:** Quality Manager

	Jan	Feb	Mar	Apr	May	Jun	Jul	Aug	Sep	Oct	Nov	Dec
Hoshin	2	4	6	8	10	12	13	15	17	19	21	23
Actual	3	6	9	10	11	11	12	13				

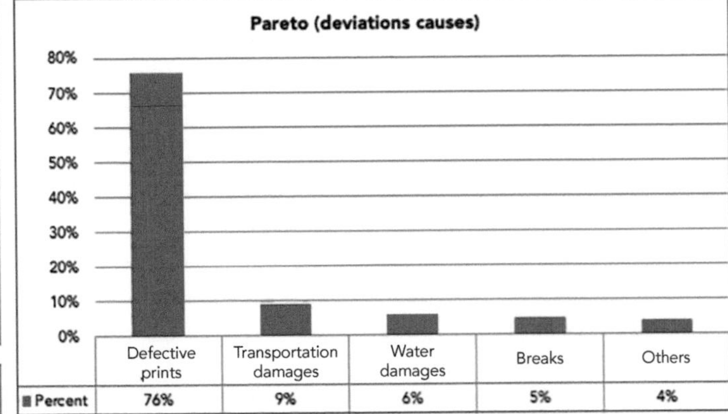

	Defective prints	Transportation damages	Water damages	Breaks	Others
Percent	76%	9%	6%	5%	4%

The CEO also wanted to underline the success in reducing inventory between June (when they had applied TMI) and August. The Logistics team had managed to reduce the inventory value from 12.3 to 11.1 million euros. Up to now it had been possible to implement 22 Kanban in Supplier #1. This was indeed good news.

"When 33 Kanban are implemented, we will reduce the inventory by another 600 thousand euros!" The CEO commented, confident that they would reach the 3 million euros inventory reduction, something that had already been assumed by the Executive Committee.

TARGETS TO ACHIEVE	Starting point	Annual target	Un.		Jan	Feb	Mar	Apr	May	Jun	Jul	Aug	Sept	Oct	Nov	Dec
Sales/FTE from 191 K€ to 200 K€ by Dec/Year 1	191.0	200.0	thousand €	***Hoshin***	191.8	192.5	193.3	194.0	194.8	195.5	196.3	197.0	197.8	198.5	199.3	200.0
				Actual	191.0	193.0	194.5	195.0	195.0	194.0	199.0	199.7	199.8			
External Services & Supplies from 17.7% to 16.4% of Sales (1 M€) by Dec/Year 1	17.7%	16.4%	%	***Hoshin***	17.6%	17.5%	17.4%	17.3%	17.2%	17.1%	16.9%	16.8%	16.7%	16.6%	16.5%	16.4%
				Actual	17.7%	17.5%	17.5%	17.4%	16.9%	16.9%	16.5%	16.9%	16.8%			
	0.0	1 035	thousand €	***Hoshin***	7.2	28.7	64.7	115.0	179.7	258.7	352.2	460.0	582.2	718.7	869.7	1 035.0
				Actual	0.0	26.5	39.8	79.6	265.4	318.5	557.3	424.6	537.4			
Planned Waste from 8% to 7% (505 K€) by Dec/Year 1	8.0%	7.0%	%	***Hoshin***	7.9%	7.8%	7.8%	7.7%	7.6%	7.5%	7.4%	7.3%	7.3%	7.2%	7.1%	7.0%
				Actual	8.1%	7.9%	9.0%	7.8%	7.7%	7.4%	7.2%	7.2%	7.1%			
	0	505	thousand €	***Hoshin***	42	84	126	168	210	253	295	337	379	421	463	505
				Actual	45	81	122	165	208	256	295	339	383			
Purchase Part Variance (PPV) from 50.5 M€ to 50 M€ by Dec/Year 1	0	500	thousand €	***Hoshin***	41.7	83.3	125.0	166.7	208.3	250.0	291.7	333.3	375.0	416.7	458.3	500.0
				Actual	0.0	0.0	55.2	110.1	184.5	294.6	336.6	368.6	400.6			
Non-quality Costs from 2 M€ to 1.52 M€ by Dec/Year 1	0	1.52	million €	***Hoshin***	0.13	0.25	0.38	0.51	0.63	0.76	0.89	1.01	1.14	1.27	1.39	1.52
				Actual	0.15	0.29	0.43	0.50	0.57	0.64	0.71	0.88	1.05			
# Customer Complaints from 84 to 42 by Dec/Year 1	0	42	#	***Hoshin***	4	7	11	14	18	21	25	28	32	35	39	42
				Actual	7	12	14	15	17	19	24	26	30			
On-Time Delivery from 75% to 82.5% by Dec/Year 1	75.0%	82.5%	%	***Hoshin***	75.6%	76.3%	76.9%	77.5%	78.1%	78.8%	79.4%	80.0%	80.6%	81.3%	81.9%	82.5%
				Actual	70.0%	71.0%	72.7%	73.0%	74.6%	75.0%	80.0%	84.0%	84.5%			
Inventory from 12.9 M€ to 9.7 M€ (6.2 to 12.3 turns) by Dec/Year 1	12.9	9.7	million €	***Hoshin***	12.6	12.4	12.1	11.8	11.6	11.3	11.0	10.8	10.5	10.2	10.0	9.7
				Actual	12.8	12.9	12.7	13.1	13.0	12.3	11.1	10.9	10.6			
Time To Market from 50 to 40 weeks until Dec/Year 1	50	40	wk	***Hoshin***	49	48	48	47	46	45	44	43	43	42	41	40
				Actual	50	49	49	45	49	46	40	44	35			
Sales from 79.6 M€ to 87.6 M€ until Dec/Year 1	0	87 575	thousand €	***Hoshin***	7 298	14 596	21 894	29 192	36 490	43 788	51 085	58 383	65 681	72 979	80 277	87 575
				Actual	6 897	13 766	20 636	27 505	34 375	41 244	48 114	54 983	61 853			
Vitality: New Customer Sales from 0 to 3 M€ by Dec/Year 1	0	3 000	thousand €	***Hoshin***	250	500	750	1 000	1 250	1 500	1 750	2 000	2 250	2 500	2 750	3 000
				Actual	203	380	525	607	871	1 016	1 245	1 367	1 427			

LESSONS LEARNED IN THE MONTH 9 REVIEW:

- "Good data = good KAIZEN™". With rigorous data collection and analysis, countermeasures are more accurate, actions are very specific and therefore can provide the desired results. This is the beginning of a Countermeasures Culture.
- The purpose of countermeasures is to eliminate deviations within a month to correct the adverse trend.

7.6 CEO's Year 2 X Matrix

With the end of the year coming, the CEO began discussing the objectives for the following year. It was necessary to complete the first version of the level 1 matrix and start the Catchball process. This would allow each level 2 manager to prepare their matrix, the Bowler and the Action Plan, together with their team. These elements were to be included in the MCR after the annual review, so that the start of the Hoshin Year 2 could proceed without delays.

7.6.1 Preparing Hoshin For Year 2

The consultant opened the session by displaying the level 1 matrix from the previous year:
"Together, we will review our progress in achieving 3-year Breakthrough Objectives and then draw up the new matrix for Year 2." He paused and continued "But first we need to estimate the end-of-year results and how much we will achieve from this year's objectives." The consultant questioned the audience "Are we going to achieve the forecasted EBITDA for the first year?"

"This will be ALFA's best year ever, but I do not think we will be able to reach our Hoshin's €7.2 million euros." the CEO quickly replied.

"What about quality, will we achieve our objectives?" the consultant asked again.

"We'll be close... But no. We will still be missing more or less 50 thousand euros." the Operations Director replied with some disappointment.

The consultant proceeded "Will we achieve our objective of on-time delivery?"

"That one, yes! It was achieved in August!" the Operations Director exclaimed, notoriously proud of his team.

The CEO concluded "Not to understate the excellent work we've done, it just means that we have not stretched this objective enough. We must change it next year!"

"And regarding time to market, how are we going to end the year?" the consultant asked.

"In September we were better than the annual objective, but then there was a problem with a project that caused a delay and spoiled the average. I think we will end the year with 44 weeks ..." the Engineering Director said.

The consultant took the opportunity to make a small reflection "What happened in this case should serve as an example to never let us relax, waiting for everything to go well. My experience says that there are unforeseen obstacles in our path; and how about our inventory objective?"

"I think we're going to hit the Hoshin, or at least we'll get very close," the Logistics Director said, in a motivated tone.

Everyone seemed excited about the results of their first year of Hoshin until the consultant asked one more question "And what about the sales growth objective?"

"We're not going to hit it at all, not even if sales promises are accounted for..." the CEO said, ironically, while the Marketing and Sales Director remained silent.

Intending to open up the discussion, the consultant asked what the Breakthrough Objectives should be for Year 2. After an exchange of ideas with his team members, the CEO concluded that EBITDA would remain his number 1 priority, but it was now essential to materialise sales growth. Therefore, improving OTD would remain a fundamental Breakthrough. As for improving quality, everyone considered that, given the level already achieved, this would no longer be an Improvement Priority. However, all its indicators would continue to be tracked in the MCR.

However, the CEO remained concerned about how to ensure sales growth the following year and so he told the team "It's not acceptable to go to Hoshin Year 2 without understanding why we cannot increase sales. I have already discussed this with the Kaizen Institute and we will focus our efforts on this subject early in the year. As a countermeasure, I want to schedule three KAIZEN™ events focused on sales growth. I would like each of you to fully participate in at least one of them, and I have already decided that I will attend two.

We need to set the dates for the Voice of Customer, Sales Order Processing and Value Selling events, and it is best to do it right now." The whole team agreed, as this was Hoshin's biggest challenge for Year 2.

7.6.2 How to Set Breakthrough Objectives for Year 2?

The consultant explained "Last year, the rule we followed was to calculate 50% of the 3-year Breakthrough Objectives and set them as objectives for the first year. We decided to do so because there was no track record to define the organisation skills in achieving 'stretched objectives'. By now, we have already completed over 100 KAIZEN™ Events in both plants and we believe this is a proven method to enable us to achieve our ambitious objectives. So, the question for Year 2 is: Why not opt for the same performance?" The consultant paused to let the team think about it. "At KAIZEN we call this "keeping the same run rate", i. e., why should we get different results if we are going to follow the same process? This means that the calculation of Objectives for Year 2 should be based on real data from the previous year's improvement run rate and not on a theoretical objective without any practical evidence."

A few minutes later, the team was divided into three analysis groups that were asked to calculate their run rates and then set the Breakthrough Objectives for Year 2. Everyone in the room was aware that these Objectives should be brave and disruptive enough to ensure the success of the objectives set for the 3 years of Hoshin. There was a strong drive on the part of some team members to set the Year 3 targets as the objectives for Year 2, but at KAIZEN™, data always comes first and emotions second. Therefore, the consultant insisted that the groups to calculate the run rate for each improvement priority. One hour later, the calculations showed that the expectation was acceptable. Assuming the obligation to perform the same number of KAIZEN™ Events as in Year 1 and be focused on their Improvement Priorities, it was fully agreed that the Breakthrough Objectives for Year 2 would be:

1. EBITDA from EUR 6,1 million to EUR 10 million.
2. OTD from 87% to 92% (objective for Year 3 reworked).
3. Free Cash Flow from EUR 7 million to 8.6 million.
4. Time to Market from 44 weeks to 34 weeks.

With everyone aligned and motivated, they completed the X Matrix for Year 2.

The CEO and his team knew that these objectives had been defined based on real facts. They had one year of results to prove it, which allowed them to be more confident regarding the success of the implementation in the second year.

LEVEL 1 X MATRIX

Time To Market fro 44 to 34 weeks by Year 2	Free Cash Flow from 7M€ to 8.6 M€ by Year 2	On-Time Delivery from 87% to 92%* by Year 2	EBITDA from 6.1 M€ to 10 M€ by Year 2	L1 Improvement priorities	Sales/ FTE from 200 K€ to 207 K€ by Dec/Year 2	Ext. Services & Supplies from 16.6% to 15.5% of Sales (914 K€) by Dec/Year 2	Planned Waste from 6.6% to 5.6% (514.9 K€) Dec/Year 2	On-Time Delivery from 87% to 92% by Dec/Year 2	Time To Market from 44 to 34 weeks by Dec/ Year 2	Inventory from 9.8 M€ to 6.8 M€ until Dec/Year 2	Mean Receipt Timeframe from 83 to 76 days by Dec/Year 2	Average Payment period (PMP) from 95 to 78 days by Dec/Year 2	Sales from 83.1 M€ to 89.3 M€ by Dec/Year 2	Vitality: New Customer Sales from 0 to 3 M€ by Dec/Year 2	# SKU of Raw Material and Finished Goods from 1500 to 900 by Dec/Year 2	Operations Manager	Engineering Manager	Materials & Logistics Manager	Marketing & Sales Manager	Human Resources Manager	Purchasing Manager	Financial Manager	IT Manager
			●	Implement a process to reduce #SKU (Raw Material and Finished Goods)											●	○	○		●		○		
	●			Implement a process to reduce Working Capital						●	●	●						●	○		○	○	
		●		Optimise a process to increase On-Time Delivery				●								○		●	○				○
			●	Implement a process to reduce Product Cost (VA/VE)			●										●						
			●	Implement a process to increase Productivity	●	●										●		○		○			○
●				Accelerate a process to reduce New Product Lead Times					●							○	●						
●			●	Accelerate a process to improve Marketing & Sales									●	●					●				○

Annual Breakthrough objectives | Targets to Improve (TTI) | 3-year Breakthrough objectives

Time To Market	Free Cash Flow	On-Time Delivery	EBITDA	3-year Breakthrough objectives
			●	EBITDA from 2.3 M€ to 12 M€ in 3 years (20% sales growth included)
		●		On-Time Delivery from 75% to 92% in 3 years
	●			Free Cash Flow from 545 K€ to 10 M € in 3 years
●				Time To Market from 50 to 30 weeks in 3 years

Resources
- ● Primary responsibility
- ○ Secondary responsibility

Level 1 X Matrix, Year 2

Hoshin Review is a key part of Strat to Action, which includes the implementation plan achievement periodic reviews of results including, whenever necessary, countermeasures for correcting deviations.

In the first year of the Hoshin implementation at ALFA, the sales results were much lower than expected: by EUR 4.5 million. The action was detailed by implementing aggressive countermeasures defined for the following year in Chapter 9, describing the three KAIZEN™ Events required to correct the sales shortfall.

Year 1

Year 1 Results

The Rewarded Effort

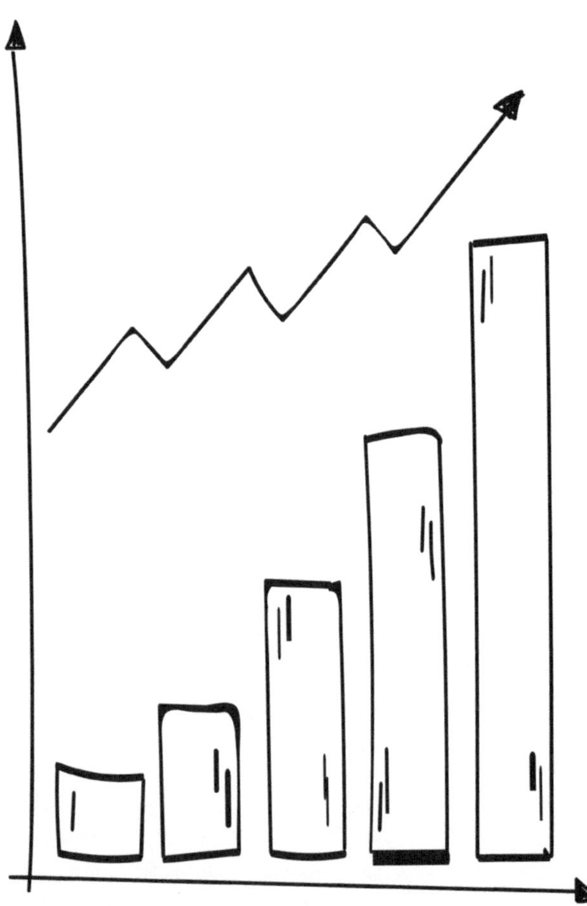

The Hoshin Review cycle ends each year with the Annual Review. This chapter describes the Year 1 review, scheduled for the same date as the usual monthly review, but instead of the standard 2 hours, the Executive Committee set aside all morning. After presenting the agenda, the consultant began by explaining the purpose of the last revision of the year in detail and its importance for subsequent years. He also shared that, in the last part of the session, they would reflect on the difficulties in integrating Hoshin into ALFA and the lessons learned that followed. It was time to acknowledge the need for further improvement and define the countermeasures to overcome them.

8.1 Review of Year 1 Results

The results analysis of the year began with the CEO's review "I invite you to look at the results we have achieved." He proceeded, pointing to his Bowler. "I want to congratulate you all for the effort and dedication shown. Without this, we would not have reached EUR 6.1 million in EBITDA." Although the accounts were not closed yet, the CEO was confident in the result.

TARGET TO ACHIEVE	Starting point	Annual target	Un.		Jan	Feb	Mar	Apr	May	Jun	Jul	Aug	Sept	Oct	Nov	Dec
Sales/FTE from 191 K€ to 200 K€ by Dec/Year 1	191.0	200.0	thousand €	**Hoshin**	191.8	192.5	193.3	194.0	194.8	195.5	196.3	197.0	197.8	198.5	199.3	200.0
				Actual	191.0	193.0	194.5	195.0	195.0	194.0	199.0	199.7	199.8	198.5	198.9	200.0
External Services & Supplies from 17.7% to 16.4% of sales (1 M€) by Dec/Year 1	17.7%	16.4%	%	**Hoshin**	17.6%	17.5%	17.4%	17.3%	17.2%	17.1%	16.9%	16.8%	16.7%	16.6%	16.5%	16.4%
				Actual	17.7%	17.5%	17.5%	17.4%	16.9%	16.9%	16.5%	16.9%	16.8%	16.7%	16.6%	16.6%
	0.0	1 035	thousand €	**Hoshin**	7.2	28.7	64.7	115.0	179.7	258.7	352.2	460.0	582.2	718.7	869.7	1 035.0
				Actual	0.0	26.5	39.8	79.6	265.4	318.5	557.3	424.6	537.4	663.4	802.8	875.8
Planned Waste from 8% to 7% (505 K€) by Dec/Year 1	8.0%	7.0%	%	**Hoshin**	7.9%	7.8%	7.8%	7.7%	7.6%	7.5%	7.4%	7.3%	7.3%	7.2%	7.1%	7.0%
				Actual	8.1%	7.9%	9.0%	7.8%	7.7%	7.4%	7.2%	7.2%	7.1%	7.4%	7.0%	6.6%
	0	505	thousand €	**Hoshin**	42	84	126	168	210	253	295	337	379	421	463	505
				Actual	45	81	122	165	208	256	295	339	383	424	470	507
Purchase Part Variance (PPV) from 50.5 M€ to 50 M€ by Dec/Year 1	0	500	thousand €	**Hoshin**	41.7	83.3	125.0	166.7	208.3	250.0	291.7	333.3	375.0	416.7	458.3	500.0
				Actual	0.0	0.0	55.2	110.1	184.5	294.6	336.6	368.6	400.6	432.6	464.6	496.6
Non-quality Costs from 2M€ to 1.52 M€ by Dec/Year 1	0	1.52	million €	**Hoshin**	0.13	0.25	0.38	0.51	0.63	0.76	0.89	1.01	1.14	1.27	1.39	1.52
				Actual	0.15	0.29	0.43	0.50	0.57	0.64	0.71	0.88	1.05	1.27	1.34	1.54
# Customer Complaints from 84 to 42 by Dec/Year 1	0	42	#	**Hoshin**	4	7	11	14	18	21	25	28	32	35	39	42
				Actual	7	12	14	15	17	19	24	26	30	35	40	42
On-Time Delivery from 75% to 82.5% by Dec/Year 1	75.0%	82.5%	%	**Hoshin**	75.6%	76.3%	76.9%	77.5%	78.1%	78.8%	79.4%	80.0%	80.6%	81.3%	81.9%	82.5%
				Actual	70.0%	71.0%	72.7%	73.0%	74.6%	75.0%	80.0%	84.0%	84.5%	85.2%	86.7%	87.0%
Inventory from 12.9 M€ to 9.7 M€ (6.2 to 12.3 turns) by Dec/Year 1	12.9	9.7	million €	**Hoshin**	12.6	12.4	12.1	11.8	11.6	11.3	11.0	10.8	10.5	10.2	10.0	9.7
				Actual	12.8	12.9	12.7	13.1	13.0	12.3	11.1	10.9	10.6	10.5	9.9	9.8
Time To Market from 50 to 40 weeks until Dec/Year 1	50	40	wk	**Hoshin**	49	48	48	47	46	45	44	43	43	42	41	40
				Actual	50	49	49	45	49	46	40	44	35	45	44	44
Sales from 79.6 M€ to 87.6 M€ until Dec/Year 1	0	87 575	thousand €	**Hoshin**	7 298	14 596	21 894	29 192	36 490	43 788	51 085	58 383	65 681	72 979	80 277	87 575
				Actual	6 897	13 766	20 636	27 505	34 375	41 244	48 114	54 983	61 853	68 722	75 592	83 056
Vitality: New Customer Sales from 0 to 3 M€ by Dec/Year 1	0	3 000	thousand €	**Hoshin**	250	500	750	1 000	1 250	1 500	1 750	2 000	2 250	2 500	2 750	3 000
				Actual	203	380	525	607	871	1 016	1 245	1 367	1 427	1 568	1 760	2 137

Level 1 Bowling chart, Year 1

The meeting continued with a detailed analysis of the main indicators shown in the MCR throughout the year:

- **PRODUCTIVITY**

The objective was to increase sales from 191 thousand to 200 thousand euros per FTE, which is exactly the result achieved at the end of Year 1. The realisation of 26 KAIZEN™ Events in both industrial units, according to the planned roadmap, had contributed to the 5% productivity gains across the organisation. The events were focused on JIT (8 events), OEE (6 events), Mizusumashi (4 events) and Daily KAIZEN™ (8 events).

- **SUPPLY AND EXTERNAL SERVICES**

The objective was to reduce the Supply and External Services costs result from 17.7% to 16.4% of sales. The value achieved was 16.6%, which represented a saving of 876 thousand euros, an amount with a high impact on EBITDA. This had largely been achieved through increased productivity of internal teams, which allowed outsourced services to be insourced in addition to the renegotiation of contracts by the Purchasing department.

- **COST OF PLANNED WASTE**

The Target to be Improved aimed to reduce this indicator from 8.0% to 7.0% for raw materials. The result of Year 1 was 6.6%, which represented 507 thousand euros of cost reduction. This was mainly due to better use of raw material, replacement by lower cost materials, effectively fulfilling the same function, and making small investments to improve the performance of cutting presses. The Engineering Department had carried out 5 VA/VE events to deliver this result.

- **COST OF RAW MATERIALS**

With the outlined objective, a saving of 500 thousand euros was anticipated on materials expenditure. The result at the end of the year was 497 thousand euros. To achieve this, the purchasing team had completed 4 PPV events in both industrial units.

- **COST OF NON-QUALITY**

This indicator had a planned reduction of 480 thousand euros, moving from the previous 2 million to 1.52 million euros. The result was very close to the target, standing at 1.54 million euros, with a saving of 460 thousand euros. The number of customer complaints had also dropped from 84 to a new record of 42. To achieve this excellent quality improvement, a series of KAIZEN™ Events focusing on Auto Quality (2 events), Poka-yoke (2 events) and Problem Solving (4 events) had been triggered by the Operations Department. The Daily KAIZEN™ also contributed decisively to the positive evolution of this indicator.

- **OTD COMPLIANCE**

The objective was to improve the OTD from 75.0% to 82.5%. This was greatly exceeded and stood at 87.0%. A very important result enabling shorter Lead times whilst improving on-time deliveries. The success of this outcome was due to the accomplishment of several KAIZEN™ Events for Pull Planning implementation (13 events) and WIP supermarket standardisation (7 events).

- **INVENTORY**

The improvement target was to reduce inventory value from 12.9 to 9.7 million euros. The result achieved by the end of the year was 9.8 million euros, representing a contribution of 3.2 million euros to free cash flow. The largest part of this figure came from the 6 TMI KAIZEN™ Events, although supermarket standardisation and the new pull planning model also contributed to the result.

- **NEW PRODUCTS - TIME TO MARKET**

The goal was to reduce the new products development lead time from 50 to 40 weeks. In December the indicator was at 44 weeks. This had been achieved after a long implementation of a 9-step New Product Development process (9 Step Gateway Review). The conditions were then created so that all those involved in the 9-step process could work in cooperation, with less rework and in compliance with planned deadlines.

- **SALES**

The goal was to increase sales from 79.6 million euros to 87.6 million euros. That is, a 10% growth which, in fact, had not materialised, leaving the annual sales value at 83.1 million euros. This had become the organisation's biggest challenge and priority for the second year of implementation. As requested by the CEO, the Director of Marketing and Sales started by presenting the countermeasures planned for the beginning of the year, which all members of the Executive Committee fully agreed to make a top priority.

With these countermeasures, it was intended to reach 87,6 million euros before the beginning of the second half of Year 2.

COUNTERMEASURES

Improvement priority:	Design a process to improve Marketing & Sales
Target to improve:	Sales from 83.1 million to 89.3 million € by Dec. Year 2

Problem definition:

The target to be improved intends an increase in sales from 79.6 to 87.6 million €. The indicator is currently at 83.1 million € and it has been the greatest organisational challenge so far. This indicator is a priority for Year 2 implementation. The Marketing & Sales Manager and the Executive Commitee have decided to implement 3 KAIZEN™ events as a countermeasure for the results achieved : (1) Voice of the Customer. (2) Value Selling and (3) Sales Order Processing.

Countermeasures

What	Who	When	How much (impact)
Voice of the Customer KAIZEN™ Event	Marketing & Sales Manager	Jan wk 3 and 4	~ 2.8M €
Value Selling KAIZEN™ Event	Marketing & Sales Manager	Feb wk 3	~ 1.2M €
Sales Order Processing Mapping KAIZEN™ Event	Orders Processing Manager	Feb wk 1	~ 200 thousand €

Review date: Jan - wk 2, Year 2	**Primary responsibility:** Marketing & Sales Manager

Sales Monthly Progress

Hoshin / Actual

Year 1 — Year 2

	Jul	Aug	Sep	Oct	Nov	Dec	Jan	Feb	Mar	Apr	May	Jun
Hoshin	51	58	66	73	80	88	07	15	22	30	37	45
Actual	48	55	62	69	76	83						

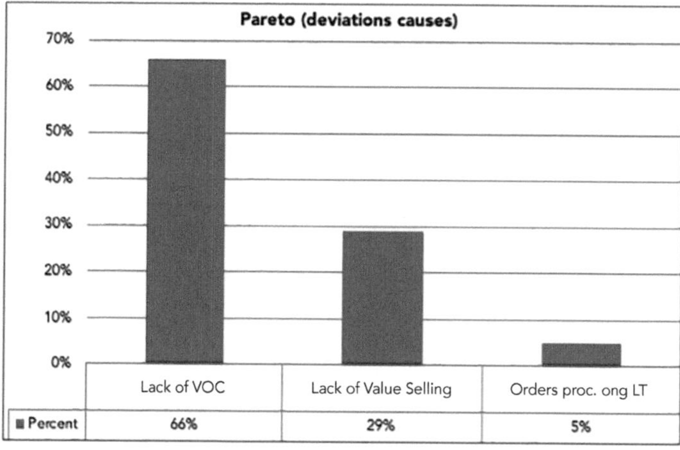

- **FREE CASH FLOW**

Free cash flow increased from 545 thousand to 7.0 million euros, basically due to the release of 3.2 million euros in inventory and the results achieved in Year 1. This objective would continue into year 2 since the TMI methodology had only been implemented in the three main suppliers.

- **EBITDA**

Hoshin's EBITDA target was to move from 2.3 million euros to 7.2 million euros. EBITDA at the end of Year 1 was 6.1 million euros.

- **KAIZEN™**

The KAIZEN™ plan for Year 1 ended with 128 events carried out in both industrial units, since the Sales Order Processing event had not been accomplished. In the first year, the workshops had focused on inventory reduction (24 events), increasing productivity (22 events) and improving quality (10 events). The return on investment in the Kaizen Institute, compared to the increase in EBITDA, was a return on investment of 3 to 1.

"And there is an indicator that we are not yet evaluating, which is the motivation and involvement of all our people, which this year was fantastic!" commented the Director of Human Resources, visibly satisfied.

"It was worth the effort!" exclaimed the Engineering Director, as he patted the Logistics Director on the back.

"Boss, we should hold a party to celebrate the results", the Operations Director said, teasing the CEO.

The consultant smiled and proposed moving forward with the agenda as he asked for calm in the noisy room. The year was not over yet. It was necessary to complete the Hoshin Review process and to ponder, as a team, what could be improved.

8.2 How to Coach the Executive Team to Reflect?

A structured way of thinking allows for the identification of essential opportunities and solutions for the success of a transformation such as the one that was intended at ALFA. The next step on the agenda was the consultant's presentation based on the Kaizen Institute's experience of organisation's most common failures in their first year of Hoshin implementation.

MAIN FAILURE MODES

The consultant posed a set of questions to evaluate the performance of ALFA within Hoshin. All of them were based on the major failures committed by companies in the early implementation stages. The Executive Board had to respond to each question in order to understand the weaknesses, and improvements that should be applied in the coming years.

1. How effective was the Hoshin Planning? Have we achieved the planned Breakthroughs?
2. How useful was the data analysis when creating a Countermeasure culture?
3. Have the Breakthroughs been standardised, now being part of the daily management processes?
4. Are we sustaining productivity gains by applying the standard or are we reallocating resources?
5. Did we apply resources effectively? Was there an even distribution of activities among all teams?
6. Have the Improvement Priorities been deployed to the appropriate level? Have we made sure that the best person in the team is responsible for the action, and not relied upon the formal hierarchy?
7. Was the Action Plan managed so that improvements could be implemented at the point of impact?
8. Is there a clear understanding of the KAIZEN™ methodologies, with application of the correct tool for each objective?
9. Were the KAIZEN™ Breakthroughs led by members of the management team?
10. Have our goals changed during the year? Have they been diverted by internal or external factors?
11. Have the Hoshin monthly review meetings been productive or do we need to improve their structuring?
12. Is Hoshin leading a real breakthrough in the organisation? Have we changed paradigms? Did we get 2-digit results?

After a few minutes of discussion on each issue, it was possible to identify the main opportunities for improving the application of the Strat to Action process at ALFA. The main conclusions were grouped into five bullets as follows:

Standardisation

- There was no alignment as to what the organisational standard was. Different Action Plan formats and Countermeasures were used, and several departments continued to insist on their own versions.
- An absence of impact calculation in planning KAIZEN™ Events was very common.

Review Meetings

- Although Level 1 meetings normally kept to the 2 hours scheduled, level 2 meetings generally lasted about 4 hours.
- There was still a tendency for the person responsible for Improvement Priorities to describe what they had done instead of presenting the data and analyses that underpinned the countermeasures.

Misson Control Rooms

- It was possible to improve Visual Management in the MCRs of both plants because there was too much information and too few charts. The improvement was aimed at identifying deviations after 5 seconds of looking at the indicators.
- There was a need to relocate the MCR location in Industrial Unit 2 since it was too far from the work areas and therefore not used for project meetings, except when the Executive Committee held their meeting in this unit.

Organisational Structure

- There was some difficulty in passing on the sense of urgency in the application of countermeasures, since the departmental structure required timely planning of all activities.
- Multidisciplinary project teams had difficulty in recruiting full-time staff during the workshop implementation period.

Variable Compensation Model

- The existing annual award model was heavily dependent on achieving the budget and did not differentiate who had achieved the Hoshin goals.
- The annual award goals were not yet fully aligned with the Improvement Priorities as defined in Hoshin.

After the presentation, the consultant agreed with the identified opportunities. He was satisfied to see how honestly everyone in the room had exposed their weaknesses. The team was determined to improve, so the Action Plan for these improvements was promptly finalised. Before concluding the exercise, the consultant commented on two aspects that he considered to be important for the success of ALFA's transformation in the coming years:

"If we look at the variable compensation method followed by several World Class Companies, we will find that they essentially reward their teams for their performance achieved at Hoshin. Thus, they are able to generate greater motivation and effort in the organisation, 'to go the extra mile', as they say." He continued after a pause. "Another aspect that ALFA will certainly have to consider is its organisational structure. As your company consolidates the improvements in value flows, you will feel the need to reduce those departmental structures with lower added value and integrate tthose functions into a dedicated and multidisciplinary model that, in KAIZEN™, we call Value Stream. It is normal that we expect ALFA to remove vertical silos over the next two years and create a horizontal organisation in Value Stream.

To conclude the morning's session, it was time for the entire team to update the Mission Control Room with the Year 2 matrices, their Bowlers and Action Plans, to continue with another year of Strat to Action.

This had been the best day since the CEO came to ALFA. The whole team was thrilled with the results. He took the opportunity to remind them that they would have to achieve even better results in the following year.

In the first year of Hoshin's implementation at ALFA, sales fell far shorter than expected, with a difference of 4.5 million euros above the target. As a result of this, a set of Countermeasures was defined for the following year. Chapter 9 describes these Countermeasures, implemented through 3 KAIZEN™ Events.

Countermeasures to Increase Sales

Customers talk, we listen

The sales objective for ALFA, in Hoshin year 1, was €87.6 million euros. However, the result was below expectations, with the year ending with sales of €83.1 million euros. This was the biggest deviation to the plan; sales growth became the Executive Committee's priority for the second year and as a countermeasure, it was agreed with the Director of Marketing and Sales that 3 KAIZEN™ Events would be carried out in the first quarter of Year 2. Their goal was to close the gap in sales and to have them totally recovered by the middle of the year.

Some suggested strategies are presented in this chapter that allow organisations to improve their performance in the Marketing and Sales processes. In this context, organisations are challenged to question how they can meet and even exceed customer expectations. This exercise will allow you to identify and act on the processes with a real impact on customer satisfaction.

9.1 The Voice of the Customer

The Voice of the Customer (VOC) methodology allows you to understand what customers think about your service levels and how your products are important for them; it also will identify their expectations and desires. It is an essential methodology for growth of sales empowerment, with a total focus on the customer feedback.

This KAIZEN™ Event consists of 4 phases:

- PHASE 1: **Internal data analysis.**
- PHASE 2: **Current state design - customer interviews.**
- PHASE 3: **Current state design - interviews with potential customers.**
- PHASE 4: **Action Plan Definition.**

The workshop was prepared by members of the Marketing and Sales team, who gathered all available information regarding clients' histories. Before starting the work, the CEO informed them that he would participate as a member of the team and that the leader of the event would be the Director of Marketing and Sales. The CEO also emphasised the importance of this and the following initiatives:
"Today we are about to begin implementing the countermeasures that I hope will bring sales back up to our forecasted sales revenue for the year."

Phase 1: Analysis of Internal Data

The Marketing and Sales Director began by thanking his team for their efforts in gathering essential information for the workshop's first phase. Good data equals a good KAIZEN™ event. Based on these data it would be possible to gain a first insight into the organisation's performance regarding the fundamental competitive factors of on-time delivery, lead time, batch size, quality, price, sales volume, and profitability. In order to carry out this analysis, the product range sold by ALFA was split in 3 distinct categories: (1) products with declining sales, (2) products with stagnant sales, and (3) products with growing sales. For all of them, data was prepared covering the previous 3 years.

Competitive Factors	Declining Sales (old products)	Stagnated Sales (core products)	Emerging Sales (breakthrough products)
OTD	<75%	<80%	85%
Lead Time	3 - 5 weeks	10 days	5 weeks
Batch	100 units	5 pallets	Make to Order
Quality	> 1% of defects	< 1% of defects	Few occurences
Price	low	average	high
Sales	16.6 M€	57.1 M€	9.4 M€
Profitability	average	average	low

Key competitive factors - assessment before VOC

After the exercise, the entire team analysed and discussed the data already collected. The CEO and the Marketing and Sales Director did not seem surprised by the findings:

"Well, last year the quality of our products and services improved substantially, but unfortunately our customers have a very good memory and they remember only our 'dark' past. - It was a self-justifying attitude from the Marketing and Sales Director.

Whilst reviewing the VOC data, the Directors kept repeating that both they and their team knew perfectly the position of ALFA in the market, as they were in constant contact with customers. "We have already made great changes in our processes and we have already explained this to our customers, so I see no benefit in going over and over what has already been done by the sales team. Honestly, I think that going to the street and interviewing customers, is a waste of time. But in any case, if this is the team's decision, I support the actions that are being proposed, and I will be open-minded to listen to our customers feedback."

Without commenting on the statement, the consultant proceeded: "We must now move on to the next step. We need to verify whether this is actually the perception that customers have of our organisation, before going on with any kind of action." That said, he went on to explain to the team how the Voice of the Customer exercise would be carried out. "Let's start by identifying the different points of customer contact in their process of buying an ALFA product. After that we will conduct a series of interviews to capture customers' expectations at each point, discovering whether we meet them or not and if not, why, and ultimately to measure customer satisfaction. And remember, the customer will give us many reasons to justify not buying our products. Listen and register, do not feel disappointed or angry because of possible negative feedback. Look at it rather as an opportunity to improve and grow."

As a result, the team would have to obtain customer feedback on each competitive factor in order to compare their perception with the information initially collected. The consultant continued. "Obviously we will not interview all our customers. We will work with a reliable sample and for this we need to identify which customers represent 80% of the category under analysis. The consultant continued his line of reasoning."After compiling the list with the target companies, we need to identify the different players in the decision-making process and their respective roles. Beware of considering that the decision maker is not always the most obvious person, such as the Purchasing Manager. My advice is to talk to your sales team colleagues who are closer to each customer, to understand the decision-making process in each organisation."

Once the interviewees were identified, the team proceeded to prepare the interview script and schedule.

Phase 2: Current State Design - Customers Interviews

The second part of the workshop took place a few days after the last interview. In the first instance, it was necessary to organise and present the information gathered during the interviews, with the already summarised results. The initial data was reviewed and the reality was more disturbing than the internal analysis indicated. The team admitted that without the interviews, a lot of pertinent information would have passed them by. As a result of the exercise, qualitative information was also collected, focusing on quality, delivery and customer relations.

The consultant explained that the observed gap was absolutely normal, remarking that the perception that organisations have of themselves does not often correspond to the reality of how customers see them.

Despite the discomfort among the sales team, everyone admitted there were several pressing gaps to be closed.

Competitive Factors	Declining Sales (old products)		Stagnated Sales (core products)		Emerging Sales (breakthrough products)	
	ALFA	**Customer Feedback**	**ALFA**	**Customer Feedback**	**ALFA**	**Customer Feedback**
OTD	<75%	<60% (delivery quality decrease; serious delays in summer period)	< 80%	<70% (several issues with container shipments; customers prefer pallet delivery; difficulties in getting a deliver deadline confirmation)	85%	30% (OTD = 30% - customer not satisfied with a 5 week delivery time; OTD = 90% - for 15 week deliveries)
Lead time	3-5 weeks	3-5 weeks	10 days	10 days	5 weeks	15 weeks
Batch	100 units	1000 units	5 pallets	20 pallets	made to order	made to order
Quality	> 1% of defects	> 10% of defects (it is decreasing; handling damage; low quality packaging materials)	< 1% of defects	< 5% of defects (great price-quality ratio)	Few occurences	High quality
Price	low	low	medium	medium	high	high
Customer relationship		Salespeople only visits customers to inform about price increase		Resistance to paying transportation costs price increases; salespeople do not update customers about new products		Good relationship between customers and suppliers

Key competitive factors - assessment after VOC

Phase 3: Current State Design - Interviews with potential Customers

The next VOC phase was to listen to the opinion of potential customers.

"Since we're not selling to any of these companies, at least for now, we must collect another kind of data in these interviews. Therefore, we must discover the value of each potential customer in the different categories, what each of them takes for granted, what they do not value, what they think no one else offers but they would like to obtain, and the reasons they are buying from other competitors rather than from ALFA," The consultant said, while writing each of these points on the flipchart.

Reflecting on the previously used methodology, the new interviews were duly prepared and carried out by the work team and, a few days later, the information was compiled and presented by the Marketing and Sales Director.

By then, the importance of VOC application was quite clear to all. The consultant emphasised the importance of regular implementation of this process, allowing organisations to listen to the customer in a structured and repeated way. This was a mandatory need due to fast market changes as well as customer expectations. The CEO agreed and asked that, from that moment on, an effort was made in order to standardise this process as soon as possible at ALFA.

Declining Sales (old products)	Stagnated Sales (core products)	Emerging Sales (breakthrough products)
Mainly end-of-life products, so changing supplier is not a solution	High cost, some customers would consider buying the product, if it was 10% less Several competitors "My current supplier works well, so I see no reason to change" One of the new customers gave up buying after the first delivery had been a disaster Poor follow-up by salespeople	The customer sees the value in these products, but they are not willing to pay high costs for it Poor or non-existent competition Some customers consider the price competitive and they would definitely buy it if the ensured Lead Time was of 3 weeks

VOC summary done to potential customers

As a next step, it was important to understand the information compiled and to outline specific actions to solve the newly identified problems.

Phase 4: The Action Plan Definition

At the beginning of the last phase, the consultant highlighted once again the importance of collecting reliable data as this was the best way to gain a deep understanding of Customer Expectation. This was exactly what the team had been focused in the previous phases - and the conclusions showed initial perception to be quite different from reality.

For the Action Plan definition, it was necessary to list the improvement opportunities identified in VOC and to prioritise them. The consultant proposed all actions be characterised in terms of implementation difficulty and impact. The easiest activities to be performed, with the greatest added value, were considered a priority.

At the end of this KAIZEN™ Event, the resulting actions were added to the Improvement Priority Action Plan "Accelerate the Process to Improve Marketing and Sales" for Year 2.

9.2 Sales Order Processing

The Marketing and Sales Director and the Sales Managers of both plants were concerned about the high absenteeism and turnover rate in the department. It was about time to improve Sales Order Processing, the KAIZEN™ Event to improve this transactional process, comprised of 3 key phases:

- **Phase 1: Ordering process mapping.**
- **Phase 2: Improvement opportunities identification and new process design.**
- **Phase 3: Implementation of the solution and results confirmation.**

Phase 1: Ordering Process Mapping

In the first phase, the current state was mapped, including all the tasks required to carry out order processing. For this, the following tools were applied:

- **Process mapping** - Task sequence identification, runtime and lead time.
- **MUDA Observation** - MUDA vs. value added in each job.
- **Spaghetti Diagram** - Graphical representation of movements made by each team member.
- **Handoff diagram** - Graphical representation of the information exchange between two people, two systems, or one person and a system (and vice versa).

- **Balance Loss** - Graphical representation of the workload imbalance among employees.
- **Right First Time (RFT)** - Rate of orders processed with no errors or locks.
- **Takt time** - The average time frame between each order entry.

Using this data, the team was able to present a solid analysis of the current process state, detailing key performance indicators and the Pareto diagram of main causes of errors in the order handling process.

Through detailed observation it was possible to measure the real added value and describe the waste in this activity (MUDA observation). Through a sample of 146 orders, the team concluded that only 10% were correctly entered into the system at the first attempt (Right First Time indicator). Therefore, there were high levels of rework, low productivity and lack of team motivation.

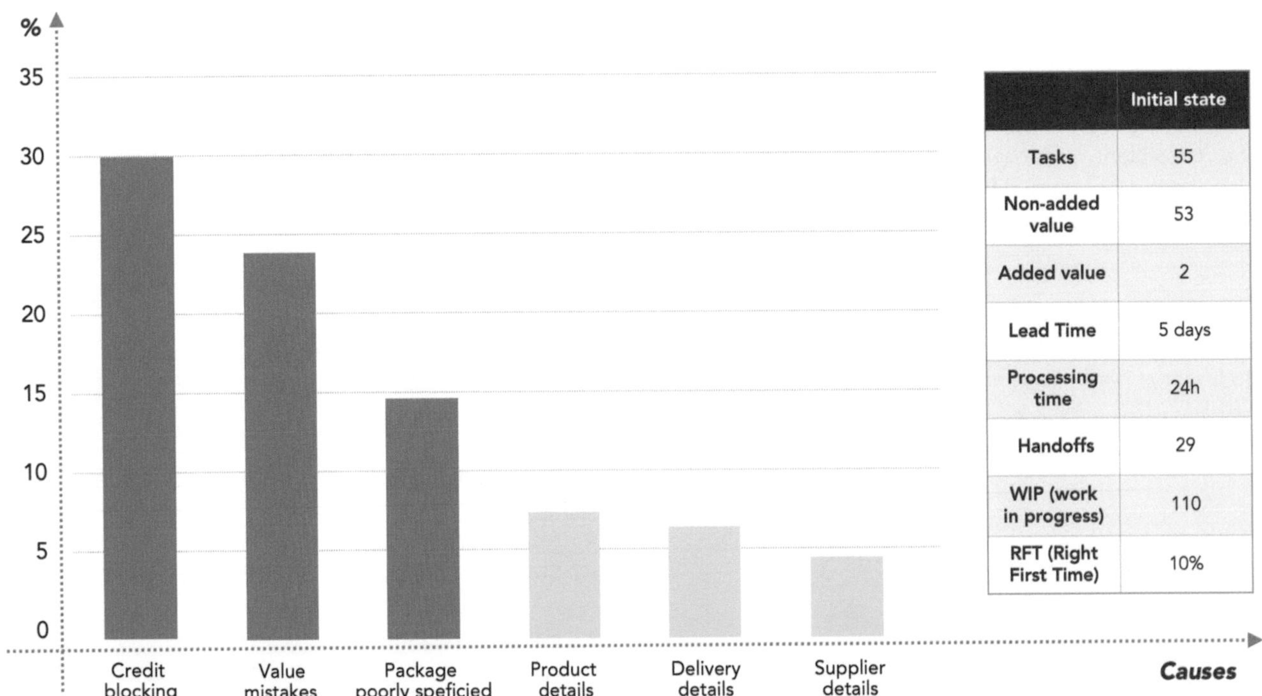

	Initial state
Tasks	55
Non-added value	53
Added value	2
Lead Time	5 days
Processing time	24h
Handoffs	29
WIP (work in progress)	110
RFT (Right First Time)	10%

Right First Time pareto diagram

In order to prioritise and channel the team effort, the 3 main causes of error in order handling were presented. Together, these 3 main causes accounted for 68% of all orders requiring rework:

1. **Customers with blocked credit** (30% of RFT).
2. **Errors in order pricing** (24% of the RFT).
3. **Unspecified packaging** (14% of RFT).

Then the consultant asked:
"How does your team solve these kinds of problems on a daily basis?"

One of the team members answered promptly:
"The only way to do it is to call the salesman that placed the order and wait for him to send us the correct information."

Another team member added:
"The problem is that when we ask them for help in solving these issues, they are always busy! It's very frustrating for us, as you can imagine."

The Marketing and Sales Director, who already knew the problem, remained silent. The CEO, on the other hand, showed a certain uneasiness regarding so much waste associated with a process that should be fast. Everyone in the room was aware that the process had very large levels of waste that needed to be eliminated.

Phase 2: Improvement Opportunities Identification and New Process Design

After the current state had been presented, what followed was the design of the solution. For this exercise, the consultant divided the team into 3 working groups, so that each of them could address one of the main causes of errors already identified in order processing.

The analysis and the conclusions reached are described below.

1. CUSTOMERS WITH BLOCKED CREDIT

After a more detailed deep dive, the group realised that customers' credit limits had been set 5 years ago and had not been reviewed since so they did not reflect the volume of existing orders, which in the meantime had doubled. This led to a situation where more than 40% of the orders needed to be approved by the Finance Department. This was not seen as a priority and orders were left to accumulate until finally someone in finance just approved a batch. Initially, the group worked on customer credit risk revaluation, having integrated the latest financial and commercial data, and the credit limits were updated accordingly. Subsequently, a procedure was developed in order to ensure that all process steps were performed in the most efficient way and without rework. In addition, a quick response was implemented in the procedure to anticipate the entry of new customers, an extraordinary increase in sales volume and a sudden increased risk with a specific customer.

2. PRICING ERRORS

Initially, the group checked the system and the price catalogue, thinking that there might be several errors in the database. However, while carrying out a more detailed analysis, they concluded that the source of the problem was related to the discounts and special conditions agreed locally by the sales team. In these situations, the order was not automatically processed by the system, being blocked and having to wait for manual input of the agreed exception. The solution adopted by the group took into account the introduction of only 4 types of discount in the order entry menu instead of the 50 initially considered.

3. UNSPECIFIED PACKAGING

The group found that the Sales team sometimes did not define all the characteristics of the intended packaging type, or the suggested packaging was not a current product and would need some slight adjustment, which made order processing difficult or impossible. In this case, the system could not process orders without manual intervention.

As a solution, a new standard was created with the Sales team, including the available packaging options for each product. All improvement proposals were discussed, tested and properly adjusted.

Phase 3: Solution Implementation and Results Confirmation

In addition, based on the KAIZEN™ concepts of "Quality First" and "One Piece Flow", the consultant introduced the whole team to the concept of **one stop cell**, according to which all transactions were carried out in the same physical space. All the order processing, from the customer queries to the delivery date confirmation would take less than 5 minutes. This was a very different approach from the existing one and the consultant scheduled a visit to a company where KAIZEN™ had already implemented this concept.

In the beginning the commercial assistants that attended the event could not imagine being able to process orders in such a short time, but observation on the ground allowed them to understand the principles supporting the "one stop cell". After the visit, they were visibly enthusiastic to implement the same concept at ALFA's.

Before changes, the handling of orders at ALFA's involved the use of 8 separate locations to complete the entire process. A One Stop Cell was designed to be used only when orders were placed. During the time when this was not happening, employees would be allocated to other functions, contributing to the overall productivity increase of the department. After reviewing the layout, it was easily concluded that it would be enough to have a person working part-time in the cell.

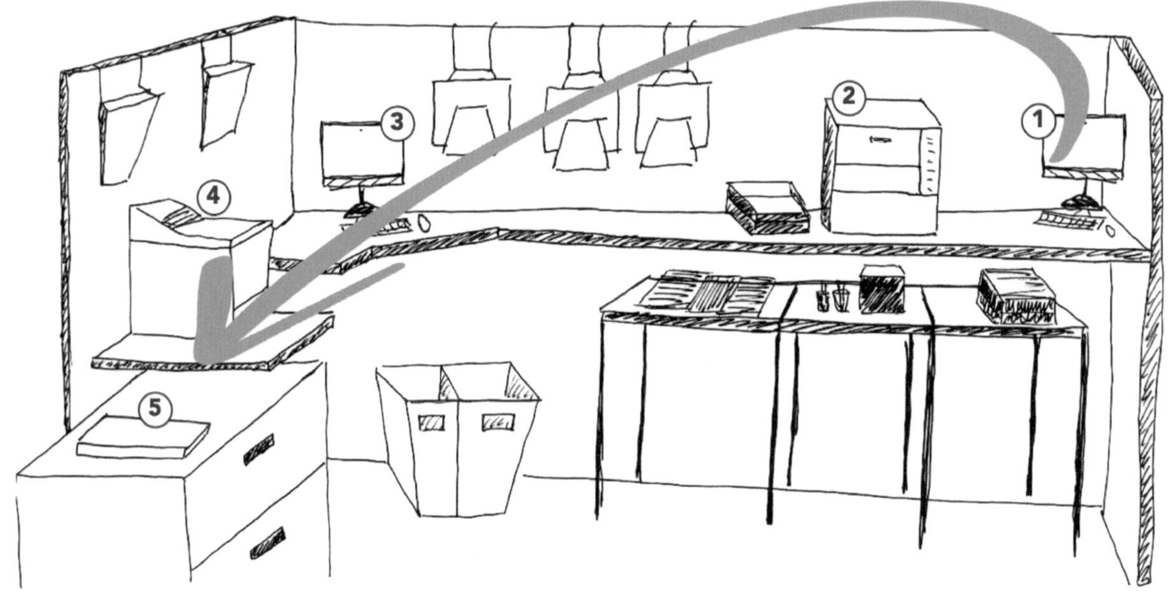

	Initial state	Final state
Tasks	55	29
Non-added value	53	27
Added value	2	2
Lead Time	5 days	5 min.
Processing time	24h	5 min.
Handoffs	29	7
WIP (work in progress)	110	19
RFT (Right First Time)	10%	90%

All-in-one work cell

This change, together with the improvement proposals previously presented, achieved excellent results after 5 days of implementation:

- Processing time reduction from 24 hours to 5 minutes.
- Number of process steps involved in order processing reduced from 8 to 1.
- Improvement in Right First Time from 10.0% to 91.3%.

Besides the quantitative results presented, there was a general increase in the motivation of the team members. In addition, the relocation of people previously associated only with the order processing task allowed a general increase in efficiency in the department. The team remained focused on identifying more sources of waste and coming up with quick solutions for their daily work.

9.3 Value Selling

The day had come for the KAIZEN™ Value Selling Event, which was expected to generate more debate among the participants. In the room were the CEO, the Operations Director, the Marketing and Sales Director, the Marketing team leader, and the Sales team leaders from both plants. The company's four most experienced salespeople and two sales assistants were also invited to attend.

Value Selling is a methodology for increasing teams' skills in converting a customer's need into an effective sale. It has an impact on the 4 main phases of the sales process: capacity management and sales funnel; sales preparation; sales meeting; sales evaluation.

The consultant introduced the Value Selling concept through a simple sports analogy:
"For a football team to win a game, it is necessary to create opportunities to shoot, and the higher the number of shots, the greater the goal scoring probability. In the same way, for a sales team to increase sales volume, it is necessary to create more customer contacts and, besides that, to convert those contacts into effective sales, for example to improve the conversion rate, or hit rate, as it is called at ALFA."

"But we cannot sell more if we continue to spend so much time at the office carrying out administrative tasks!" One of the salespeople interjected.

"Furthermore, we have little room to negotiate prices, compared to our competitors!" Added another sales team member.

The Operations Director replied,"By listening to you, it seems that the significant improvements we have achieved make no sense to you, both in terms of delivery and quality. Internally this year, for the first time, we improved our margins by increasing our operating efficiency, and not price increases. But even so, sales remain the same."

The consultant finished the discussion, by saying:
"I agree with what was said, and like any other department, Marketing and Sales should also practice continuous improvement. And that's why we're here today. Recalling what was said at the beginning of the session, our aim for this KAIZEN™ Event is to achieve more contact time with the customer and more efficiency during that time."

The KAIZEN™ Event continued as planned, with the current state description and subsequent future state design. The first part was for gathering all the necessary information of the current state mapping, which described the sales process at ALFA.

9.3.1 A Typical Week of a Sales Person

By shadowing ALFA's salespeople over a week and identifying all their activities and the associated time, the group started to illustrate the concept of added value for a sales team. They concluded that a salesperson would only add value when in the customer's presence with a well-prepared sales argument. To ensure a successful sale it would be necessary to meticulously prepare the value proposition for each customer, a method that would allow the creation of countermeasures against them buying from other players in the market.

The daily analysis of ALFA's salespeople showed that their time was distributed as follows:

- 70% was devoted to maintenance of existing customer portfolios, i.e., the sale of the same products to the same customers.
- 30% was dedicated to customer portfolio growth or new products sales, both to existing and new customers.

The consultant questioned the group as to whether this was the best time distribution for salespeople, saying that they would return to this discussion when designing solutions.

9.3.2 The Sale Moment

Afterwards, the group proceeded to describe the factors that influenced a salepeople's performance in face-to-face contact with the customer. For this they used a set of role-plays in which the Director of Marketing and Sales assumed the role of the customer, with whom the sales force tried to simulate a sale. The exercise was useful to show that there was a great variability in the selling approach, either between different salespeople with the same type of customer or for the same salesperson selling to different customers with similar needs.

After completing the various role-plays, the Marketing and Sales Director spoke to his team:
"I'm seriously disappointed. In the role-play it became clear that we do not believe in our products. We are not able to show our customers why they should buy from us and not the competition, and we do not know how to highlight our distinctive features. In view of this we lose self-confidence and are not prepared to counter-argue. Our only defence is to criticise our competitors! I know we do not have a process to help us in this situation, but we should be able to at least quantify the value of our offer." The director stopped for a few seconds and resumed. "But what worries me the most now is the lack of capacity to surprise the customer. We need to be able to present our products and services at every visit as things that add value."

After this summary, some comments of concern were heard among those present. Although aware of their weaknesses, the team felt that, with the help of a consistent process, they could achieve much more satisfactory results.

9.3.3 Solutions Design

Following the analysis and mapping of the initial state, the team discussed the actions to improve the sales process, with the challenge of maximising the number of visits and increasing the conversion rate.

"MORE SHOTS": Maximising the Number of Visits

Up to that point the consultant looked at the time distribution of salespeople, followed by the company and commented that this was far and away from the best in class. That said, he commented that excellent sales teams typically used the Rule 30-60-10, which consisted of:

- 30% of the time spent maintaining the existing customer portfolio.
- 60% of the time dedicated growing the client portfolio in traditional sectors.
- 10% of the time dedicated to differentiation, that is, to the sale of the same products outside of traditional sectors, or innovative products in traditional sectors.

In order to achieve this distribution without losing sales to existing customers, two paradigm shifts would have to be achieved by drastically reducing the time spent on administrative activities, and significantly increasing visit effectiveness. Thus, salespeople could spend more time prospecting new customers as well as penetrating new markets in which they had never thought it would be possible to sell.

The team concluded that to maximise the number of visits, it would be necessary to develop 3 key activities:

- Create a client ranking: Classify all clients by relevance, to assign an appropriate visit frequency.
- Define geographic sales areas and reallocate salespeople to customers by region, to reduce the time wasted on travel. Some exceptions were made due to some special customer relationships and technical requirements.
- Optimise the routes of the sales force in their geographical sales area.

In addition, the team decided to use the information gathered in the VOC to identify new customer segments, specifically identifying their individual needs. Customers in these segments would be the target of ALFA's salespeople.

Having that in mind, the following processes were implemented:

- Identification of "customer interests" by market segment.
- Information collection and updating the database, allowing the identification of potential customers.
- These potential customers should be included and followed in the sales funnel, generating new opportunities for increased sales.

One of the paradigms that needed to be broken was the need for salespeople to spend too much time on administrative tasks.

After some discussion, the team concluded that this could be achieved by implementing the following improvements:

- Optimisation of the administrative processes carried out by salespeople.
- Creation of a working procedure and support guide for commercial assistants, administrative tasks.
- Transfer of tasks from salespeople to sales assistants, such as opening new customers, tracking orders, informing customers of possible quality issues or delays in delivery, and increasing autonomy in billing management.

To ensure alignment, control and training of the sales teams, a Daily KAIZEN™ Level 1 was implemented with the following work order:

- Analysis of performance indicators.
- Sales funnel management and conversion follow-up into new opportunities.
- Seller allocation to new customers.
- Planning of visits to be carried out in the next cycle.
- Development of new value propositions for clients.
- Value Selling training.
- Training on new products.
- Ideation of new offers with customisation of existing products or new services.

"MORE GOALS": Increase of Conversion Rate

With the team being more motivated and with much more positive energy, they needed to look at how to increase the conversion rate, another paradigm the team had to break.

After reflecting on the necessary solutions, they concluded that it would be essential to act in 3 areas, namely:

- **"Get information"** - Gathering and sharing relevant customer data, such as purchasing potential, current suppliers, decision process, customer profile, etc.
- **"Give information"** - Presenting the value proposition, setting challenges and sharing useful knowledge with the customer.
- **"Ask for commitment"** - Obtain a commitment to action from the client according to the request.

The team quickly realised that it would have to make every effort to develop a Working Procedure as A Guide to Creating and Using the Value Proposition, which should include:

- Step-by-step description of the intended dialogue with the customer, including the arguments for the most common objections, and questions about the evolution trends of their products.
- Differentiating aspects of the value proposition.
- Facilitating questions able to expose the weaknesses of competition when compared to ALFA's value proposition, such as: "Are you satisfied with the current quality/price ratio?"; "What about the deadline? What do you have to say?"; "In case of emergency, is your supplier responsive?".

For a correct monetisation of the value proposition, it was also suggested to train the sales force in identifying the reasons why a customer buys from a more expensive supplier (see example), creating a template for a quick benefits calculation and definition of cross selling/upselling strategies for products and services.

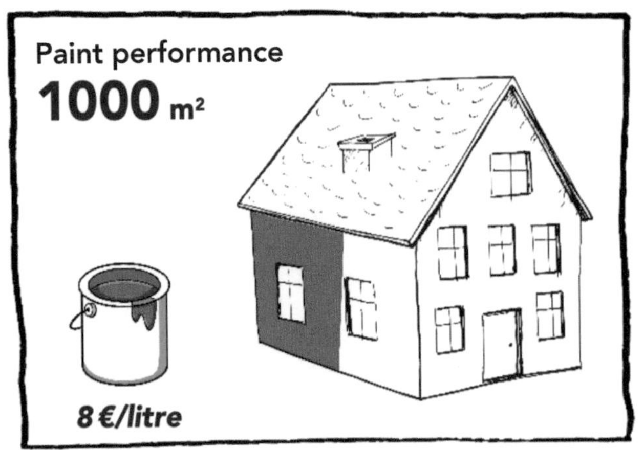

ABC PAINT		XYZ PAINT
8	Necessary litres	4
x 8 €	Value/litre	x 12 €
= 64 €	Paint full cost	**= 48 €**

To ensure success it was essential that the sales team got the technical know-how regarding products and services and understood which solution would best suit the needs of each customer.

Following the development of some examples of the Standard Guide to Creating and Using the Value Proposition and its training materials, the Marketing and Sales Director assigned full responsibility to sales managers for rolling out all these initiatives. For each sales team, the relevant manager had to ensure the training of salespeople, supervision of the value proposition preparation and observation of customer visits, providing coaching until the salesperson had acquired the new skills. They were also responsible for sharing structured feedback to salespeople and evaluating their progress by updating a Skills Matrix.

After completing the KAIZEN™ Event, the consultant commented to the Marketing and Sales Director that the intensity of implementation of these new processes would expose weaknesses of some of his sales team, which would require prompt action.

As a final note, he reinforced the importance of the Daily KAIZEN™ meeting and monitoring the salespeople's performance in realising increased sales.

Year 2

Year 2 End Results

The Turning Point

10.1 Year 2 Results Review

Having finished the Year 2 and at the beginning of January, the Executive Committee met to review the results achieved with the Hoshin implementation. This chapter describes this meeting, which took place with the final Bowler analysis and acknowledgment of the main reasons leading to the end of year results.

TARGET TO ACHIEVE	Starting point	Annual target	Un.		Jan	Feb	Mar	Apr	May	Jun	Jul	Aug	Sept	Oct	Nov	Dec
Sales/FTE from 200 K€ to 207 K€ by Dec/Year 2	200.0	207.0	thousand €	**Hoshin**	200.6	201.2	201.8	202.3	202.9	203.5	204.1	204.7	205.3	205.8	206.4	207.0
				Actual	200.0	201.7	201.9	203.0	203.4	203.1	204.2	204.0	206.7	209.8	210.4	211.0
External Services & Supplies from 16.6% to 15.5% of Sales (914 K€) by Dec/Year 2	16.6%	15.5%	%	**Hoshin**	16.5%	16.4%	16.3%	16.2%	16.1%	16.1%	16.0%	15.9%	15.8%	15.7%	15.6%	15.5%
				Actual	16.6%	16.5%	16.5%	16.3%	16.3%	16.2%	16.1%	15.9%	15.8%	15.3%	15.1%	15.0%
	0.0	914	thousand €	**Hoshin**	76.2	152.3	228.5	304.7	380.8	457.0	533.2	609.3	685.5	761.7	837.8	914.0
				Actual	0.0	13.8	20.8	83.1	103.8	166.1	242.2	387.6	498.3	899.8	1 142.0	1 328.9
Planned Waste from 6.6% to 5.6% (514.9 K€) Dec/Year 2	6.6%	5.6%	%	**Hoshin**	6.5%	6.4%	6.4%	6.3%	6.2%	6.1%	6.0%	5.9%	5.9%	5.8%	5.7%	5.6%
				Actual	6.8%	6.6%	6.5%	6.5%	6.3%	6.2%	6.0%	5.8%	6.0%	5.7%	5.6%	5.6%
	0.0	514.9	thousand €	**Hoshin**	42.9	85.8	128.7	171.6	214.6	257.5	300.4	343.3	386.2	429.1	472.0	514.9
				Actual	41.2	80.0	120.9	167.0	201.3	250.6	320.0	353.0	370.0	431.0	475.0	515.0
On-Time Delivery from 87% to 92% by Dec/Year 2	87.0%	92.0%	%	**Hoshin**	87.4%	87.8%	88.3%	88.7%	89.1%	89.5%	89.9%	90.3%	90.8%	91.2%	91.6%	92.0%
				Actual	87.0%	87.4%	87.5%	88.0%	89.2%	89.5%	90.0%	89.9%	89.9%	90.0%	91.0%	91.5%
Time-To-Market from 44 to 34 weeks by Dec/Year 2	44	34	Wk	**Hoshin**	43	42	42	41	40	39	38	37	37	36	35	34
				Actual	44	43	43	42	41	40	39	37	36	35	36	35
Inventory from 9.8 M€ to 6.8 M€ by Dec/Year 2	9.8	6.8	million €	**Hoshin**	9.6	9.3	9.1	8.8	8.6	8.3	8.1	7.8	7.6	7.3	7.1	6.8
				Actual	9.7	9.6	9.6	9.5	9.3	8.9	8.7	8.3	7.9	7.5	7.3	7.1
Mean Receipt Timeframe from 83 to 76 days by Dec/Year 2	83	76	days	**Hoshin**	82	82	81	81	80	80	79	78	78	77	77	76
				Actual	83	83	82	80	79	79	77	76	76	75	74	73
Average Payment Period from 95 to 78 days by Dec/Year 2	95	78	days	**Hoshin**	94	92	91	89	88	87	85	84	82	81	79	78
				Actual	95	95	92	91	90	88	88	87	84	82	80	78
Sales from 83.1 M€ to 89.3 M€ by Dec/Year 2	0	89 300	thousand €	**Hoshin**	7 442	14 883	22 325	29 767	37 208	44 650	52 092	59 533	66 975	74 417	81 858	89 300
				Actual	6 921	14 788	22 263	29 727	37 552	44 642	51 896	58 938	67 847	74 957	82 179	89 758
Vitality: New Customer Sales from 0 to 3 M€ by Dec/Year 2	0	3 000	thousand €	**Hoshin**	250	500	750	1 000	1 250	1 500	1 750	2 000	2 250	2 500	2 750	3 000
				Actual	0	123	300	706	1 260	1 509	1 890	2 013	2 500	2 789	2 900	3 170
#SKU of Raw Material and Finished Goods from 1500 to 900 by Dec/Year 2	1 500	900	#	**Hoshin**	1 450	1 400	1 350	1 300	1 250	1 200	1 150	1 100	1 050	1 000	950	900
				Actual	1 500	1 504	1 380	1 331	1 242	1 198	1 198	1 170	998	954	923	892

Level 1 Bowling chart, Year 2

The CEO lead the meeting and, addressing his team, said:
"Today we will review our performance for last year. I would like to take this opportunity to congratulate you on the extraordinary results of €10.5 million euros in EBITDA. Although it is still a provisional number, I am very confident about this result!" The CEO continued to highlight the performance of the Marketing and Sales department: "As you know, in Year 1 we went through some difficulties and did not reach our goal for sales. I am very pleased with the impact of the improvements implemented in the Marketing and Sales processes over the last few months. I believe they will guarantee the sustainability and growth of sales at ALFA."

The meeting continued with a comprehensive analysis of the main indicators:

- **PRODUCTIVITY**

The goal was to improve productivity from 200 to 207 thousand euros of sales per FTE. The result achieved at the end of the year was 211 thousand euros per FTE, which represented an increase of 5.5%. This was achieved mainly through 9 KAIZEN™ Events held in production and focusing on Working Procedures and OEE. For instance the Ennis line moulding machine in Unit 1 had improved its OEE from 67% to 92%. This could only have happened due to the joint effort between the Engineering and Production teams. Only by working together were they able to solve the complex issues.

- **SUPPLY AND EXTERNAL SERVICES**

The objective was to reduce the cost of outsourced services from 16.6% to 15.5% of sales. The value achieved was 15.0%, which represented a saving of 1.3 million euros, that contributed greatly to reinforce the EBITDA result.

- **COST OF PLANNED WASTE**

The goal was to reduce planned waste from 6.6% to 5.6%. The result achieved by the end of the year was 5.6%, or 515 thousand euros in cost reduction, through a better material utilisation.

- **COMPLIANCE WITH DELIVERY DEADLINES**

The goal was to improve OTD from 87.0% to 92.0%. The result for this indicator was surprising, reaching 91.5% at the end of December. Customer satisfaction was increasingly noticeable not only in the increase in sales, but also in the last Voice of the Customer analysis. This improvement allowed ALFA to continue to shorten delivery times.

- **NEW PRODUCTS - TIME TO MARKET**

This indicator was to reduce the new products Time to Market from 44 to 34 weeks. In December ALFA had achieved 35 weeks and, whilst missing the target, this excellent result had made it possible to create a new vision in the Engineering team, where it was possible for them to foresee a one digit time to market, to aim for less than 10 weeks time to market for every new product.

- **INVENTORY**

To reduce inventory from €9.8 to €6.8 million euros of stock. The result achived at the end of the year was €7.1 million euros, which represented a reduction of €2.7 million euros in working capital. The extension of the TMI process together with the implementation of Just-in-Time and Pull Planning events had provided opportunities for inventory optimisation.

- **PAYABLES AND RECEIVABLES AVERAGE TERM**

In this case, the defined objective was to increase PMP to 17 days, which had occurred. The projected reduction in the PMR was exceeded, because it had managed to gain 10 days. It was also worth pointing out, once again, the remarkable team work of the Purchasing, Sales and Financial teams in having achieved successful results in these indicators.

- **SALES**

The target was to increase sales from €83.1 million euros to €89.3 million euros. The amount reached was €89.8 million euros, which represented a significant increase of 7.5% in the year. Major changes and the implementation of new processes in the Marketing and Sales teams would continue this growth.

- **REDUCTION OF SKU NUMBER IN RAW MATERIALS AND FINISHED PRODUCTS**

In the previous year, the target to improve was to reduce the number of SKUs of raw materials and finished products by 600 references. The team had eliminated 511 finished product references, with most customers migrating to alternative products. In addition, 97 references were removed from the list of raw materials. These actions had a significant impact on flexibility and margin, continuing to be a priority for the organisation in the coming years.

- **EBITDA**

Hoshin's EBITDA target was €10 million, up from €6.1 million. The result obtained at the end of the year was €10.5 million euros, which represented a new record at ALFA.

- **FREE CASH FLOW**

Once again, it was possible to make a significant improvement in free cash flow, increasing it from €7.0 to €8.7 million euros. To reach this value, in addition to the improvements in operating results, the continuous reduction of stocks proved to be decisive.

- **KAIZEN™**

The KAIZEN™ roadmap for Year 2 successfully completed 115 Events held at both ALFA plants. In terms of sales growth, this increased free cash flow and continued consolidation of improvements in Daily KAIZEN™, OEE and stock management. The ROI in consulting was also higher than expected with a ratio of 4 to 1 in relation to the obtained increase in EBITDA.

After the annual review, the team discussed further opportunities for improving the Hoshin process. It was time to put an end to Year 2 and renew the Mission Control Room for the following year. After the CEO introduced the final version of his X-Matrix, all those responsible for Improvement Priorities set out their Bowlers and Action Plans in the Mission Control Room.

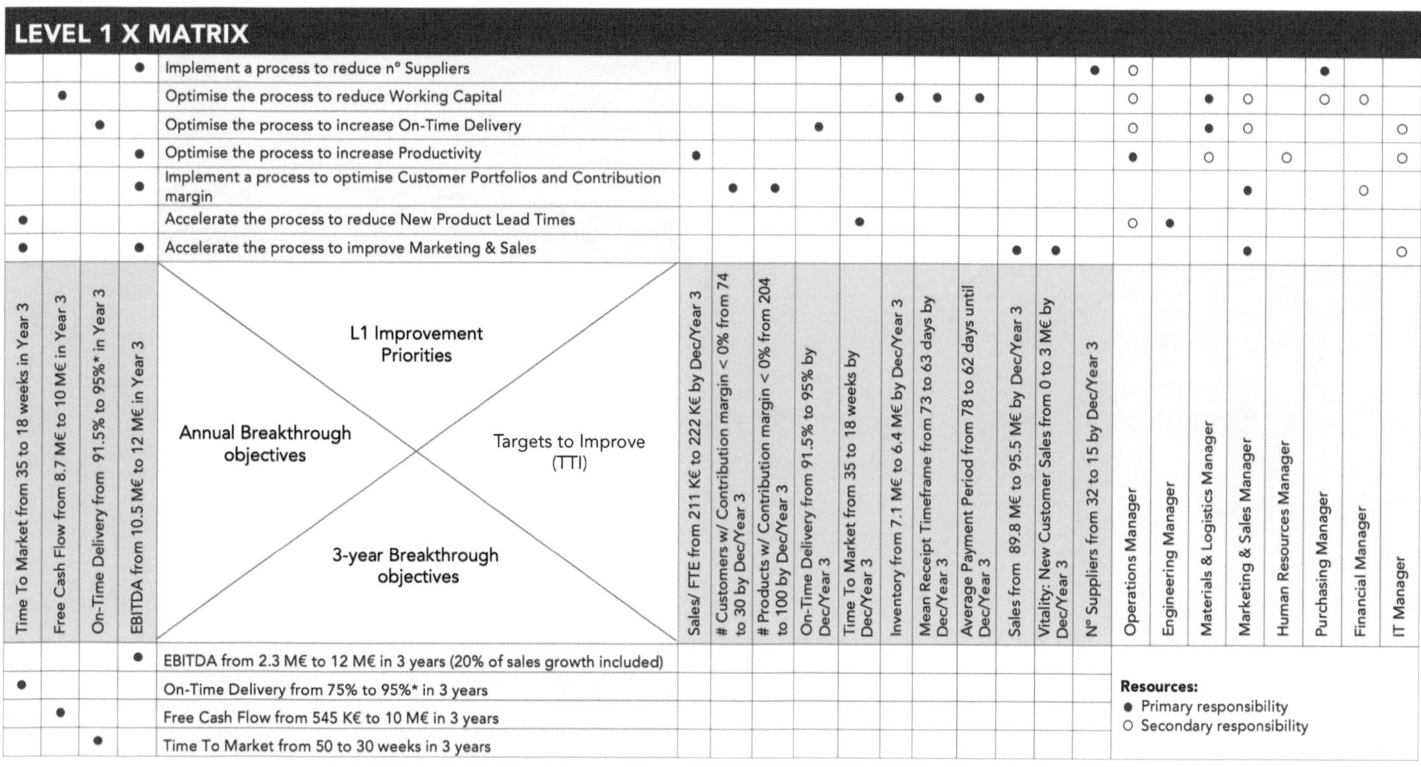

LEVEL 1 X MATRIX

Time To Market from 35 to 18 weeks in Year 3	Free Cash Flow from 8.7 M€ to 10 M€ in Year 3	On-Time Delivery from 91.5% to 95%* in Year 3	EBITDA from 10.5 M€ to 12 M€ in Year 3	L1 Improvement Priorities	Sales/ FTE from 211 K€ to 222 K€ by Dec/Year 3	# Customers w/ Contribution margin < 0% from 74 to 30 by Dec/Year 3	# Products w/ Contribution margin < 0% from 204 to 100 by Dec/Year 3	On-Time Delivery from 91.5% to 95% by Dec/Year 3	Time To Market from 35 to 18 weeks by Dec/Year 3	Inventory from 7.1 M€ to 6.4 M€ by Dec/Year 3	Mean Receipt Timeframe from 73 to 63 days by Dec/Year 3	Average Payment Period from 78 to 62 days until Dec/Year 3	Sales from 89.8 M€ to 95.5 M€ by Dec/Year 3	Vitality: New Customer Sales from 0 to 3 M€ by Dec/Year 3	Nº Suppliers from 32 to 15 by Dec/Year 3	Operations Manager	Engineering Manager	Materials & Logistics Manager	Marketing & Sales Manager	Human Resources Manager	Purchasing Manager	Financial Manager	IT Manager
			●	Implement a process to reduce nº Suppliers											●	○					●		
	●			Optimise the process to reduce Working Capital						●	●	●				○		●	○		○	○	
		●		Optimise the process to increase On-Time Delivery				●								○		●	○				○
			●	Optimise the process to increase Productivity	●											●		○		○			○
			●	Implement a process to optimise Customer Portfolios and Contribution margin		●	●												●			○	
●				Accelerate the process to reduce New Product Lead Times					●							○	●						
●			●	Accelerate the process to improve Marketing & Sales									●	●					●				○

Annual Breakthrough objectives / Targets to Improve (TTI) / 3-year Breakthrough objectives

Time To Market	Free Cash Flow	On-Time Delivery	EBITDA	3-year Breakthrough objectives
			●	EBITDA from 2.3 M€ to 12 M€ in 3 years (20% of sales growth included)
●				On-Time Delivery from 75% to 95%* in 3 years
	●			Free Cash Flow from 545 K€ to 10 M€ in 3 years
		●		Time To Market from 50 to 30 weeks in 3 years

Resources:
● Primary responsibility
○ Secondary responsibility

Level 1 X Matrix, Year 3

At the end of the meeting, there was an atmosphere of enthusiasm driven by results after two years of applying Strat to Action. The Executive Committee was motivated for the challenges of the new year and committed to repeating again. All ALFA teams had already enjoyed their taste of victory and it was about time to broaden horizons and challenge previously unthinkable paradigms.

In the following chapters, we will describe how ALFA felt the need to transform its organisational structure in order to deliver a better service for their customers, as well as simplify the entire process of preparing the annual Budget.

The new way of Budgeting

Budgeting with No Effort

Chapter 11

The last quarter of the year is synonymous with budgeting. Usually considered to be a headache, it is still a mandatory management tool. Is there a better process that can be applied, delivering better results with less effort?

11.1 The Way we have always done it

Most top managers recognise that the traditional process of annual budgeting is subject to repeated amendments, too much time and effort spent generating costs that are not accounted for or even realistic. However, despite all these limitations, the process is seen as robust and necessary. In the absence of an alternative, they opt to live with this paradigm.

At the beginning of September of Year 2, the consultant scheduled a meeting with the CEO and the Financial Director, to present the KAIZEN™ budgeting method for Year 3, very different from the approach currently used in the company.

"Now that we are about to start another budgeting cycle, after two years of Hoshin, rethinking this process makes all the more sense. How much compliance have we achieved with the budget? Last year, we achieved much more than we anticipated and this year everything indicates that we are continuing along the same path. So, I ask: What added value is present in the current budgeting process?" The consultant continued: "There is an alternative that simply uses a whole year of Hoshin process results to prepare the budget. We all know the effort our teams have to commit to the current budgeting process at this time of year, which represents a huge opportunity for improvement at ALFA!"

After a few seconds in silence, the CEO replied:
"I'm willing to think about it. The truth is that, in the years before we implemented Hoshin, we were always under budget. Now that we have followed the Hoshin process we also failed, by being over budget. Nevertheless, I want to understand this new paradigm you are proposing. I've never seen the budget done in another way and, I've been through many companies!"

The Financial Director, visibly concerned, addressed the consultant:
"Are you suggesting improving the way we develop the budget, or radically change the process?"

The consultant replied:
"The fact is the traditional budgeting process can only make reliable predictions about business sustainability, but it cannot anticipate the components of growth and improvement." He continued: "But before I introduce you to this new concept, I would like you to explain to me how the current process works."

"Budgeting usually begins in the first week of September and we try to finish it by December 15th." While speaking, the Financial Director showed the annual budget schedule. "Between these dates, several revisions of the document are made: Two with the CEO and two with the Executive Committee."

The consultant asked:
"Can we calculate the time and people involved in each activity, and then estimate the preparation and execution time of the annual budget?"

PLANNING & OWNERS OF ALFA'S ANNUAL BUDGET ELABORATION		DATE	ENGAGED PEOPLE
Guidelines & Assumptions	Executive Committee general guidelines for budget Year N+1 to the CEO: sales, EBITDA, Capex, strategic orientations	wk 1 Sep	Executive Committee and CEO
	General guidelines for salary mass increase in Year N+1	wk 2 Sep	CEO/HR/Controllers
	CEO's general guidelines for Year N+1 budget to Plant Managers and Corporate Managers: sales, EBITDA, capex, salary mass increase, etc.	wk 2 Sep	CEO/CFO/Plant Managers/Corporate Manager/Controllers
	Assumptions for raw material level prices, average sales prices, transports prices, energy prices and other significant prices, inflation estimated level, exchange rate, holding fees, etc.	By 30th Sep	CEO/CFO/Plant Managers/ Purchasing Manager/ Commercial Manager
Year N closing forecast (P&L), at plant level	P&L forecast from august to december in Year N	wk 3 Sep	Plant Manager/Manager/Controllers
	Sales forecast from august to december in Year N	wk 3 Sep	Plant Manager/Commercial Manager/Controllers
	Costs forecast from august to december in Year N	wk 3 Sep	Plant Manager/Managers/Controllers
	Human resources costs forecasts and people number for Year N	wk 3 Sep	Plant Manager/ Managers/HR/Controllers
Budget elaboration at plant level for Year N+1	Sales budget per customer, product or salesperson	wk 2 Sep	Commercial Manager/Salespeople/Controller
	Production budget per machine (capacity, efficiency, productivity, shifts number, people number, etc.)	wk 3 Sep	Production Manager/Controller
	Personnel expenses, per employee, work overtimes included, external temporary staff, headcount variation, (entering and leaving employees),variable premiums, estimated costs of potential compensations, etc.	wk 3 Sep	Production Manager/HR/Controller
	Raw material costs per product, according to sales budget and purchasing estimated prices	wk 3 Sep	Purchasing Manager/Production Manager/Controllers
	Other variable costs considering: sales budget, historical data and price assumptions for year N+1	wk 3 Sep	Production Manager/ Logistics Manager/Controllers
	Maintenance costs considering: production budget, historical data and price assumptions for year N+1	wk 3 Sep	Purchasing Manager/Production Manager/Maintenance Manager/Controllers
Plant Manager Approval	Capex and other improvement projects proposal for Year N+1	wk 3 Oct	Plant Manager/Managers/Controllers
	Plant first version budget approval from the Plant Manager	By 31th Oct	Plant Manager/ Managers/HR/Controllers
Approval & presentation to the CEO	Plant Manager presentation to the CEO	wk 1 Nov	CEO/Plant Managers/Corporate Managers/Controllers
	Budget review and plant Capex with the CEO observations and the final version resend to the CEO	wk 2 Nov	Plant Managers/Controllers
	ALFA's consolidated budget elaboration (plant 1 + plant 2 + corporation) and Capex	wk 2 Nov	CEO/Executive Committee/Controllers
Approval & presentation to the Executive Committee	ALFA's budget and Capex presentation to the Executive Committee	wk 3 Nov	CEO/Executive Committee
	ALFA's budget and Capex review with the Executive Committee observations	wk 4 Nov	CEO/Executive Committee
	ALFA's Budget final approval and Capex by the Executive Committee and the Executive Board	By 15th Dec	CEO/Executive Committee / Executive Board

After a few calculations, it was possible to estimate that an average of 56 hours were consumed per employee involved in the preparation of the document, which meant 400 working days in total. Although they knew it was a process with many interactions, both the CEO and the CFO were surprised by the result. They acknowledged that this was an opportunity for the company to analyse the process and make it much more responsive, but they remained reluctant to make any change, since the budget brought them a sense of reassurance and security for the year to come.

The CEO and Financial Director agreed on the need to maintain the same framework for the budget, as it was an input needed for other business-critical processes.

11.2 The Hoshin to guarantee the Budget

In general, the Board of Directors pushes down for an aggressive budget and expects the Executive Committee to be able to achieve the projected results. However, when all the demands and aspirations come together, the uncertainty in the budget increases dramatically, causing the team to lose sight of the real risks involved. The consequence is budget approval without the organisation knowing how it can be achieved, putting them into constant countermeasure mode.

"While the traditional budgeting method only seeks to know HOW MUCH (results), Hoshin focuses on HOW FAR (goals) and, especially, on HOW - how to get there." The consultant reinforced.

Traditionally, the budget includes two distinct elements: **(1)** to sustain current performance and **(2)** to increase sales and improve QCD. This adds a level of uncertainty as a result of joining the two objectives of maintaining the results achieved, with the strategic objectives of growth and improvement of the company. However, it is necessary to understand that these two strands are like water and oil: they do not mix and should not be brought together in the same document. The budget should be based on a model of minimum error, capable of generating confidence about the organisation's ability to deliver the result.

Before introducing the new budgeting paradigm, the consultant began by reiterating the fundamental concepts that everyone already knew:

"With KAIZEN™, the current performance support, and QCD improvement and sales growth are managed through a consistent and structured methodology, which we call Strat to Action. In this methodology, the action is accomplished through the improvement or creation of new processes, which is the best guarantee of sustainability. On the other hand, future developments are achieved through the definition of Breakthrough Objectives and application of KAIZEN™ tools to achieve new levels of performance." He continued, introducing the new budget concept. "Why can't we use year 1 Hoshin results for the following year as these are not aspirational but already achieved?"

A budget is only prudent if it is established with results that the organisation can already achieve. Hoshin requires the improvements to be based on the company's processes (in the matrix North Box), which necessarily guarantees its sustainability. That is, the expected minimum performance for the following year should be estimated based only on its current performance. Thus, the budget is no longer based on aspirations, but on real data.

This concept is reflected in the following chart, where it is possible to observe that the budget for the following year is the result (sustained) from the previous year. The growth and improvement achieved are the difference of budgets of consecutive years.

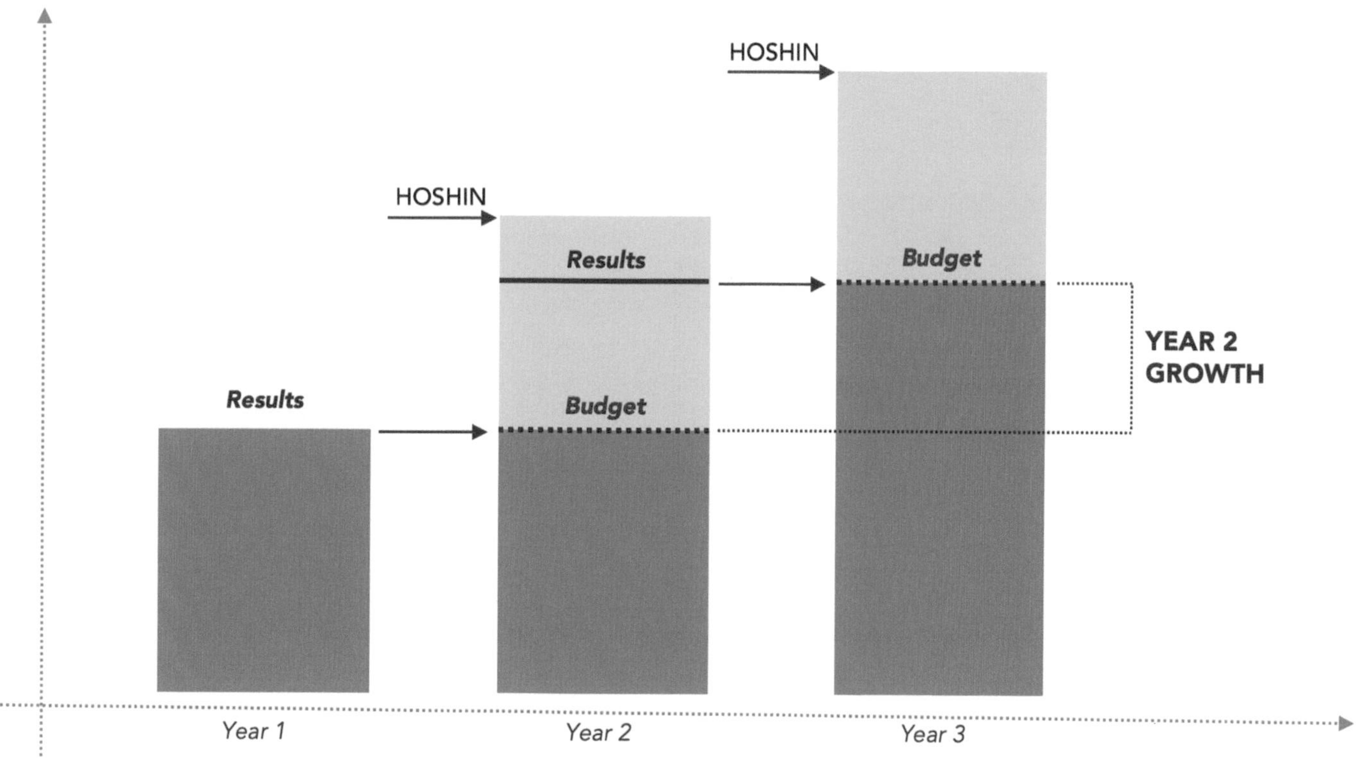

Then the Financial Director, who had already understood the new concept, promptly proposed to illustrate this paradigm using the example of the last Income Statement available (August, Year 2), changing the values of the YTD Budget column by the amounts of the expected impact of the Hoshin up to the month of August (YTD Hoshin), and placing the values of the YTD August column from the previous year (Year 1) as values for the budget of the current year (Year 2).

Example of the Current Results Account:

BALANCE SHEET - TRADITIONAL METHOD	Cumulative until August			Cumulative Variance			
	Year 2	Year 2	Year 1	YTD Aug Year 2 vs. budget		YTD Aug Year 2 vs. Aug Year 1	
	YTD August	YTD budget	YTD August	value	%	value	%
Sales and services provided	**58 938 102**	**56 698 454**	**54 517 744**	**2 239 648**	**4.0%**	**4 420 358**	**8.1%**
Consumable supplies and materials costs	36 070 118	35 039 645	33 801 001	1 030 474	2.9%	2 269 117	6.7%
Supply and external services	9 371 158	9 298 546	9 213 499	72 612	0.8%	157 659	1.7%
Personnel expenses	7 249 387	7 540 894	7 632 484	-291 508	-3.9%	-383 098	-5.0%
EBITDA	**6 247 439**	**4 819 369**	**3 870 760**	**1 428 070**	**29.6%**	**2 376 679**	**61.4%**
Depreciation & amortisation	2 009 789	1 927 747	1 853 603	82 042	4.3%	156 186	8.4%
EBIT	**4 237 650**	**2 891 621**	**2 017 157**	**1 346 028**	**46.5%**	**2 220 493**	**110.1%**
Financial results	182 708	170 095	163 553	12 613	7.4%	19 155	11.7%
Pre-tax results	**4 054 941**	**2 721 526**	**1 853 603**	**1 333 416**	**49.0%**	**2 201 338**	**118.8%**

Example of the Results Account with Hoshin:

BALANCE SHEET - HOSHIN METHOD	Cumulative until August			Cumulative Variance			
	Year 2	Year 2	Year 2	YTD Aug year 2 vs. Hoshin		YTD Aug year 2 vs. budget	
	YTD August	**YTD Hoshin**	YTD budget	value	%	value	%
Sales and services provided	**58 938 102**	**59 533 000**	**54 517 744**	**-594 898**	**-1.0%**	**4 420 358**	**8.1%**
Consumable supplies and materials costs	36 070 118	35 243 536	33 801 001	826 582	2.3%	2 269 117	6.7%
Supply and external services	9 371 158	9 465 747	9 213 499	-94 589	-1.0%	157 659	1.7%
Personnel expenses	7 249 387	7 441 625	7 632 484	-192 238	-2.6%	-383 098	-5.0%
EBITDA	**6 247 439**	**7 382 092**	**3 870 760**	**-1 134 653**	**-15.4%**	**2 376 679**	**61.4%**
Depreciation & amortisation	2 009 789	2 024 122	1 853 603	-14 333	-0.7%	156 186	8.4%
EBIT	**4 237 650**	**5 357 970**	**2 017 157**	**-1 120 320**	**-20.9%**	**2 220 493**	**110.1%**
Financial results	182 708	178 599	163 553	4 109	2.3%	19 155	11.7%
Pre-tax results	**4 054 941**	**5 179 371**	**1 853 603**	**-1 124 430**	**-21.7%**	**2 201 338**	**118.8%**

"I've got it! The new method completely simplifies budgeting, which is used as a baseline to measure our performance over the previous year. Hoshin tells us where we want to go and how. The budget tells us from where we left off." The CEO concluded.

The meeting ended in a constructive environment and with the decision to test the new budgeting method for the following year.

A few days later, the Financial Director and Executive Committee met in the Mission Control Room for the presentation of this new model to the whole team. The news was received with inquisitiveness.

The Financial Director highlighted:
"Presenting a budget without growth may seem unacceptable to the Board of Directors. However, this new paradigm must be seen in the light of what we have achieved over the last two years, resulting from all the dynamics imposed by Hoshin. If we increase EBITDA every year by more than two digits, as we have been doing, what is the problem of not forecasting growth in the budget? What this means is that we will start using the budget as a basis to measure how much we can grow annually, and Hoshin as a lever to make us improve and continue to grow." There were comments among the members of the Executive Committee, who had already realised that the method would change substantially. "Thus, in the first days of January, after the provisional closing of the annual accounts, we will meet in this room with the Board of Directors for the budget validation and presentation of Hoshin's new year. Now, the important thing is to devote part of the time gained to improving Hoshin's annual review."

The Kaizen Institute recommends streamlining the budgeting process in organisations with a track record of performance and excellence within a minimum of 3 years of applying Strat to Action with exponential results.

A Value Stream Organisation

How to Measure an Organisation's Maturity

Chapter 12

As already explained in the **Strat to Action process**, it is from Strategic Goals that Breakthroughs must be deployed to the point of impact with the application of KAIZEN™ Events to ensure that changes do happen. These usually start with the highest priority operational value streams.

After several improvement cycles in value streams, it is normal to begin recognising the massive amounts of waste that still exist in the organisation. This can be compared to an iceberg; you can only see 10% with 90% being submerged. The more you repeat the mapping and eliminating of waste cycle, the easier it will be to identify the deeply embedded waste. This action will create a thorough awareness of how much waste still exists in the processes, and the resources spent on managing that waste. Usually, after two KAIZEN™ cycles in the same value stream, usually consisting of 10 to 15 individual KAIZEN™ Events, the team acquires the knowledge and experience to continuously optimise the flow. This improvement process, once learned, can be deployed to every organisation's value streams.

In an ideal organisation, each person will be aligned to achieving the strategic goals. This means that the strategic objectives should include all people in an organisation, but what usually happens is that the improvement processes only start in Operations, and all other areas, such as Sales and Marketing, Engineering, Supply Chain, are excluded. However, it is reasonable to assume that there is the same amount of waste in these management processes as in the operational value streams. Therefore, the opportunity for continuing to improve quality, cost and customer satisfaction is even greater. Generally, in the third and fourth cycles of KAIZEN™, the improvement in the value streams extends upstream to the customer and downstream into the supply chain. At this point it becomes necessary to integrate other indirect business functions.

But the challenge is to think further. So, we need to start to define and implement a Value Stream Organisation that creates value streams that provide excellence in customer's satisfaction. This is the fundamental reason that drives the change from a traditional departmentalised structure to a value flow model, called a Value Stream.

A simplest way to visualise this is, for instance, to analyse a value stream that has been transformed from a batch production system to a One-Piece Flow system. Invariably, the results are better quality, lower cost and improved flexibility, which translates into much higher customer satisfaction. It is well recognised in manufacturing that one-piece flow is efficient, and that batching is an expensive inefficient method for process organisation, so why not organise the whole business to flow? Value Stream Organisation has the ability to achieve this bringing together of all the company functions.

Although it seems natural and obvious, the truth is that when mapping cross-management processes, they are traditionally organised around departments or silos. Consequently, information is received and moves forward in batches, with very little flow and a large amount of rework and duplication. To transform management processes, it is necessary to break these silos down and create flow using the same methods applied to Operations Value Streams.

In view of the above, this chapter describes the fundamentals and opportunities associated with organising around Value Stream. As an example, it presents the restructuring carried out at ALFA during the Year 3 of the Hoshin implementation.

12.1 A simple example of Organisational Change

In an industrial company, the Production Manager is generally responsible for all production activities within the factory. But in a Value Steam organisation this no longer happens, as there is a Value Steam manager responsible all the way from order placement to the delivery to the customer. This allows managers to develop an in-depth knowledge of people, processes and performance of their Value Stream, as well as leading the continuous waste elimination. In this type of organisational model each Value Stream can develop its own Improvement Priorities based on customer experiences. In a traditional model, the Production Manager has the responsibility to manage several Value Streams which gives him no chance to develop deep knowledge in each of them and the customer experience gets compromised.

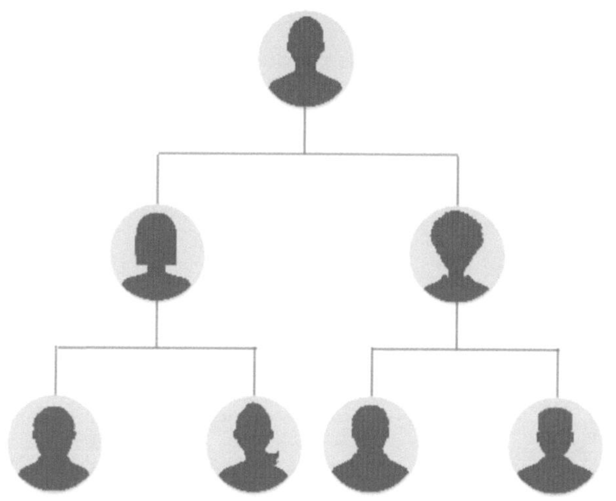

In a vertical hierarchy model, the departmental **rules and procedures create predictability** and make **coordination easier,** but they eliminate the "voice of the customer" and the **need for creativity, memory, and perception,** as people limit themselves to the responsibility of performing repetitive departmental tasks.

In a Value Stream model, there is **collective intelligence.** The group, with its many **connections between members,** will become **smarter** and **more innovative** than a traditional company organisation.

This can be seen when analysing successful small businesses with 10 to 50 people. These tend to be well organised, be under control and have a high sense of Quality, Cost and Service. This is because the leader can virtually "embrace the whole organisation." Communication is direct and immediate, cross-functional teams do what is necessary without having complex and inefficient structures, which usually add a lot of cost with little value.

To implement a Value Stream structure the company must be reorganised into "small business units" of 10 to 50 people, who manage their own value stream, focused on the client. This allows them to have greater sensitivity, a characteristic that is lost in a larger organisation.

Team members become **less productive** as **group size increases** (Ringelmann Effect). Therefore, teams **must remain small,** but large enough to cover Value Stream.

12.2 How to implement a Value Stream Organisation?

The implementation of organisational change into Value Streams must start from current value streams and ask what functions should be included in order to fully serve customers' expectations. This may include Logistics, Maintenance, Engineering, Sales, Finance or Human Resources as examples of existing cross-cutting functions. This way, there is no silo structure, all the transactional and operational management resources are organised in a Value Stream. It soon becomes possible to see the contribution to the profit from each Value Stream as each becomes a small business within the larger business, with its own P & L. This allows a whole new world of opportunities to be opened up regarding waste identification and elimination.

In a Value Stream organisation, it is possible to observe multi-functional teams being responsible for the entire value stream, from product or service ordering to delivery in the shortest possible time, with the best quality and lowest cost.

1 P&L - Profit and Loss account - Results demonstration

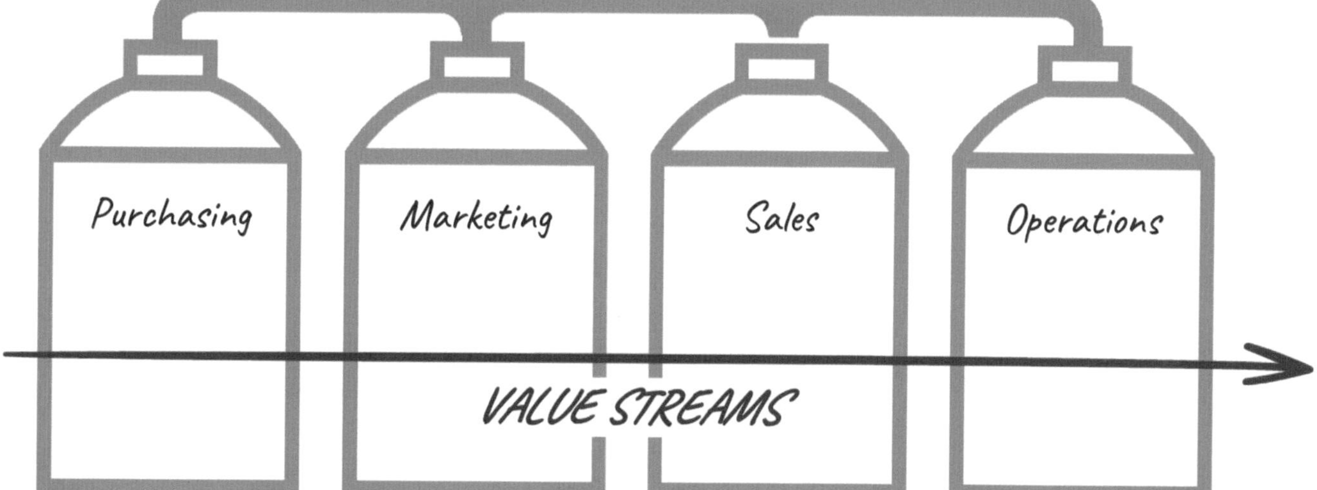

The team gets only what is needed from each of the silos to run its Value Stream efficiently, working in groups and communicating freely to provide total customer satisfaction. Each team can improve and create its own business processes, such as Supply Chain Management, Product Management and all the necessary development to satisfy demand. As the reorganisation around the value streams progresses, more services are allocated to the Value Stream, which results in demolishing the silos.

12.3 Value Stream Management Power

If a company recognises that organising their products and services in a Value Stream is the most efficient way to reduce cost and improve quality, then it will not be a huge leap to admit that support process integration is also going to be a more efficient organisation. To begin this integration the value streams maps need to be extended, not only including Operations but covering other functions. Value Streams break down barriers created by functional departments, simplify communication, align objectives, and create a high focus on customer satisfaction.

A Value Stream organisational model simplifies business, restores everything that is really needed and removes everything that isn't. To reduce complexity, the business is split into smaller pieces, where it becomes possible to have a real sense of cause and effect. These become the natural Value Streams.

Silos, or traditional departments, rarely evaluate customer experience. They are usually focused on managing interdepartmental conflicts and daily performance. A Value Stream gives the team a real sense of customer expectation and satisfaction.

The benefits identified by those companies that had been organised by Value Stream are compelling. They achieved greater growth, greater profitability, shorter lead times, better customer experience and knowledge, and a greater ability to adapt to changes on demand.

Once you can envisage a completely Value Stream structured organisation, imagine the reverse.

To **organise** people into **multifunctional teams,** around each value stream

You have organised people into multifunctional teams, around each value stream, now you will divide them into functional teams and separate them physically so that they are no longer able to communicate easily, only using email, sitting in daily quality and service improvement meetings. They also start using a complex ERP system to access all data and meet customer requirements and needs. At this point, this idea will surely seem to be total nonsense.

It is up to the leader to take the initiative and show the direction his company should take. Therefore, it is only natural for the next step to be as a consequence of Breakthrough Objectives, "create a process to allocate all resources in Value Stream" and "a process to measure the contribution of each Value Stream to profit". The impact will be to drastically reduce centralised high cost resources, which have been accumulated at the organisation headquarters.

Perhaps some leaders will think: "If my company is generating returns according to the shareholders' expectations, why take the risk? The answer is simple: the status quo will be short lived. More than ever it is necessary to turn waste into a superior performance to keep pace with competition. World Class Companies have this clear strategy and include the reorganisation into Value Stream in their Strat to Action process."

12.4 Reorganisation of ALFA's Structure

INITIAL STRUCTURE - YEAR 0

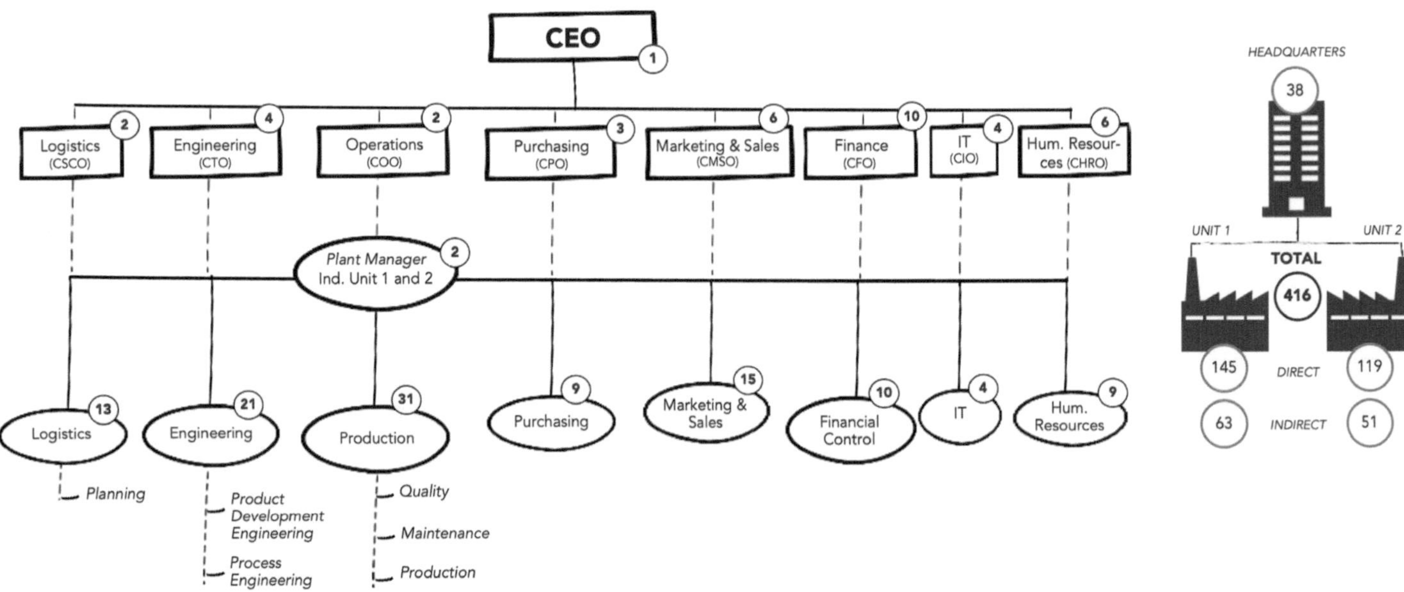

STRUCTURE IN VALUE STREAM

It was in Year 3 of Strat to Action implementation that ALFA reorganised itself into a Value Stream model and, by doing so, centralised functions were drastically reduced, releasing 14 resources, equivalent to 840 thousand euros in cost reduction. The number of direct and indirect employees increased to 430. If we compare this with Year 0, although there was a 3.4% increase in staff, justified by sales growth around 26%, the wage bill reduced by around 10% in this period.

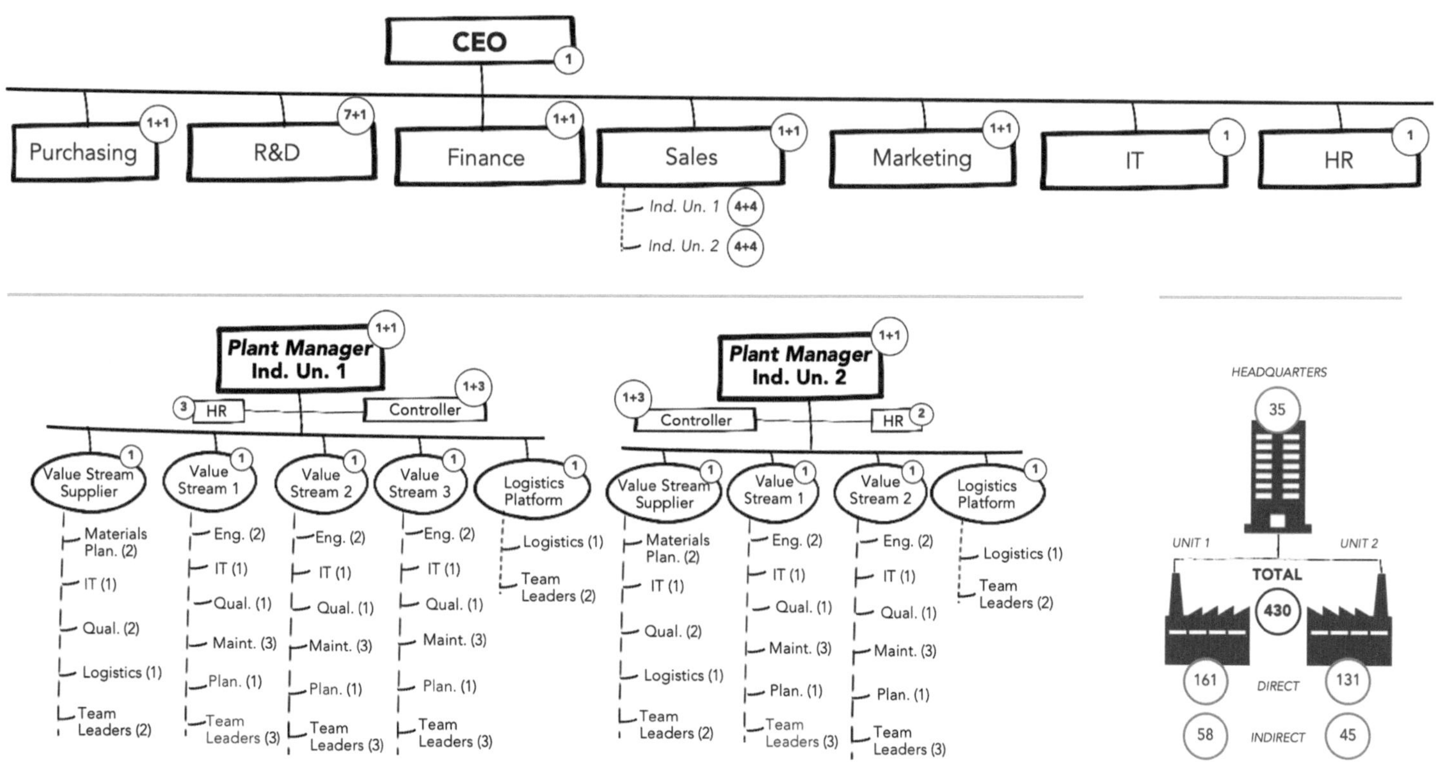

12.5 *Nagamichi* KAIZEN™ - The Organisational Transformation Model

It is natural that in the early years of applying Strat to Action, an organisation is focused on business operational aspects rather than on organisational issues. Problems such as matrix structures, multiple interfaces, functions and responsibilities proliferation or a structure that fails to provide the required speed, flexibility, and cost, are left behind. However, as the company begins to achieve its strategic objectives by applying the KAIZEN™ tools, it can identify more opportunities to transform its traditional departmental structure and create a Value Stream, customer-focused organisation.

The experience of the few companies that have achieved the status of World Class Companies shows that a process can be established to carry out the transformation to a level of excellence in the entire business. For this to be done effectively, each organisation must evaluate its progress against a long-term maturity plan in terms of continuous improvement.

The Kaizen Institute has an auditing model that allows companies to measure their transformation process over 10 to 15 years, helping them to keep their perspective on their objectives. In addition, there is such a level of detail, that progress can be audited every 6 months. This assessment program is called Nagamichi KAIZEN™.

Nagamichi evaluates 4 stages of Human Development, and 3 phases of Organisational Transformation. The following diagram explains this concept in detail:

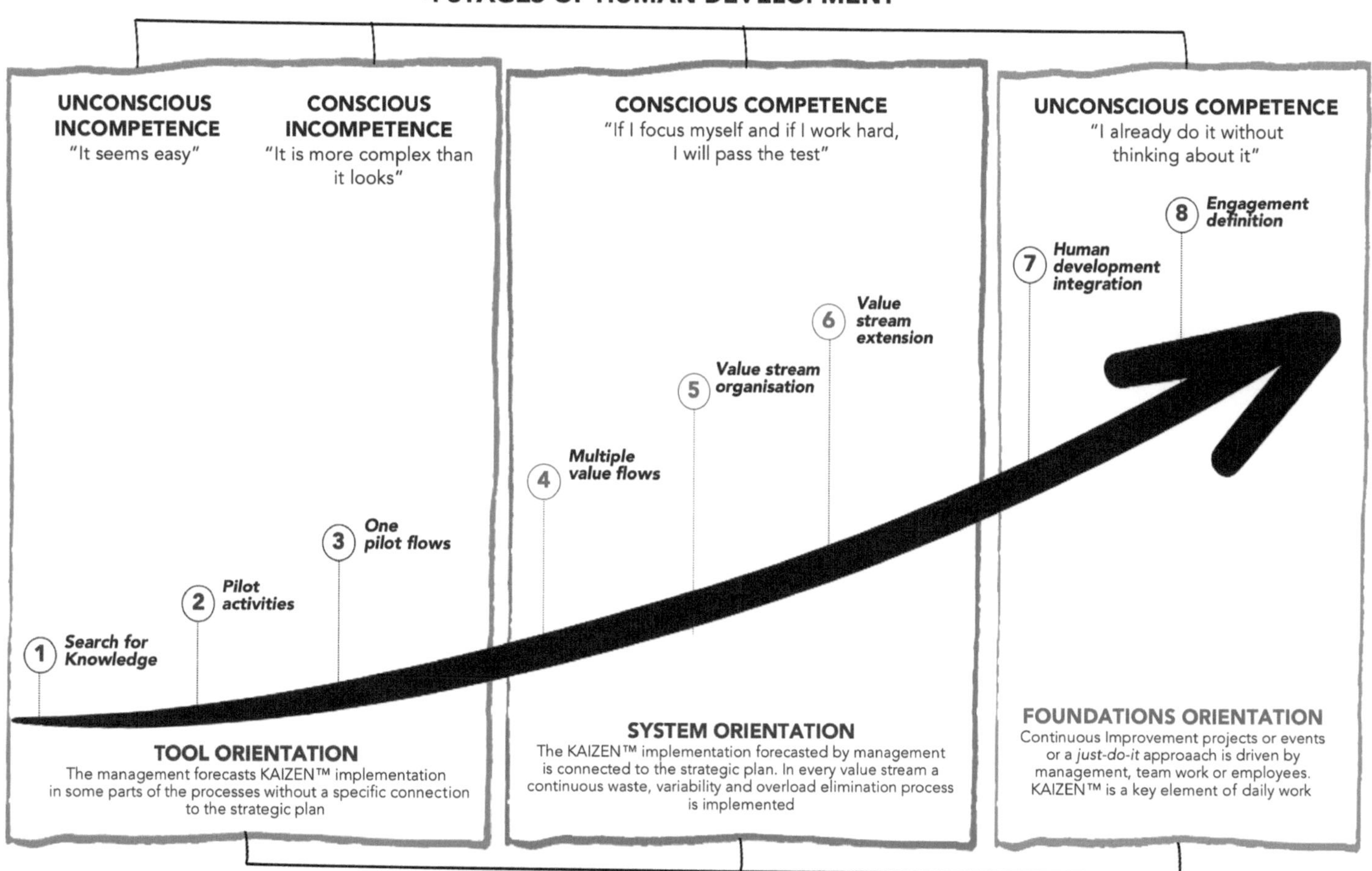
4 STAGES OF HUMAN DEVELOPMENT
UNCONSCIOUS INCOMPETENCE
"It seems easy"
CONSCIOUS INCOMPETENCE
"It is more complex than it looks"
CONSCIOUS COMPETENCE
"If I focus myself and if I work hard, I will pass the test"
UNCONSCIOUS COMPETENCE
"I already do it without thinking about it"
1 Search for Knowledge
2 Pilot activities
3 One pilot flows
4 Multiple value flows
5 Value stream organisation
6 Value stream extension
7 Human development integration
8 Engagement definition
TOOL ORIENTATION
The management forecasts KAIZEN™ implementation in some parts of the processes without a specific connection to the strategic plan
SYSTEM ORIENTATION
The KAIZEN™ implementation forecasted by management is connected to the strategic plan. In every value stream a continuous waste, variability and overload elimination process is implemented
FOUNDATIONS ORIENTATION
Continuous Improvement projects or events or a just-do-it approaach is driven by management, team work or employees. KAIZEN™ is a key element of daily work
3 PHASES OF ORGANISATIONAL TRANSFORMATION

The four stages of Human Development, initially known as the "4 Skill States", were originally proposed by Noel Burch. The current learning model describes the psychological states involved in transforming inability into ability or absolute mastery.

The four stages of Skills Development are a model that describes the process as how humans acquire a new skill. This model shows that humans are originally unaware of their skills. Once they become aware of an incompetence, they try to develop that skill. When an individual is dedicated to enhancing competence, through repetitive practice and formal training, they will be able to reach a consciously competent level. Over time, this acquired competence is effectively used without realising it. This happens as the individual acquires experience and knowledge, reaching the stage of unconscious competence, that is, they do not need to think about the activity that they are very good at.

Regarding the progress in organisational transformation, Nagamichi KAIZEN™ uses the levels of improvement proposed by Shigeo Shingo. According to Shingo, as organisations start their transformation, it usually occurs at the level of improvement techniques and **tools** application. In some **organisations**, this transformation proceeds to the **system** level, creating a more integrated and sustained improvement model. Eventually, the company reaches a third level, when all employees develop a deep understanding of the principles (the "whys"), enabling the organisation to develop and implement methodologies and practices of excellence.

In the Nagamichi KAIZEN™ model, the 3 transformation phases are described as follows:

- **Phase 1 - Tool-oriented:** described by starting to implement KAIZEN™ occasionally in parts of processes, with any connection to the strategic plan. Often assumed to be the "learning by doing" phase, using that methodology.

- **Phase 2 - System-oriented:** managers plan improvement activities linked to the business strategic needs. They use Hoshin Planning to define Improvement Priorities, and KAIZEN™ to systematically eliminate waste in value streams.

- **Phase 3 - Principle-oriented:** In addition to using KAIZEN™ to achieve the goals of each Improvement Priority as defined in Hoshin Planning, the Culture of Countermeasures is also widespread. Leaders "lead by example", actively participating in KAIZEN™ events. Continuous improvement is practiced every day in all areas and by all people.

In its long process of transformation, the Nagamichi KAIZEN™ model evaluates 8 levels of maturity, namely:

1. **Knowledge search:** there is an active search for improvement methods, through books, training, media and benchmark visits. It is well known that other organisations have performance improvements, and there is a desire to understand "why" and "how" they have achieved those results.

2. **Pilot activities:** there is recognition that it is necessary to "learn by doing", and the desire to test actions in a pilot area. It is expected to obtain results indicating the reason why the competitors present a superior performance.

3. **First value stream:** there is an awareness of the need to define value from a customer perspective, identifying waste at every step in the value chain. So it is necessary to implement

actions to improve the value stream, passing it to be pulled by the customer. It is also essential to develop a structured method to continually deepen the quality, cost and customer satisfaction improvements by eliminating new layers of waste.

4. **Multiple value streams:** business organisation around natural product groups and customers, with the creation of multiple value streams. A Strat to Action implementation to achieve excellence in performance.

5. **Organisation by Value Streams:** integration of support functions in each value stream and elimination of departmental silos. Creation of an organisational structure by Value Streams with multifunctional teams associated with Quality, Engineering, Sales, Finance, and all the functions necessary to satisfy customer need.

6. **Value Streams Extension:** there is a need to "further" extend the improvement of value streams from customers to suppliers. The company becomes a customer-oriented organisation, developing a strong relationship with its suppliers, building End-to-End Value Streams.

7. **Incorporation of Human Development:** Knowledge of KAIZEN™ practice is widespread among everyone in the organisation. KAIZEN™ becomes the way of life and executives lead KAIZEN™. There is a deep understanding and confidence in the results of KAIZEN™ methods and these are incorporated into everything that is done.

8. **Engagement definition:** the organisation implements KAIZEN™ methodologies across all business units, drawing a strategic plan, implemented with Strat to Action. These activities extend to mergers and acquisitions.

The assessment proposed in the Ngamichi model, evaluates the expected characteristics of an organisation in detail, as it progresses through each of the 8 levels of maturity.

The main criteria for this assessment are:

- **General perspective:** what you see and feel throughout the organisation, in terms of defining KAIZEN™ principles of improvement objectives and application. Ability to achieve significant QCD results - Quality, Cost and Delivery.
- **Human Development:** evaluation of the right measure of "Learn by doing" and "Going to GEMBA", applied to Executives, Directors, Supervisors and Collaborators.
- **Organisational Model:** evolution from departmental silos to an organisation by Value Streams.
- **Tools and Methodologies:** use of the correct tool for the purpose. Application of KAIZEN™ principles in all management, transactional and operational processes.
- **Results:** KAIZEN™ activities translate into financial results and customer experience. The return on investment ratios are at least greater than 3:1.

First, the organisation carries out its self-assessment to identify deviations from the assessment carried out by Kaizen Institute. These deviations should be included in the next Hoshin Planning.

This chapter aimed to demonstrate the potential of an organisational structure by Value Streams, making its agility and the achieved productivity boom evident, also the level of maturity acquired in this transformation process can be evaluated by the Nagamichi KAIZEN™ model.

The following chapter shows the results achieved in Year 3 of Hoshin implementation.

Year 3

Year 3 End Results

A Rising Star

By the end of the third year of Strat to Action development in the company, the time had arrived for the Annual Review. The Executive Committee met to evaluate the results.

This chapter describes that meeting, which followed the usual agenda, including Bowler's analysis of that year and identification of the main causes and countermeasures, followed by reflection on opportunities for improvement.

13.1 Review of Results achieved in Year 3

The CEO began by recalling the main objectives set for the year currently ending:
"The major milestones of Year 3 were the reorganisation of ALFA's structure into a Value Stream model and we continued to drive

TARGET TO ACHIEVE	Starting point	Annual target	Un.		Jan	Feb	Mar	Apr	May	Jun	Jul	Aug	Sept	Oct	Nov	Dec
Sales/FTE from 211 K€ to 222 K€ by Dec/Year 3	211.0	222.0	thousand €	Hoshin	211.9	212.8	213.8	214.7	215.6	216.5	217.4	218.3	219.3	220.2	221.1	222.0
				Actual	211.0	210.0	210.0	214.0	216.0	218.5	220.3	221.3	222.8	223.4	228.0	232.7
# Customers w/ Contribution Margin < 0% from 74 to 30 by Dec/Year 3	74	30	#	Hoshin	70	67	63	59	56	52	48	45	41	37	34	30
				Actual	74	74	74	65	63	60	50	44	32	28	28	28
# Products w/ Contribution Margin < 0% from 204 to 100 by Dec/Year 3	204	100	#	Hoshin	195	187	178	169	161	152	143	135	126	117	109	100
				Actual	200	190	184	177	175	174	170	123	111	98	96	93
On-Time Delivery from 91.5% to 95% by Dec/Year 3	91.5%	95.0%	%	Hoshin	91.8%	92.1%	92.4%	92.7%	93.0%	93.3%	93.5%	93.8%	94.1%	94.4%	94.7%	95.0%
				Actual	89.0%	91.0%	89.5%	91.5%	91.3%	92.3%	92.8%	92.1%	93.0%	93.5%	94.2%	94.7%
Time-To-Market from 35 to 18 weeks by Dec/Year 3	35	18	wk	Hoshin	34	32	31	29	28	27	25	24	22	21	19	18
				Actual	36	34	34	33	31	28	26	25	23	22	20	20
Inventory from 7.1 M€ to 6.4 M€ by Dec/Year 3	7.1	6.4	million €	Hoshin	7.0	7.0	6.9	6.9	6.8	6.8	6.7	6.6	6.6	6.5	6.5	6.4
				Actual	7.1	7.2	7.0	7.4	7.5	7.3	7.0	6.6	6.6	6.5	6.4	6.4
Mean Receipt Timeframe from 73 to 63 days by Dec/Year 3	73	63	days	Hoshin	72	71	71	70	69	68	67	66	66	65	64	63
				Actual	73	74	73	72	70	69	70	67	65	62	61	60
Average Payment Period from 78 to 62 days by Dec/Year 3	78	62	days	Hoshin	77	75	74	73	71	70	69	67	66	65	63	62
				Actual	77	77	78	76	73	70	70	65	66	64	63	62
Sales from 89.8 M€ to 95.5 M€ by Dec/Year 3	0	95 537	thousand €	Hoshin	7 961	15 923	23 884	31 846	39 807	47 769	55 730	63 691	71 653	79 614	87 576	95 537
				Actual	7 848	15 729	24 024	32 558	41 119	49 540	57 754	66 282	74 624	83 042	91 632	100 024
Vitality: New Customer Sales from 0 to 3 M€ by Dec/Year 3	0	3 000	thousand €	Hoshin	250	500	750	1 000	1 250	1 500	1 750	2 000	2 250	2 500	2 750	3 000
				Actual	176	467	770	1 029	1 250	1 609	1 980	2 134	2 489	2 876	3 017	3 254
Nr. Suppliers from 32 to 15 by Dec/Year 3	32	15	#	Hoshin	31	29	28	26	25	24	22	21	19	18	16	15
				Actual	32	32	32	27	27	27	23	22	20	20	17	17

Level 1 Bowling chart, Year 3

improvements in our profitability. If you all recall, we have achieved this, especially due to the elimination of products with a negative contribution margin. Reducing the number of suppliers was, of course, also vital to the simplification of our processes and to negotiate better prices and services." After the opening summary, the team looked at the Bowler.

Together, the team reflected on the values achieved:

- **PRODUCTIVITY**

The Hoshin Objective was to improve productivity from 211 thousand euros to 222 thousand euros in sales per FTE. The actual result at the end of the year was 233 thousand euros per FTE. This was due to the continuous improvement of OEE and Standard Work by completing 7 KAIZEN™ Events.

- **MARGIN ENHANCEMENT**

The goal was to reduce the number of customers showing a negative contribution margin (including direct costs) from 74 to 30. In December, this goal had been exceeded, with only 28 customers remaining. Also reducing the number of references (SKUs) of finished products with a negative contribution margin, in this case from 204 to 100. By the end of the year, this disruptive objective had also been exceeded, reaching 93 references.

- **ON TIME DELIVERY (OTD) COMPLIANCE**

The target for Year 3 of Hoshin implementation predicted an increase in OTD from 91.5% to 95.0%. By the end of the year, ALFA had reached 94.7%. This excellent result had proven to be a pivotal differentiating factor in relation to competitive advantage, having contributed to the increase in sales to existing customers and in new customers.

- **NEW PRODUCTS - TIME TO MARKET**

The Target to be Improved was to reduce the development time of new products from 35 to 18 weeks. The actual results showed a reduction in time to market to 20 weeks. This has been very important in attracting new customers. Furthermore, the ALFA engineers' motivation was to reach 10 weeks in the near future.

- **INVENTORY**

The objective was to reduce the value of total stocks from 7.1 to 6.4 million euros, by reducing ALFA's working capital requirements. By the end of the year, despite the achieved increase in sales, it had been possible to reach the target set.

- **PAYABLES AND RECEIVABLES AVERAGE TERM**

In this case, the objective was to continue correcting the excessive payment terms from 78 to 62 days, while the average deadline for receivables was to be reduced from 73 to 63 days. By the end of the year, the average payment terms were already being met, as predicted in Hoshin. In the average deadline for receivables it was possible to achieve the outstanding result of 60 days, due to the first-rate work carried out by the multidisciplinary teams of each Value Stream working with customers and suppliers in chasing cash.

- **SALES**

The target was to achieve an improvement in sales from 89.8 to 95.5 million euros. This figure had been surpassed by €4.5 million, reaching a record of 100 million euros. Sales of 3.3 million euros to new customers had also contributed to this result. Finally, the potential for improvement, identified in many KAIZEN™ Events and actions carried out in the Marketing and Sales processes, had been materialised.

- **SUPPLIER REDUCTION**

ALFA aimed to reduce the number of suppliers of raw materials from 32 to 15, seeking to achieve better prices through the volume effect, as well as stronger trust relationships and partnerships. By the end of the year, there were 17 suppliers, a lower number than expected, but acceptable due to the introduction of new products that required the purchase of different components.

- **FREE CASH FLOW**

In Year 3, the target set was to raise free cash flow from 8.7 to 10.2 million euros. The excellent operating performance and the maintenance of the investment restraint policy, together with the reduction in stock and the average deadline for receivables, allowed a remarkable figure of 11.6 million euros by the end of the year.

- **EBITDA**

ALFA's 3-Year Breakthrough Objectives aimed to reach 12 million euros in EBITDA. Although many believed it to be possible, they had never considered the possibility of reaching 15 million euros. This remarkable value of 15% on sales was considered as Best in Class in this area of activity.

- **KAIZEN™**

The decision to continue with the same KAIZEN™ Event run rate proved to be a good bet. The 127 events carried out at both industrial units had focused on restructuring the organisation, improving margins and reducing suppliers. The return on investment in consultancy remained at a ratio of 4 to 1, in relation to the achieved increase in EBITDA.

At the end of the meeting, the entire Executive Committee was proud of the results accomplished, but conscious of the responsibility to maintain the continuous requirement to improve processes and people, not only to consolidate these gains, but also to perpetuate growth, year upon year.

The next chapter presents the overall results of the three years of Hoshin implementation at ALFA.

Results after 3 Years Transformation

Consistent Processes lead to Expected Results

Chapter 14

At the CEO's request, the Board of Directors joined the Executive Committee for the presentation of the results of ALFA's 3-Year transformation. It was an important milestone for the company and its executive team. In order to make the recovery visible, a presentation was prepared with the 3-year evolution of the main performance indicators, the analysis of which is described in this chapter.

As the members of the Board of Directors arrived, the CEO greeted them and took the opportunity to explain the importance of the information displayed on the walls of the Mission Control Room. The mood was one of expectation and some anxiety among those present. The members of the Executive Committee recalled the difficulties experienced throughout the change process.

As transformation leader, the CEO kicked the session off: "Firstly, I would like to thank the members of the Board of Directors for your presence at this meeting. In the next 60 minutes we will talk about the long journey we have made over the last 3 years. Do you remember the situation in January of Year 1?" The CEO paused and then proceeded "At that time, ALFA was in a serious situation, EBITDA had fallen year on year and the company could not generate free cash flow to fuel the required growth. This was a trend that we and our teams had to correct rapidly. As you know, the involvement of all of us and our teams was fundamental in this change process. We defined disruptive goals which challenged us to go beyond what we were used to. The pressure was high, but it made us get out of our comfort zones and strive to go farther, every step of the way. After transforming all business areas of this company, we now have a profitable ALFA, supported by solid processes and continuous improvement methodologies. This is what gives us very promising prospects for the future. So, I would like to share the results of this transformation with you in detail."

- **SALES AND EBITDA**

Over the 3 years of Strat to Action, sales had increased from 80 to 100 million euros, while EBITDA had increased from 2.9% to 15% of sales, reaching a remarkable value of 15 million euros.

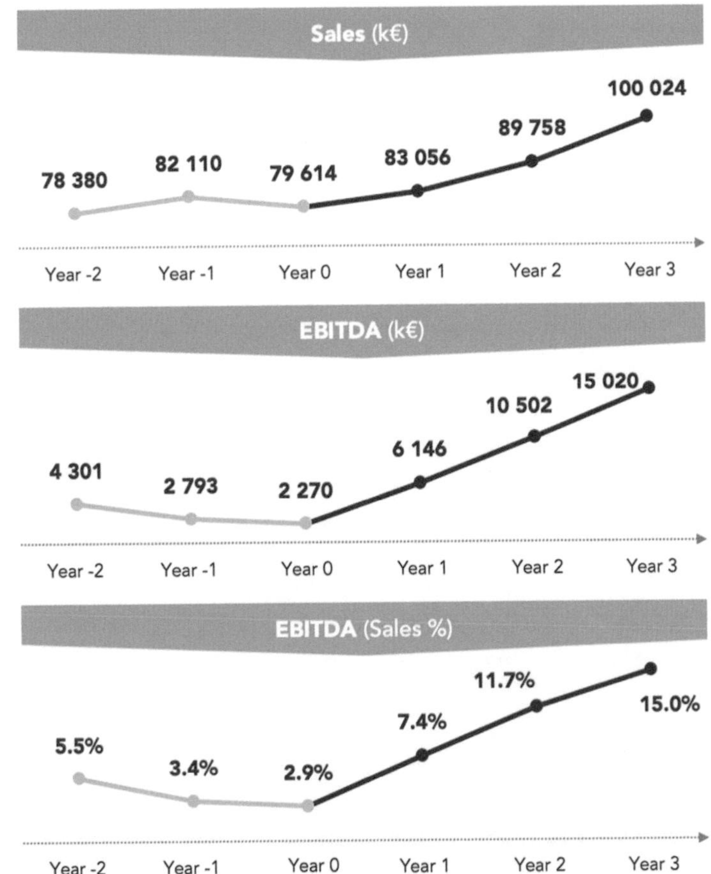

- **FREE CASH FLOW**

Free cash flow had increased from 0.5 million euros to 11.6 million euros, driven by a 50% reduction in inventory value, as well as an improvement obtained in average payment terms from 83 to 60 days. Even with an increase in sales, it was possible to reduce the inventory value from 12.9 to 6.4 million euros.

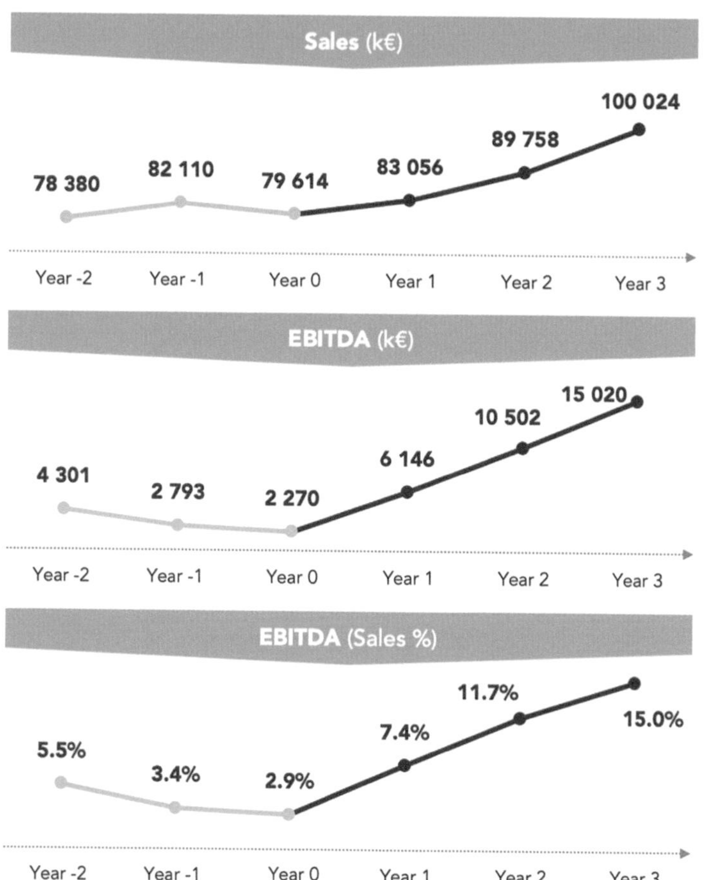

- **SUPPLY AND EXTERNAL SERVICES**

With the support team's efficiency improvements, it was possible to substantially reduce dependence on subcontracting. Furthermore, the introduction of the PPV methodology and the consequent improvement in contracting with suppliers had contributed greatly to the reduction of supply and external services costs, from 17.7% to 14.5% of sales. This result represented a saving of 3.1 million euros.

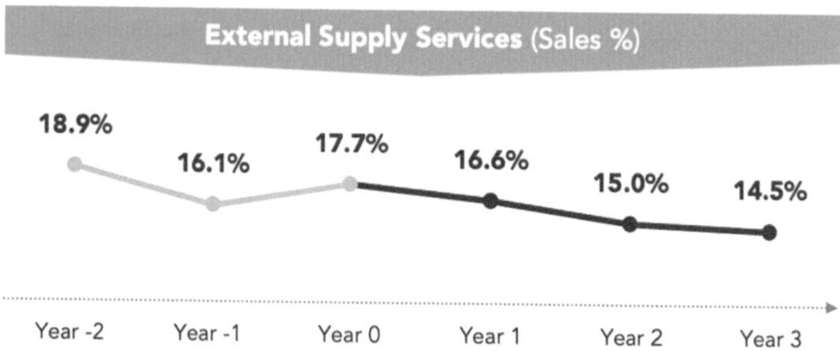

- **PRODUCTIVITY**

Overall productivity gains, measured by sales over the total number of employees, represented an increase of 22%, taking the indicator from 191 to 233 thousand euros per employee in 3 years. This increase in productivity, associated with the increase in sales volume, allowed staff costs to be reduced to 11.3%, from a starting level of 15.7%.

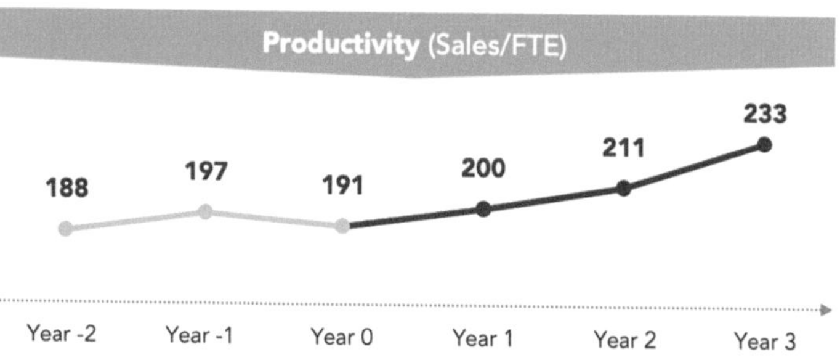

Year	Sales (k€)	Personnel Expenses (k€)	Sales %	N° employ.	Costs/ FTE (€)	Sales/ FTE (k€)
Year 0	79 614	12 538	15.7%	416	30 138	191
Year 1	83 056	11 628	14.0%	415	28 019	200
Year 2	89 758	10 861	12.1%	425	25 555	211
Year 3	100 024	11 303	11.3%	430	26 285	233
Variance Year 0 - 3	25.6%	-9.8%		3.4%	-12.8%	21.5%

- **QUALITY**

With the creation of a countermeasure culture and structured problem solving, it was possible to eliminate the causes of problems at their root. This improvement in processes quality had been extended to the customer. Consequently, the reduction in the number of complaints reached 71%, with associated savings of 1.4 million euros in scrap and rework costs.

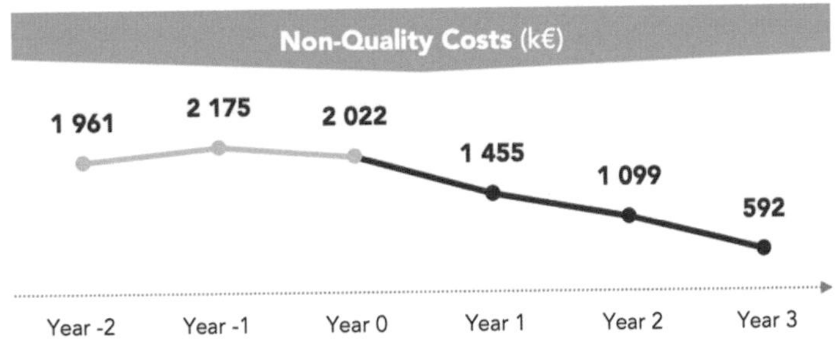

- **OTD - ON TIME DELIVERY**

The drastic inventory reduction, achieved with the implementation of JIT on the production lines, together with a planning model based on real customer demand (pull), improved On Time Delivery from 75.0 % to 94.7%.

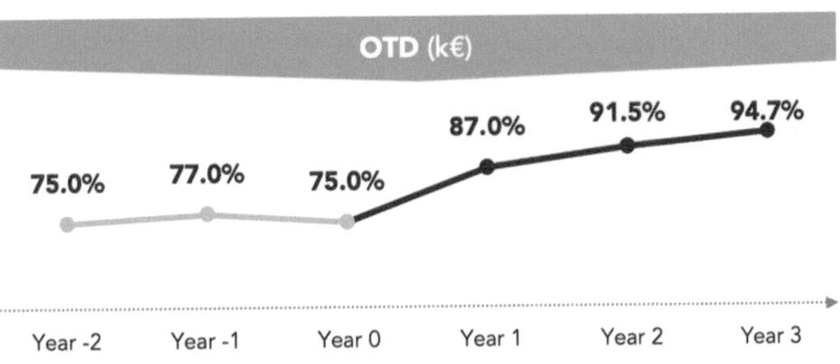

- **TIME TO MARKET**

The time to market for new product development was significantly reduced from 50 to 20 weeks. This was mainly supported by the introduction of a Stage Gate Review process, responsible for controlling and accelerating different development stages. It also reduced Engineering rework and established the ability to resolve problems quickly.

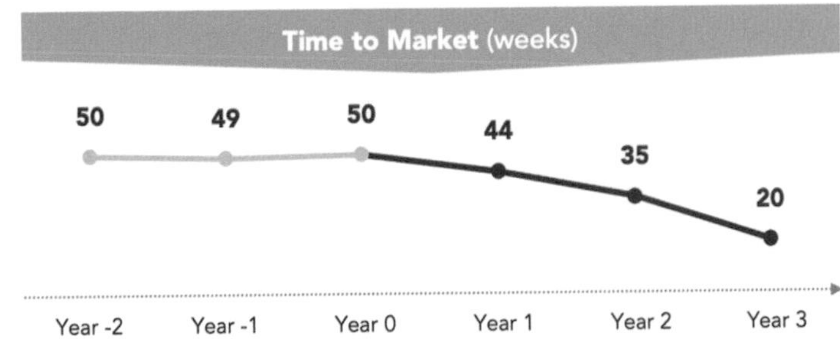

In addition, the CEO highlighted the results achieved in reducing the number of raw material SKUs, suppliers and technical waste, which had greatly contributed to increased profitability. As had reducing the number of SKU with a negative margin.

- **KAIZEN™ EVENTS**

In 3 years of Continuous Improvement, ALFA had completed 370 KAIZEN™ Events. Year 1 focused on productivity, quality, inventory and customer service. Year 2 had prioritised sales growth and increased free cash flow. Year 3 focused on improving margins, product innovation and restructuring by Value Stream.

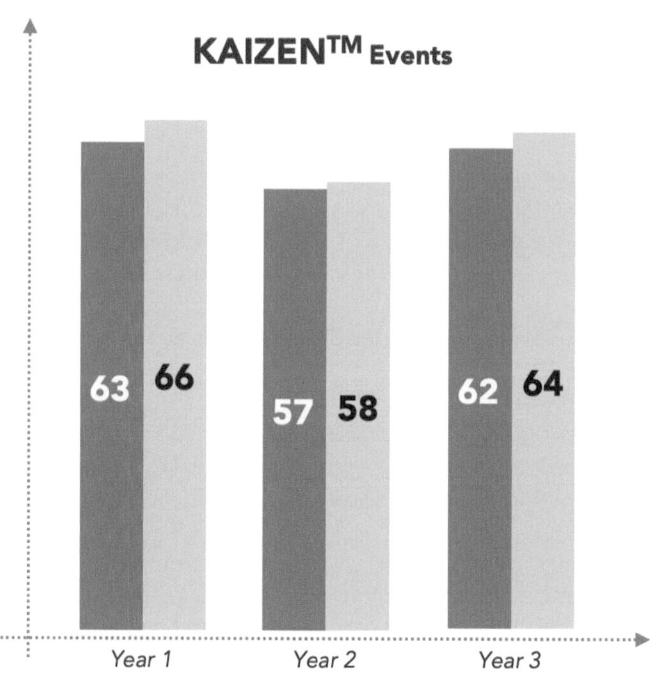

- **NAGAMICHI KAIZEN™: A CULTURAL TRANSFORMATION**

Cultural change had begun by being guided in the technique and use of KAIZEN™ as a tool. The need to focus on Voice of the Customer improvement activities led ALFA to the creation and optimisation of its Value Streams. The use of Strat to Action as a methodology to define and implement strategic goals allowed the organisation to begin advancing toward a system culture. The organisation of the business around natural product groups and customers, and the creation of multiple Value Streams, had also contributed to this improvement system culture. In addition, the inclusion of support functions in each Value Stream and the elimination of departmental silos, with the consequent creation of a new organisational structure by Value Stream, had enhanced the culture of improvement system at ALFA.

In conclusion to the presentation of its 3-year of leadership results at the company, the CEO thanked, particularly, the members of his executive team for their commitment and perseverance in this path of organisational transformation:
"Today, we have teams with a much higher level of maturity in terms of continuous improvement, with high autonomy and a great capacity for generating results," The CEO continued: "So, from now on we will take full advantage of the lessons learned by us all. If we have succeeded in transforming ALFA, imagine what we can do in the future. In terms of the application of continuous improvement, best-in-class organisations have been able to achieve results, for decades, that are similar to those presented today. This must be our ambition. Count on me to continue to challenge and follow you on this successful journey."

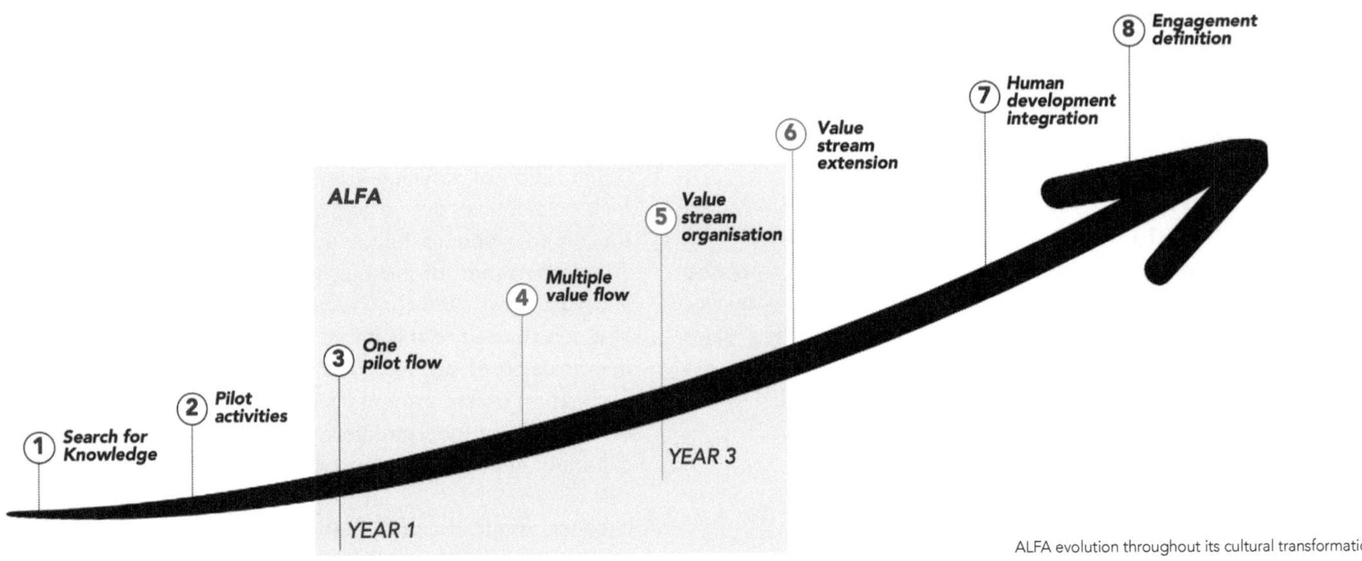

ALFA evolution throughout its cultural transformation

Often, in the search for Continuous Improvement, organisations do not lack new ideas, but lack focus instead. In an attempt to implement all the initiatives being considered, there is a loss of capacity in the execution, monitoring and obtaining of sustained results. It is in this context that the Strat to Action methodology plays a key role in organisations, able to focus decision makers on the most critical processes, those with a real impact on results and customer value creation.

In this constant search for improvement in processes, managers often forget that processes are managed and optimised by people. Thus, permanent improvement requires a team motivated and fully aligned with the organisation's purposes. So it is crucial to have a culture of leadership by example, an approach far from the well-known traditional reality. "Leading by example" makes leaders fundamental to the change process, due to their active participation in improvement initiatives alongside their teams.

At KAIZEN™ we know that the greatest barriers to Continuous Improvement are inherent to the organisation itself and reside in the paradigms that have been created throughout its existence. By agreeing to commit to truly disruptive objectives, organisational leaders are creating the conditions to break current paradigms, challenging their people to set different limits and meet the new paradigms.

Once these strategic objectives have been defined, the next step aims to transpose them from paper to reality, which is often ineffective, due to the absence of a structured management process.

Strat to Action transforms strategy into action, challenging and preparing organisations for the future, through methodical management focused on process improvement, commitment from leaders and everyone's engagement.

Appendices

1. Level 1 and Level 2 Matrices and respective Bowler Charts

APPENDIX 1.1 - LEVEL 1 X MATRIX, YEAR 1

LEVEL 1 X MATRIX

Time To Market from 50 to 40 weeks in Year 1	Free Cash Flow from 545 K€ to 5.3 M€ in Year 1	On-Time Delivery from 75% to 82.5% in Year 1	EBITDA from 2.3 to 7.2 M€ in Year 1	L1 Improvement Priorities	Sales/ FTE from 191 K€ to 200 K€ by Dec/Year 1	Ext. Services & Supplies from 17.7% to 16.4% of sales (1 M€) by Dec/Year 1	Planned Waste from 8.0% to 7% (505 K€) by Dec/Year 1	Purchase Part Variance (PPV) from 50.5 M€ to 50 M€ Dec/Year 1	Non-quality Costs from 2 M€ to 1.52 M€ by Dec/Year 1	# Customer Complaints from 84 to 42 by de Dec/ Year 1	On-Time Delivery from 75% to 82.5% by Dec/ Year 1	Inventory from 12.9 M€ to 9.7 M€ (6.2 to 12.3 turns) Dec/Year 1	Time To Market from 50 to 40 weeks by Dec/ Year 1	Sales from 79.6 M€ to 87.6 M€ by Dec/Year 1	Vitality: Sales to New Customers from 0 to 3 M€ by Dec/Year 1	Operations Manager	Engineering Manager	Materials and Logistics Manager	Marketing & Sales Manager	Human Resources Manager	Purchasing Manager	Financial Manager	IT Manager
●			●	Design a process to improve Marketing & Sales										●	●				●				○
●				Implement a process to reduce New Product Lead Times									●			○	●						
	●			Implement a process to reduce Working Capital								●						●			○	○	
		●		Implement a process to increase On-Time Delivery							●					○		●	○				○
			●	Implement a process to reduce Non Compliances					●	●						●							
			●	Design a process to reduce Product Cost (VA/VE,PPV)			●	●									●				○		
			●	Implement a process to increase Productivity	●	●										●		○		○			○

Annual Breakthrough objectives | Targets to Improve (TTI) | 3-year Breakthrough objectives

Time To Market	Free Cash Flow	On-Time Delivery	EBITDA	3-year Breakthrough objectives
			●	EBITDA from 2.3 M€ to 12 M€ in 3 years (20% of sales growth included)
		●		On-Time Delivery from 75% to 90% in 3 years
	●			Free Cash Flow from 545 K€ to 10 M€ in 3 years
●				Time To Market from 50 to 30 weeks in 3 years

Resources:
- ● Primary responsibility
- ○ Secondary responsibility

APPENDIX 1.2 - LEVEL 1 BOWLER CHART, YEAR 1

TARGET TO ACHIEVE	Starting point	Annual target	Un.		Jan	Feb	Mar	Apr	May	Jun	Jul	Aug	Sept	Oct	Nov	Dec
Sales/FTE from 191 K€ to 200 K€ by Dec/Year 1	191.0	200.0	thousand €	**Hoshin**	191.8	192.5	193.3	194.0	194.8	195.5	196.3	197.0	197.8	198.5	199.3	200.0
				Actual	191.0	193.0	194.5	195.0	195.0	194.0	199.0	199.7	199.8	198.5	198.9	200.0
External Services & Supplies from 17.7% to 16.4% of sales (1 M€) by Dec/Year 1	17.7%	16.4%	%	**Hoshin**	17.6%	17.5%	17.4%	17.3%	17.2%	17.1%	16.9%	16.8%	16.7%	16.6%	16.5%	16.4%
				Actual	17.7%	17.5%	17.5%	17.4%	16.9%	16.9%	16.5%	16.9%	16.8%	16.7%	16.6%	16.6%
	0.0	1 035	thousand €	**Hoshin**	7.2	28.7	64.7	115.0	179.7	258.7	352.2	460.0	582.2	718.7	869.7	1 035.0
				Actual	0.0	26.5	39.8	79.6	265.4	318.5	557.3	424.6	537.4	663.4	802.8	875.8
Planned Waste from 8% to 7% (505 K€) by Dec/Year 1	8.0%	7.0%	%	**Hoshin**	7.9%	7.8%	7.8%	7.7%	7.6%	7.5%	7.4%	7.3%	7.3%	7.2%	7.1%	7.0%
				Actual	8.1%	7.9%	9.0%	7.8%	7.7%	7.4%	7.2%	7.2%	7.1%	7.4%	7.0%	6.6%
	0	505	thousand €	**Hoshin**	42	84	126	168	210	253	295	337	379	421	463	505
				Actual	45	81	122	165	208	256	295	339	383	424	470	507
Purchase Part Variance (PPV) from 50.5 M€ to 50 M€ by Dec/Year 1	0	500	thousand €	**Hoshin**	41.7	83.3	125.0	166.7	208.3	250.0	291.7	333.3	375.0	416.7	458.3	500.0
				Actual	0.0	0.0	55.2	110.1	184.5	294.6	336.6	368.6	400.6	432.6	464.6	496.6
Non-quality Costs from 2M€ to 1.52 M€ by Dec/Year 1	0	1.52	million €	**Hoshin**	0.13	0.25	0.38	0.51	0.63	0.76	0.89	1.01	1.14	1.27	1.39	1.52
				Actual	0.15	0.29	0.43	0.50	0.57	0.64	0.71	0.88	1.05	1.27	1.34	1.54
# Customer Complaints from 84 to 42 by Dec/Year 1	0	42	#	**Hoshin**	4	7	11	14	18	21	25	28	32	35	39	42
				Actual	7	12	14	15	17	19	24	26	30	35	40	42
On-Time Delivery from 75% to 82.5% by Dec/Year 1	75.0%	82.5%	%	**Hoshin**	75.6%	76.3%	76.9%	77.5%	78.1%	78.8%	79.4%	80.0%	80.6%	81.3%	81.9%	82.5%
				Actual	70.0%	71.0%	72.7%	73.0%	74.6%	75.0%	80.0%	84.0%	84.5%	85.2%	86.7%	87.0%
Inventory from 12.9 M€ to 9.7 M€ (6.2 to 12.3 turns) by Dec/Year 1	12.9	9.7	million €	**Hoshin**	12.6	12.4	12.1	11.8	11.6	11.3	11.0	10.8	10.5	10.2	10.0	9.7
				Actual	12.8	12.9	12.7	13.1	13.0	12.3	11.1	10.9	10.6	10.5	9.9	9.8
Time To Market from 50 to 40 weeks until Dec/Year 1	50	40	wk	**Hoshin**	49	48	48	47	46	45	44	43	43	42	41	40
				Actual	50	49	49	45	49	46	40	44	35	45	44	44
Sales from 79.6 M€ to 87.6 M€ until Dec/Year 1	0	87 575	thousand €	**Hoshin**	7 298	14 596	21 894	29 192	36 490	43 788	51 085	58 383	65 681	72 979	80 277	87 575
				Actual	6 897	13 766	20 636	27 505	34 375	41 244	48 114	54 983	61 853	68 722	75 592	83 056
Vitality: New Customer Sales from 0 to 3 M€ by Dec/Year 1	0	3 000	thousand €	**Hoshin**	250	500	750	1 000	1 250	1 500	1 750	2 000	2 250	2 500	2 750	3 000
				Actual	203	380	525	607	871	1 016	1 245	1 367	1 427	1 568	1 760	2 137

APPENDIX 1.3 - LEVEL 2 X MATRIX, OPERATIONS, IND. UNIT 1, YEAR 1

LEVEL 2 X MATRIX- OPERATIONS

L2 Improvement priorities

L1 Improvement priorities

Targets to Improve (TTI)

Annual Breakthrough objectives

L2 Improvement priorities	Implement a process to reduce Non-compliances	Implement a process to increase Productivity	Sales / FTE Ennis line from 192 K€ to 202 K€ by Dec/Year 1	Ennis Line OEE from 74% to 85% by Dec/Year 1	Ennis Line Setup Time from 30 to 15 min by Dec/Year 1	Ferguson Line Sales / FTE from 233 K€ to 245 K€ by Dec/Year 1	Ferguson Line OEE from 68% to 77% by Dec/Year 1	Ferguson Line Setup Time from 25 to 15 min by Dec/Year 1	Maintenance Specialised Services from 4% to 3.5% of sales by Dec/Year 1	Several External Services from 4.7% to 4.4% of sales by Dec/Year 1	Non-quality Costs from 1.2 M€ to 0.88 M€ by Dec/Year 1	# Customer Complaints from 46 to 23 by Dec/Year 1	Plant Manager	Production Manager	Purchasing Manager	Quality Engineer	Process Engineer
Implement a Poka-yoke process	●										●	●				○	●
Implement a Problem Solving process	●										●	●				●	○
Implement an Auto-quality process	●										●	●				●	○
Implement a process to reduce External Services		●							●	●			○		●		
Implement a process to increase Ferguson Line Productivity		●				●	●	●						●			
Implement a process to increase Ennis Line Productivity		●	●	●	●									●			

Annual Breakthrough objectives	Implement a process to reduce Non-compliances	Implement a process to increase Productivity
EBITDA from 2.3 to 7.2 M€ in Year 1	●	●
On-Time Delivery from 75% to 82.5% in Year 1		
Free Cash Flow from 545 K€ to 5.3 M€ in Year 1		
Time To Market from 50 to 40 weeks in Year 1		

Resources:
- ● Primary responsibility
- ○ Secondary responsibility

APPENDIX 1.4 - LEVEL 2 BOWLING CHART, OPERATIONS, IND. UNIT 1, YEAR 1

TARGET TO ACHIEVE	Starting point	Annual target	Un.		Jan	Feb	Mar	Apr	May	Jun	Jul	Aug	Sept	Oct	Nov	Dec
Ennis Line Sales/FTE from 192 K€ to 202 K€ by Dec/Year 1	192	202	thousand €	**Hoshin**	192.8	193.7	194.5	195.3	196.2	197.0	197.8	198.7	199.5	200.3	201.2	202.0
				Actual	194.0	196.0	197.5	198.0	198.0	197.0	199.0	199.7	199.8	198.5	198.9	200.0
Ennis Line OEE from 74% to 85% by Dec/Year 1	74%	85%	%	**Hoshin**	75%	76%	77%	78%	79%	80%	80%	81%	82%	83%	84%	85%
				Actual	74%	73%	74%	75%	76%	79%	81%	82%	80%	81%	84%	85%
Ennis Line Setup Time from 30 to 15 min by Dec/Year 1	30	15	min	**Hoshin**	29	28	26	25	24	23	21	20	19	18	16	15
				Actual	30	35	29	31	32	29	20	20	18	17	17	15
Ferguson Line Sales/FTE from 233 K€ to 245 K€ by Dec/Year 1	233	245	thousand €	**Hoshin**	234	235	236	237	238	239	240	241	242	243	244	245
				Actual	233	234	237	238	240	238	239	241	243	245	244	245
Ferguson Line OEE from 68% to 77% by Dec/Year 1	68%	77%	%	**Hoshin**	69%	70%	70%	71%	72%	73%	73%	74%	75%	76%	76%	77%
				Actual	68%	69%	67%	66%	69%	70%	72%	68%	69%	70%	72%	74%
Ferguson Line Setup Time from 25 to 15 min by Dec/Year 1	25	15	min	**Hoshin**	24	23	23	22	21	20	19	18	18	17	16	15
				Actual	25	24	26	26	20	21	20	20	19	22	15	17
Maintenance Specialised Services from 4% to 3.5% of sales by Dec/Year 1	4.0%	3.5%	%	**Hoshin**	4.0%	3.9%	3.9%	3.8%	3.8%	3.8%	3.7%	3.7%	3.6%	3.6%	3.5%	3.5%
				Actual	4.0%	4.1%	4.0%	3.9%	4.0%	3.9%	3.8%	3.8%	3.7%	3.7%	3.5%	3.5%
Other Services from 4.7% to 4.4% of sales by Dec/Year 1	4.7%	4.4%	%	**Hoshin**	4.7%	4.7%	4.6%	4.6%	4.6%	4.6%	4.5%	4.5%	4.5%	4.5%	4.4%	4.4%
				Actual	4.8%	4.9%	4.8%	4.8%	4.7%	4.7%	4.6%	4.7%	4.6%	4.6%	4.5%	4.4%
Non-quality Costs from 1.2 M€ to 0.88 M€ by Dec/Year 1	0	880	thousand €	**Hoshin**	73	147	220	293	367	440	513	587	660	733	807	880
				Actual	77	163	249	289	329	369	409	449	561	735	811	878
Nr. Customer Complaints from 46 to 23 by Dec/Year 1	0	23	#	**Hoshin**	2	4	6	8	10	12	13	15	17	19	21	23
				Actual	3	6	9	10	11	11	12	13	15	19	19	24

APPENDIX 1.5 - LEVEL 2 X MATRIX, ENGINEERING, YEAR 1

LEVEL 2 X MATRIX - ENGINEERING

		Implement a process to reduce new products lead time	Design a process to reduce product cost (VA/VE,PPV)	L2 Improvement priorities / L1 Improvement priorities / Targets to Improve (TTI) / Annual Breakthrough objectives	Cost Reduction with VA/VE of 300 K€ until Dec/Year 1	Sales/ FTE from 191 K€ to 200 K€ by Dec./Year 1	Purchase Part Variance (PPV) from 50.5 M€ to 50 M€ by Dec/Year 1	FSE from 17.7% (5.1 M€) to 16.4% (4.7 M€) by Dec/Year 1	Capex expenses from 2.4 M€ maximum by Dec/ Year 1	New products lead-time from 50 to 40 weeks by Dec/Year 1	New products defect costs from 200 K€ to 100 K€ by Dec/Year 1					New Product Development Engineer	Process Engineer	Maintenance Engineer	Purchasing Manager	Quality Engineer	
		●		Implement a process to do a Stage Gate Review in new product development						●	●					●	○	○	○	○	
		●		Implement a process to accelerate new product development						●						●	○	○	○	○	
			●	Implement Lean Line Design in capex process					●								●	○			
			●	Implement a PPV process to services and materials supply			●	●											●		
			●	Implement a VA/VE process	●	●										●				○	
			●	EBITDA from 2.3 to 7.2 M€ in Year 1																	
				On-Time Delivery from 75% to 82.5% in Year 1																	
				Free Cash Flow from 545 K€ to 5.3 M€ in Year 1																	
		●		Time To Market from 50 to 40 weeks in Year 1																	

Resources:
- ● Primary responsibility
- ○ Secondary responsibility

APPENDIX 1.6 - LEVEL 2 BOWLING CHART, ENGINEERING, YEAR 1

TARGET TO ACHIEVE	Starting point	Annual target	Un.		Jan	Feb	Mar	Apr	May	Jun	Jul	Aug	Sept	Oct	Nov	Dec
Cost Reduction with VA/VE of 300 K€ until Dec/Year 1	0	300	thousand €	*Hoshin*	25	50	75	100	125	150	175	200	225	250	275	300
				Actual	24	45	74	96	120	155	181	205	230	276	289	327
Sales/FTE from 191 K€ to 200 K€ by Dec/Year 1	191	200	thousand €	*Hoshin*	191.8	192.5	193.3	194.0	194.8	195.5	196.3	197.0	197.8	198.5	199.3	200.0
				Actual	191.0	193.0	194.5	195.0	195.0	194.0	199.0	199.7	199.8	198.5	198.9	200.0
Purchase Part Variance (PPV) from 50.5 M€ to 50 M€ by Dec/Year 1	0	500	thousand €	*Hoshin*	41.7	83.3	125.0	166.7	208.3	250.0	291.7	333.3	375.0	416.7	458.3	500.0
				Actual	0.0	0.0	55.2	110.1	184.5	294.6	336.6	368.6	400.6	432.6	464.6	496.6
External Services & Supplies from 17.7% (5.1 M€) to 16.4% (4.7 M€) by Dec/Year 1	0	400	thousand €	*Hoshin*	33	67	100	133	167	200	233	267	300	333	367	400
				Actual	30	65	96	132	174	207	242	245	267	331	355	398
Capex Expenses of 2.4 M€ maximum by Dec/Year 1	0	2 400	thousand €	*Hoshin*	200	400	600	800	1 000	1 200	1 400	1 600	1 800	2 000	2 200	2 400
				Actual	398	756	935	1 109	1 293	1 356	1 400	1 590	1 780	1 989	2 178	2 224
New Products Lead Time from 50 to 40 weeks by Dec/Year 1	50	40	wk	*Hoshin*	49	48	48	47	46	45	44	43	43	42	41	40
				Actual	50	49	49	45	49	46	40	44	35	45	44	44
New Products Defect Costs from 200 K€ to 100 K€ by Dec/Year 1	0	100	thousand €	*Hoshin*	8	17	25	33	42	50	58	67	75	83	92	100
				Actual	19	23	28	45	48	52	57	64	73	82	90	90

APPENDIX 1.7 - LEVEL 2 X MATRIX, MARKETING & SALES, YEAR 1

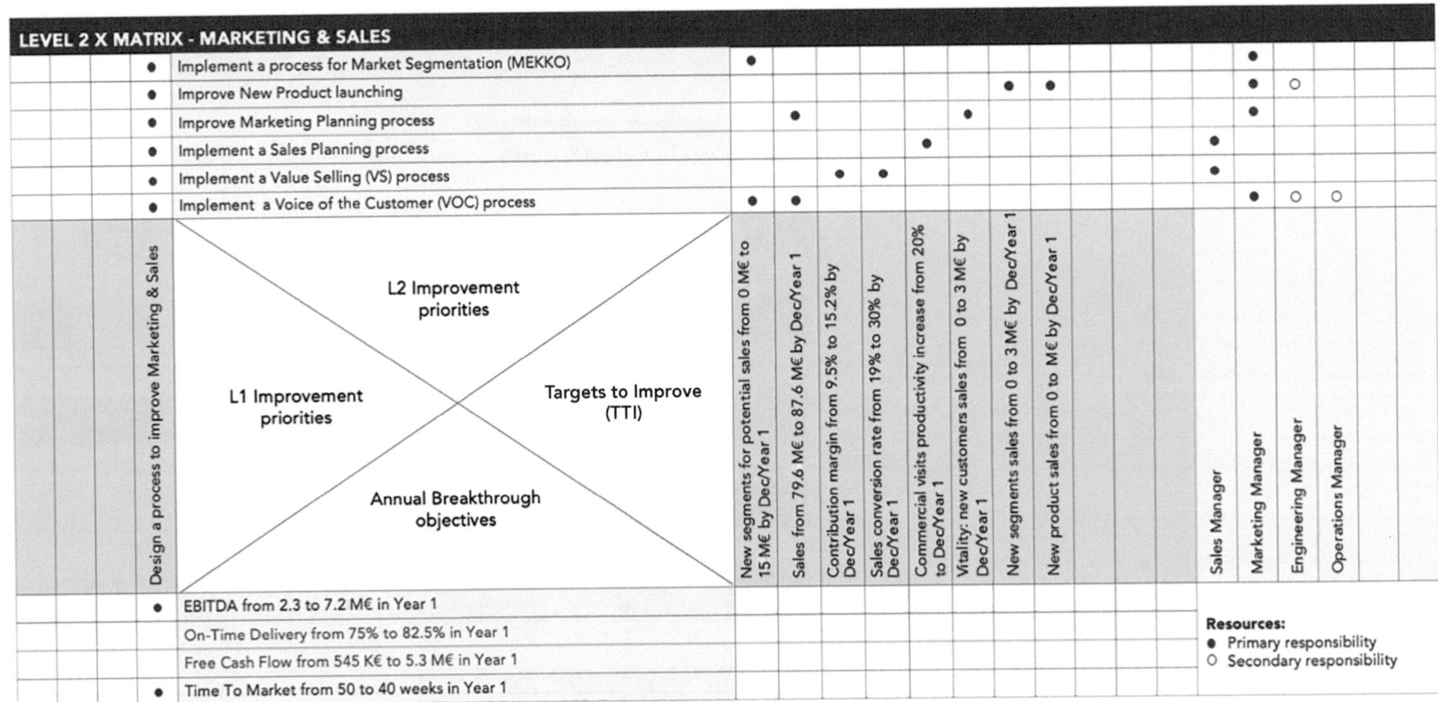

APPENDIX 1.8 - LEVEL 2 BOWLING CHART, MARKETING & SALES, YEAR 1

TARGET TO ACHIEVE	Starting point	Annual target	Un.		Jan	Feb	Mar	Apr	May	Jun	Jul	Aug	Sept	Oct	Nov	Dec
New Segments Potential Sales from 0 M€ to 15 M€ by Dec/Year 1	0	15	million €	**Hoshin**	1	3	4	5	6	8	9	10	11	13	14	15
				Actual	0	1	2	3	4	5	9	11	12	17	28	45
Sales from 79.6 M€ to 87.6 M€ by Dec/Year 1	0	87 575	thousand €	**Hoshin**	7 298	14 596	21 894	29 192	36 490	43 788	51 085	58 383	65 681	72 979	80 277	87 575
				Actual	6 897	13 766	20 636	27 505	34 375	41 244	48 114	54 983	61 853	68 722	75 592	83 056
New Segments Sales from 0 to 3 M€ by Dec/Year 1	0	3 000	thousand €	**Hoshin**	250	500	750	1 000	1 250	1 500	1 750	2 000	2 250	2 500	2 750	3 000
				Actual	0	245	459	989	1 029	1 245	1 340	1 549	1 756	1 934	2 150	2 450
New Products Sales from 0 to 1 M€ by Dec/Year 1	0	1 000	thousand €	**Hoshin**	83	167	250	333	417	500	583	667	750	833	917	1 000
				Actual	0	89	130	176	256	316	489	670	802	856	978	1 219
Commercial Visits Productivity Increase from 20% by Dec/Year 1	0.0%	20.0%	%	**Hoshin**	1.7%	3.3%	5.0%	6.7%	8.3%	10.0%	11.7%	13.3%	15.0%	16.7%	18.3%	20.0%
				Actual	1.6%	3.0%	4.9%	7.0%	7.5%	9.0%	12.0%	13.4%	14.8%	18.3%	19.8%	21.2%
Contribution Margin from 9.5% to 15.2% by Dec/Year 1	9.5%	15.2%	%	**Hoshin**	10.0%	10.5%	10.9%	11.4%	11.9%	12.4%	12.8%	13.3%	13.8%	14.3%	14.7%	15.2%
				Actual	9.8%	10.2%	10.7%	11.0%	11.8%	12.3%	12.8%	13.4%	13.7%	13.9%	14.5%	14.4%
Sales Conversion Rate from 19% to 30% by Dec/Year 1	19.2%	30.0%	%	**Hoshin**	20.1%	21.0%	21.9%	22.8%	23.7%	24.6%	25.5%	26.4%	27.3%	28.2%	29.1%	30.0%
				Actual	19.5%	20.1%	20.6%	22.0%	23.0%	22.5%	23.0%	22.5%	23.5%	27.4%	29.5%	30.5%
Vitality: New Customer Sales from 0 to 3 M€ by Dec/Year 1	0	3 000	thousand €	**Hoshin**	250	500	750	1 000	1 250	1 500	1 750	2 000	2 250	2 500	2 750	3 000
				Actual	203	380	525	607	871	1 016	1 245	1 367	1 427	1 568	1 760	2 137

APPENDIX 1.9 - LEVEL 2 X MATRIX, LOGISTICS & MATERIALS MANAGEMENT, YEAR 1

LEVEL 2 X MATRIX - MATERIALS AND LOGISTICS MANAGEMENT

	EBITDA from 2.3 to 7.2 M€ in Year 1	Implement a process to reduce working capital	Implement a process to increase On-Time Delivery	L2 Improvement priorities	Finished Goods with SDLT from 0 to 1499 by Dec/Year 1	Ongoing Inventory (WIP) from 1289 K€ to 970 K€ by Dec/Year 1	Finished Goods Inventory from 2.6 M€ to 1.9 M€ by Dec/Year 1	On-Time Delivery from 75% to 82.5% by Dec/Year 1	90% Stoppages for lack of Supply Reduction by Dec/Year 1	Raw Material Inventory from 9 M€ to 6.8 M€ by Dec/Year 1	# A items with Kanban from 0 to 70 by Dec/Year 1	Order processing Lead Tiime from 2 d to 2 h by Dec/Year 1	# Finished Goods references from 1499 to 1050 by Dec/Year 1	Airfreights Costs from 400 K€ to 100 K€ by Dec/Year 1	Warehouse Manager	Materials Manager	Planning Manager	Order Processing Team Manager	Sales Manager	IT Manager	Engineering Manager
	●			Implement a process to reduce Air Freights Costs										●	●						
		●	●	Implement a process to reduce # Finished Goods references									●				○		●		○
		●	●	Implement a process to reduce Order Processing lead time								●						●			
			●	Implement a Theory of Minimum Inventory (TMI) process						●	●					●	○				
			●	Implement a standardised Internal Logistics process (MIZU)					●						●						
		●	●	Implement a Pull Planning process		●	●	●									●				
		●		Implement a Standard Delivery Lead Time (SDLT) process	●												●		○	○	

L2 Improvement priorities

L1 Improvement priorities

Targets to Improve (TTI)

Annual Breakthrough objectives

	EBITDA from 2.3 to 7.2 M€ in Year 1	Implement a process to reduce working capital	Implement a process to increase On-Time Delivery	Annual Breakthrough objectives
	●			EBITDA from 2.3 to 7.2 M€ in Year 1
			●	On-Time Delivery from 75% to 82.5% in Year 1
		●		Free Cash Flow from 545 K€ to 5.3 M€ in Year 1
				Time To Market from 50 to 40 weeks in Year 1

Resources:
- ● Primary responsibility
- ○ Secondary responsability

APPENDIX 1.10 - LEVEL 2 BOWLING CHART, LOGISTICS & MATERIALS MANAGEMENT, YEAR 1

TARGET TO ACHIEVE	Starting point	Annual target	Un.		Jan	Feb	Mar	Apr	May	Jun	Jul	Aug	Sept	Oct	Nov	Dec
# Finished Goods of SDLT from 0 to 1499 by Dec/Year 1	0	3004	#	Hoshin	250	501	751	1 001	1 252	1 502	1 752	2 003	2 253	2 503	2 754	3 004
				Actual	202	498	753	987	1 210	1 501	1 845	1 989	2 354	2 760	2 923	3 102
On Going Inventory (WIP) from 1 289 K€ to 970 K€ by Dec/Year 1	1 289	970	thousand €	Hoshin	1 263	1 236	1 210	1 183	1 156	1 130	1 103	1 076	1 050	1 023	997	970
				Actual	1 153	1 421	1 143	1 311	1 170	1 107	1 170	1 225	1 093	957	990	882
Finished Goods Inventory from 2.6 M€ to 1.9 M€ by Dec/Year 1	2 579	1 940	thousand €	Hoshin	2 526	2 472	2 419	2 366	2 313	2 259	2 206	2 153	2 100	2 046	1 993	1 940
				Actual	2 690	2 455	2 667	2 622	2 730	2 583	2 340	2 116	2 186	2 232	1 980	2 058
On-Time Delivery from 75% to 82.5% by Dec/Year 1	75.0%	82.5%	%	Hoshin	75.6%	76.3%	76.9%	77.5%	78.1%	78.8%	79.4%	80.0%	80.6%	81.3%	81.9%	82.5%
				Actual	70.0%	71.0%	72.7%	73.0%	74.6%	75.0%	80.0%	84.0%	84.5%	85.2%	86.7%	87.0%
90% of Stoppages for Lack of Supply Reduction by Dec/Year 1	0	82	h	Hoshin	7	14	21	27	34	41	48	55	62	68	75	82
				Actual	8	15	20	32	39	40	48	57	63	64	74	85
Raw Material Inventory from 9 M€ to 6.8 M€ by Dec/Year 1	9 026	6 790	#	Hoshin	8 840	8 654	8 467	8 281	8 094	7 908	7 722	7 535	7 349	7 163	6 976	6 790
				Actual	8 966	9 044	8 890	9 178	9 100	8 610	8 191	7 795	7 651	7 441	6 931	6 861
# A items with Kanban from 0 to 70 by Dec/Year 1	0	70	#	Hoshin	6	12	18	23	29	35	41	47	53	58	64	70
				Actual	2	5	8	9	13	35	42	50	65	71	86	86
Order Processing Lead Time from 2 days for 2 hours by Dec/Year 1	16	2	h	Hoshin	15	14	13	11	10	9	8	7	6	4	3	2
				Actual	16	16	16	16	16	16	16	16	16	16	16	16
# Finished Goods References from 1 499 to 1 050 by Dec/Year 1	1 499	1 050	#	Hoshin	1 462	1 424	1 387	1 349	1 312	1 275	1 237	1 200	1 162	1 125	1 087	1 050
				Actual	1 495	1 495	1 440	1 362	1 305	1 305	1 262	1 195	1 145	1 115	1 073	1 016
Air Freights from 400 K€ to 100 K€ by Dec/Year 1	0	100	thousand €	Hoshin	8	17	25	33	42	50	58	67	75	83	92	100
				Actual	9	20	30	45	56	65	60	65	65	72	83	83

APPENDIX 1.11 - LEVEL 1 X MATRIX, YEAR 2

LEVEL 1 X MATRIX

L1 Improvement priorities

Annual Breakthrough objectives

Targets to Improve (TTI)

3-year Breakthrough objectives

L1 Improvement priorities	Time To Market fro 44 to 34 weeks by Year 2	Free Cash Flow from 7M€ to 8.6 M€ by Year 2	On-Time Delivery from 87% to 92%* by Year 2	EBITDA from 6.1 M€ to 10 M€ by Year 2
Implement a process to reduce #SKU (Raw Material and Finished Goods)				●
Implement a process to reduce Working Capital		●		
Optimise a process to increase On-Time Delivery			●	
Implement a process to reduce Product Cost (VA/VE)				●
Implement a process to increase Productivity				●
Accelerate a process to reduce New Product Lead Times	●			
Accelerate a process to improve Marketing & Sales	●			●

L1 Improvement priorities	Sales/ FTE from 200 K€ to 207 K€ by Dec/Year 2	Ext. Services & Supplies from 16.6% to 15.5% of Sales (914 K€) by Dec/Year 2	Planned Waste from 6.6% to 5.6% (514.9 K€) Dec/Year 2	On-Time Delivery from 87% to 92% by Dec/Year 2	Time To Market from 44 to 34 weeks by Dec/ Year 2	Inventory from 9.8 M€ to 6.8 M€ until Dec/Year 2	Mean Receipt Timeframe from 83 to 76 days by Dec/Year 2	Average Payment period (PMP) from 95 to 78 days by Dec/Year 2	Sales from 83.1 M€ to 89.3 M€ by Dec/Year 2	Vitality: New Customer Sales from 0 to 3 M€ by Dec/Year 2	# SKU of Raw Material and Finished Goods from 1500 to 900 by Dec/Year 2
Implement a process to reduce #SKU (Raw Material and Finished Goods)											●
Implement a process to reduce Working Capital						●	●	●			
Optimise a process to increase On-Time Delivery				●							
Implement a process to reduce Product Cost (VA/VE)			●								
Implement a process to increase Productivity	●	●									
Accelerate a process to reduce New Product Lead Times					●						
Accelerate a process to improve Marketing & Sales									●	●	

L1 Improvement priorities	Operations Manager	Engineering Manager	Materials & Logistics Manager	Marketing & Sales Manager	Human Resources Manager	Purchasing Manager	Financial Manager	IT Manager
Implement a process to reduce #SKU (Raw Material and Finished Goods)	○	○		●		○		
Implement a process to reduce Working Capital			●	○		○	○	
Optimise a process to increase On-Time Delivery	○		●	○				○
Implement a process to reduce Product Cost (VA/VE)		●						
Implement a process to increase Productivity	●		○		○			○
Accelerate a process to reduce New Product Lead Times	○	●						
Accelerate a process to improve Marketing & Sales				●				○

3-year Breakthrough objectives	Time To Market fro 44 to 34 weeks by Year 2	Free Cash Flow from 7M€ to 8.6 M€ by Year 2	On-Time Delivery from 87% to 92%* by Year 2	EBITDA from 6.1 M€ to 10 M€ by Year 2
EBITDA from 2.3 M€ to 12 M€ in 3 years (20% sales growth included)				●
On-Time Delivery from 75% to 92% in 3 years			●	
Free Cash Flow from 545 K€ to 10 M € in 3 years		●		
Time To Market from 50 to 30 weeks in 3 years	●			

Resources
- ● Primary responsibility
- ○ Secondary responsibility

APPENDIX 1.12 - LEVEL 1 BOWLING CHART, YEAR 2

TARGET TO ACHIEVE	Starting point	Annual target	Un.		Jan	Feb	Mar	Apr	May	Jun	Jul	Aug	Sept	Oct	Nov	Dec
Sales/FTE from 200 K€ to 207 K€ by Dec/Year 2	200.0	207.0	thousand €	**Hoshin**	200.6	201.2	201.8	202.3	202.9	203.5	204.1	204.7	205.3	205.8	206.4	207.0
				Actual	200.0	201.7	201.9	203.0	203.4	203.1	204.2	204.0	206.7	209.8	210.4	211.0
External Services & Supplies from 16.6% to 15.5% of Sales (914 K€) by Dec/Year 2	16.6%	15.5%	%	**Hoshin**	16.5%	16.4%	16.3%	16.2%	16.1%	16.1%	16.0%	15.9%	15.8%	15.7%	15.6%	15.5%
				Actual	16.6%	16.5%	16.5%	16.3%	16.3%	16.2%	16.1%	15.9%	15.8%	15.3%	15.1%	15.0%
	0.0	914	thousand €	**Hoshin**	76.2	152.3	228.5	304.7	380.8	457.0	533.2	609.3	685.5	761.7	837.8	914.0
				Actual	0.0	13.8	20.8	83.1	103.8	166.1	242.2	387.6	498.3	899.8	1 142.0	1 328.9
Planned Waste from 6.6% to 5.6% (514.9 K€) Dec/Year 2	6.6%	5.6%	%	**Hoshin**	6.5%	6.4%	6.4%	6.3%	6.2%	6.1%	6.0%	5.9%	5.9%	5.8%	5.7%	5.6%
				Actual	6.8%	6.6%	6.5%	6.5%	6.3%	6.2%	6.0%	5.8%	6.0%	5.7%	5.6%	5.6%
	0.0	514.9	thousand €	**Hoshin**	42.9	85.8	128.7	171.6	214.6	257.5	300.4	343.3	386.2	429.1	472.0	514.9
				Actual	41.2	80.0	120.9	167.0	201.3	250.6	320.0	353.0	370.0	431.0	475.0	515.0
On-Time Delivery from 87% to 92% by Dec/Year 2	87.0%	92.0%	%	**Hoshin**	87.4%	87.8%	88.3%	88.7%	89.1%	89.5%	89.9%	90.3%	90.8%	91.2%	91.6%	92.0%
				Actual	87.0%	87.4%	87.5%	88.0%	89.2%	89.5%	90.0%	89.9%	89.9%	90.0%	91.0%	91.5%
Time-To-Market from 44 to 34 weeks by Dec/Year 2	44	34	Wk	**Hoshin**	43	42	42	41	40	39	38	37	37	36	35	34
				Actual	44	43	43	42	41	40	39	37	36	35	36	35
Inventory from 9.8 M€ to 6.8 M€ by Dec/Year 2	9.8	6.8	million €	**Hoshin**	9.6	9.3	9.1	8.8	8.6	8.3	8.1	7.8	7.6	7.3	7.1	6.8
				Actual	9.7	9.6	9.6	9.5	9.3	8.9	8.7	8.3	7.9	7.5	7.3	7.1
Mean Receipt Timeframe from 83 to 76 days by Dec/Year 2	83	76	days	**Hoshin**	82	82	81	81	80	80	79	78	78	77	77	76
				Actual	83	83	82	80	79	79	77	76	76	75	74	73
Average Payment Period from 95 to 78 days by Dec/Year 2	95	78	days	**Hoshin**	94	92	91	89	88	87	85	84	82	81	79	78
				Actual	95	95	92	91	90	88	88	87	84	82	80	78
Sales from 83.1 M€ to 89.3 M€ by Dec/Year 2	0	89 300	thousand €	**Hoshin**	7 442	14 883	22 325	29 767	37 208	44 650	52 092	59 533	66 975	74 417	81 858	89 300
				Actual	6 921	14 788	22 263	29 727	37 552	44 642	51 896	58 938	67 847	74 957	82 179	89 758
Vitality: New Customer Sales from 0 to 3 M€ by Dec/Year 2	0	3 000	thousand €	**Hoshin**	250	500	750	1 000	1 250	1 500	1 750	2 000	2 250	2 500	2 750	3 000
				Actual	0	123	300	706	1 260	1 509	1 890	2 013	2 500	2 789	2 900	3 170
#SKU of Raw Material and Finished Goods from 1500 to 900 by Dec/Year 2	1 500	900	#	**Hoshin**	1 450	1 400	1 350	1 300	1 250	1 200	1 150	1 100	1 050	1 000	950	900
				Actual	1 500	1 504	1 380	1 331	1 242	1 198	1 198	1 170	998	954	923	892

APPENDIX 1.13 - LEVEL 1 X MATRIX, YEAR 3

LEVEL 1 X MATRIX

Time To Market from 35 to 18 weeks in Year 3	Free Cash Flow from 8.7 M€ to 10 M€ in Year 3	On-Time Delivery from 91.5% to 95%* in Year 3	EBITDA from 10.5 M€ to 12 M€ in Year 3	L1 Improvement Priorities	Sales/ FTE from 211 K€ to 222 K€ by Dec/Year 3	# Customers w/ Contribution margin < 0% from 74 to 30 by Dec/Year 3	# Products w/ Contribution margin < 0% from 204 to 100 by Dec/Year 3	On-Time Delivery from 91.5% to 95% by Dec/Year 3	Time To Market from 35 to 18 weeks by Dec/Year 3	Inventory from 7.1 M€ to 6.4 M€ by Dec/Year 3	Mean Receipt Timeframe from 73 to 63 days by Dec/Year 3	Average Payment Period from 78 to 62 days until Dec/Year 3	Sales from 89.8 M€ to 95.5 M€ by Dec/Year 3	Vitality: New Customer Sales from 0 to 3 M€ by Dec/Year 3	N° Suppliers from 32 to 15 by Dec/Year 3	Operations Manager	Engineering Manager	Materials & Logistics Manager	Marketing & Sales Manager	Human Resources Manager	Purchasing Manager	Financial Manager	IT Manager
			●	Implement a process to reduce n° Suppliers											●	○					●		
	●			Optimise the process to reduce Working Capital						●	●	●				○		●	○		○	○	
		●		Optimise the process to increase On-Time Delivery				●								○		●	○				○
			●	Optimise the process to increase Productivity	●											●		○		○			○
			●	Implement a process to optimise Customer Portfolios and Contribution margin		●	●												●			○	
●				Accelerate the process to reduce New Product Lead Times					●							○	●						
●			●	Accelerate the process to improve Marketing & Sales									●	●					●				○

Annual Breakthrough objectives — L1 Improvement Priorities — Targets to Improve (TTI) — 3-year Breakthrough objectives

Time To Market (annual)	Free Cash Flow (annual)	On-Time Delivery (annual)	EBITDA (annual)	3-year Breakthrough objectives
			●	EBITDA from 2.3 M€ to 12 M€ in 3 years (20% of sales growth included)
●				On-Time Delivery from 75% to 95%* in 3 years
	●			Free Cash Flow from 545 K€ to 10 M€ in 3 years
		●		Time To Market from 50 to 30 weeks in 3 years

Resources:
- ● Primary responsibility
- ○ Secondary responsibility

APPENDIX 1.14 - LEVEL 1 BOWLING CHART, YEAR 3

TARGET TO ACHIEVE	Starting point	Annual target	Un.		Jan	Feb	Mar	Apr	May	Jun	Jul	Aug	Sept	Oct	Nov	Dec
Sales/FTE from 211 K€ to 222 K€ by Dec/Year 3	211.0	222.0	thousand €	**Hoshin**	211.9	212.8	213.8	214.7	215.6	216.5	217.4	218.3	219.3	220.2	221.1	222.0
				Actual	211.0	210.0	210.0	214.0	216.0	218.5	220.3	221.3	222.8	223.4	228.0	232.7
# Customers w/ Contribution Margin < 0% from 74 to 30 by Dec/Year 3	74	30	#	**Hoshin**	70	67	63	59	56	52	48	45	41	37	34	30
				Actual	74	74	74	65	63	60	50	44	32	28	28	28
# Products w/ Contribution Margin < 0% from 204 to 100 by Dec/Year 3	204	100	#	**Hoshin**	195	187	178	169	161	152	143	135	126	117	109	100
				Actual	200	190	184	177	175	174	170	123	111	98	96	93
On-Time Delivery from 91.5% to 95% by Dec/Year 3	91.5%	95.0%	%	**Hoshin**	91.8%	92.1%	92.4%	92.7%	93.0%	93.3%	93.5%	93.8%	94.1%	94.4%	94.7%	95.0%
				Actual	89.0%	91.0%	89.5%	91.5%	91.3%	92.3%	92.8%	92.1%	93.0%	93.5%	94.2%	94.7%
Time-To-Market from 35 to 18 weeks by Dec/Year 3	35	18	wk	**Hoshin**	34	32	31	29	28	27	25	24	22	21	19	18
				Actual	36	34	34	33	31	28	26	25	23	22	20	20
Inventory from 7.1 M€ to 6.4 M€ by Dec/Year 3	7.1	6.4	million €	**Hoshin**	7.0	7.0	6.9	6.9	6.8	6.8	6.7	6.6	6.6	6.5	6.5	6.4
				Actual	7.1	7.2	7.0	7.4	7.5	7.3	7.0	6.6	6.6	6.5	6.4	6.4
Mean Receipt Timeframe from 73 to 63 days by Dec/Year 3	73	63	days	**Hoshin**	72	71	71	70	69	68	67	66	66	65	64	63
				Actual	73	74	73	72	70	69	70	67	65	62	61	60
Average Payment Period from 78 to 62 days by Dec/Year 3	78	62	days	**Hoshin**	77	75	74	73	71	70	69	67	66	65	63	62
				Actual	77	77	78	76	73	70	70	65	66	64	63	62
Sales from 89.8 M€ to 95.5 M€ by Dec/Year 3	0	95 537	thousand €	**Hoshin**	7 961	15 923	23 884	31 846	39 807	47 769	55 730	63 691	71 653	79 614	87 576	95 537
				Actual	7 848	15 729	24 024	32 558	41 119	49 540	57 754	66 282	74 624	83 042	91 632	100 024
Vitality: New Customer Sales from 0 to 3 M€ by Dec/Year 3	0	3 000	thousand €	**Hoshin**	250	500	750	1 000	1 250	1 500	1 750	2 000	2 250	2 500	2 750	3 000
				Actual	176	467	770	1 029	1 250	1 609	1 980	2 134	2 489	2 876	3 017	3 254
Nr. Suppliers from 32 to 15 by Dec/Year 3	32	15	#	**Hoshin**	31	29	28	26	25	24	22	21	19	18	16	15
				Actual	32	32	32	27	27	27	23	22	20	20	17	17

2. Financial Statements Complementary to Benchmark Analysis

APPENDIX 2.1 - ALFA'S INCOME STATEMENT, YEAR 0, -1 AND -2

ALFA'S INCOME STATEMENT	YEAR 0		YEAR -1		YEAR -2	
Income and expenses (Euros)	**Euros**	**Sales %**	**Euros**	**Sales %**	**Euros**	**Sales %**
Sales and services provided	79 613 782		82 109 809		78 380 205	
Operational subsidies	0		0		0	
Gains / losses credited to subsidiaries, assoc. and joint ventures	0		0		0	
Changes in production inventory	-238 723		110 229		179 581	
Works for own company	64 531		163 527		44 639	
Costs of goods sold and materials consumed	50 554 710	63.5%	54 379 108	66.2%	49 029 236	62.6%
Supply and external services	14 059 838	17.7%	13 199 275	16.1%	14 826 036	18.9%
Personnel expenses	12 537 518	15.7%	12 631 954	15.4%	10 982 554	14.0%
Other incomes	92 857		908 910		1 048 139	
Other expenses	110 445		289 166		513 980	
EBITDA	2 269 937	2.9%	2 792 972	3.4%	4 300 759	5.5%
Expenses / reversals of depreciations and amortisations	3 019 585	3.8%	2 642 212	3.2%	2 912 736	3.7%
EBIT - Operating result (before financial expenses and taxes)	-749 648	-0.9%	150 759	0.2%	1 388 023	1.8%
Interest and similar income obtained	0		0		0	
Interest and similar expenses covered	251 188		354 474		119 493	
Results before taxes	-1 000 836	-1.3%	-203 715	-0.2%	1 268 530	1.6%
Income tax for the financial period	-272 676		-1 813 371		266 971	
Net result for the financial period	-728 160	-0.9%	1 609 656	2.0%	1 001 559	1.3%

APPENDIX 2.2 - ALFA'S BALANCE SHEET, YEAR 0, -1 AND -2

ALFA'S BALANCE SHEET		YEAR 0	YEAR -1	YEAR -2
ASSET				
Non-current asset				
	Fixed tangible assets	19 543 165	19 975 579	15 001 455
	Investment properties	0	0	0
	Intangible assets	43 873	82 662	113 013
	Shareholdings	223 409	223 409	223 409
	Other financial assets	6 330	1 763	533
	Assets by Deferred Taxes	547 554	523 422	455 846
	Financial investments	0	0	0
Total non-current assets		20 364 332	20 806 835	15 794 257
Current asset				
	Inventory	12 894 678	13 851 763	14 429 291
	Customers	9 003 643	15 341 153	4 753 947
	Advances to suppliers	0	0	1 869
	State and other public organisations	2 702 742	3 913 863	0
	Shareholders	9 025 000	0	2 393 580
	Other receivables	175 007	660 851	372 521
	Deferrels	125 995	13 316	0
	Other financial assets	0	0	0
	Other current assets	0	0	0
	Cash flow and bank deposits	5 740 546	5 739 878	12 225 446
Total current assets		39 667 611	39 520 822	34 176 653
Total assets		**60 031 943**	**60 327 657**	**49 970 909**
EQUITY AND LIABILITY				
Equity				
	Paid-up capital	11 875 000	11 875 000	11 875 000
	Own shares	0	0	0
	Other equity instruments	0	0	0
	Legal reserves	1 263 095	1 182 612	1 132 534
	Other reserves	753 582	652 278	2 196 056
	Profit / Loss Carried Forward	-1 305 288	-2 430 902	-3 499 965
	Adjustments in financial assets	0	101 304	0
	Revaluation surplus	1 442 474	1 442 474	0
	Other equity variations	0	0	0
	Total	14 028 863	12 822 766	11 703 625
	Net result for the financial period	-728 160	1 609 656	1 001 559
Total equity		13 300 703	14 432 422	12 705 184
Liability				
Non-current liability				
	Provisions	0	631 211	0
	Financing obtained	2 399 512	2 399 512	353 109
	Post-employment benefit liabilities	1 886 638	1 397 182	1 569 454
	Liabilities by Deferred Taxes	2 962	3 105	3 251
	Other payables	1 052 195	0	17 271
Total non-current liability		5 341 308	4 431 011	1 943 086
Current liability				
	Suppliers	16 852 389	14 987 440	15 692 259
	Advances to customers	0	0	7 040
	State and other public organisations	1 165 284	1 625 014	1 720 240
	Shareholders	0	0	0
	Financing obtained	20 694 129	21 479 519	15 408 968
	Other payables	2 678 130	2 320 055	2 494 132
	Deferrels	0	1 052 195	0
	Other financial liabilities	0	0	0
	Other current liabilities	0	0	0
	Total current liability	41 389 932	41 464 224	35 322 639
Total liability		46 731 240	45 895 235	37 265 725
Total equity and liability		**60 031 943**	**60 327 657**	**49 970 909**

APPENDIX 2.3 - ALFA'S CASH FLOW STATEMENT, YEAR 0, -1 AND -2

ALFA'S CASH FLOW STATEMENT	YEAR 0	YEAR -1	YEAR -2
CASH FLOW OF OPERATIONAL ACTIVITIES			
Customer receivables	77 077 471	71 506 436	80 252 478
Payments to suppliers	59 313 924	67 598 892	64 524 092
Personnel payments	12 988 033	12 244 621	12 425 581
Cash flow generated by operations	4 775 514	-8 337 078	3 302 805
Income tax paid/received	1 570 747	411 802	1 085 067
Other payments/receipts	-1 240 557	129 118	813 129
Cash flow of operational activities (A)	5 105 703	-7 796 158	5 201 001
CASH FLOW OF INVESTMENT ACTIVITIES			
Payments referring to:			
Tangible fixed assets	2 224 365	8 518 498	3 859 663
Intangible assets	0	0	0
Financial investments	0	1 230	530
Other assets	0	0	0
Receipts referring to:			
Tangible fixed assets	418	1 112 490	212 324
Intangible assets	0	0	0
Financial investments	0	0	0
Other assets	0	0	0
Investment subsidies	0	2 939 274	353 109
Interest and similar income	4 903	14 061	11 327
Dividends	0	0	0
Cash flow of investment activities (B)	-2 219 044	-4 453 904	-3 283 432
CASH FLOW OF FINANCIAL ACTIVITIES			
Receipts referring to:			
Financing obtained	0	11 801 951	0
Paid-up capital and other equity instruments	0	0	0
Loss coverage	0	0	0
Contributions	0	0	0
Other financial operations	0	0	0
Payments referring to:			
Financing obtained	8 093 041	0	204 377
Interest and similar income	303 913	306 057	272 301
Dividends	0	0	0
Paid-up capital and other equity instruments	0	0	0
Other financing operations	0	0	0
Cash flow of financing activities (C)	-8 396 954	11 495 894	-476 678
Net variance and its equivalents (A+B+C)	-5 510 295	-754 168	1 440 891
Exchange rate effect	0	0	0
Cash and its equivalents - start period	2 313 999	3 068 167	1 627 276
Cash and its equivalents - end period	-3 196 296	2 313 999	3 068 167

APPENDIX 2.4 - SECTOR'S COMPANIES INCOME STATEMENT, YEAR 0

INCOME STATEMENT BY NATURE - YEAR 0												
COMPANY	ALFA		BETA		DELTA		GAMA		ZETA		SIGMA	
Income and expenses (Euros)	**Euros**	**Sales %**	**Euros**	**Sales %**	**Euros**	**Sales %**	**Euros**	**Sales %**	**Euros**	**Sales %**	**Euros**	**Sales %**
Sales and services provided	79 613 782		69 264 375		29 943 828		35 737 514		39 252 597		26 304 396	
Operational subsidies	0		2 668		1 085		2 057		0		17 865	
Gains / losses credited to subsidiaries, assoc. and joint ventures	0		1 022 238		0		30 053		103 619		0	
Changes in production inventory	-238 723		-116 511		-47 482		11 894		-90 320		18 909	
Works for own company	64 531		0		0		0		0		0	
Costs of goods sold and materials consumed	50 554 710	63.5%	43 239 864	62.4%	17 913 686	59.8%	22 158 875	62.0%	20 741 045	52.8%	16 550 971	62.9%
Supply and external services	14 059 838	17.7%	10 412 905	15.0%	6 946 735	23.2%	5 771 003	16.1%	9 124 998	23.2%	2 337 663	8.9%
Personnel expenses	12 537 518	15.7%	8 953 761	12.9%	3 684 780	12.3%	2 386 324	6.7%	4 448 751	11.3%	3 687 717	14.0%
Other income	92 857		1 664 390		392 552		568 616		322 644		826 142	
Other expenses	110 445		414 474		201 706		627 301		365 443		186 810	
EBITDA	2 269 937	2.9%	8 816 156	12.7%	1 543 076	5.2%	5 406 633	15.1%	4 908 304	12.5%	4 404 151	16.7%
Expenses / reversals of depreciations and amortisations	3 019 585	3.8%	1 499 600	2.2%	915 785	3.1%	2 994 792	8.4%	1 839 552	4.7%	1 223 142	4.6%
EBIT - Operating result	-749 648	-0.9%	7 316 556	10.6%	627 291	2.1%	2 411 841	6.7%	3 068 752	7.8%	3 181 010	12.1%
Interest and similar income obtained	0		3 772		0		37 744		78 971		0	
Interest and similar expenses covered	251 188		1 845		186 970		438 327		16 586		157 480	
Results before taxes	-1 000 836	-1.3%	7 318 484	10.6%	440 321	1.5%	2 011 258	5.6%	3 131 136	8.0%	3 023 530	11.5%
Income tax for the financial period	-272 676	-0.3%	-1 000 795	-1.4%	211 306	0.7%	366 938	1.0%	781 280	2.0%	298 102	1.1%
Net result for the financial period	-728 160	-0.9%	8 319 279	12.0%	229 015	0.8%	1 644 320	4.6%	2 349 856	6.0%	2 725 427	10.4%

APPENDIX 2.5 - SECTOR'S COMPANIES BALANCE SHEET, YEAR 0

BALANCE SHEET - YEAR 0							
COMPANY		ALFA	BETA	DELTA	GAMA	ZETA	SIGMA
ASSET							
Non-current asset							
	Fixes tangible assets	19 543 165	22 636 281	6 855 037	14 562 657	6 464 742	6 328 372
	Investment properties	0	0	0	1 141 802	0	0
	Goodwill	0	0	0	0	0	0
	Tangible assets	43 873	8 991	276 427	7 043	131 898	207 177
	Biological assets	0	0	0	0	0	0
	Shareholdings	223 409	6 255 449	0	87 803	3 005 071	25 200
	Shareholders	0	0	0	0	0	0
	Other financial assets	6 330	13 405	0	159 883	0	1 452
	Assets by Deferred Taxes	547 554	3 973 068	1 437	2 031 857	0	278 384
	Financial investments	0	0	2 900	0	0	0
Total non-current asset		20 364 332	32 887 194	7 135 800	17 991 046	9 601 710	6 840 585
	Inventory	12 894 678	4 708 109	880 379	3 108 895	4 860 535	4 098 206
	Biological assets	0	0	0	0	0	0
	Customers	9 003 643	17 231 439	4 610 664	13 580 740	10 390 441	8 697 125
	Advances to suppliers	0	0	0	0	0	0
	State and other public organisations	2 702 742	501 046	0	33 667	19 718	328 007
	Shareholders	9 025 000	0	0	0	0	0
	Other receivables	175 007	1 117 571	0	1 007 090	888 104	173 107
	Deferrals	125 995	73 245	0	3 215	658 960	30 670
	Financial assets retained for neg.	0	0	0	0	0	0
	Other financial assets	0	0	0	0	1 333	0
	Non-current assets retained for sales	0	0	0	0	0	0
	Other current assets	0	0	0	0	0	0
	Cash flow and bank deposits	5 740 546	881 165	52 544	1 080 497	8 154 523	4 241 626
Total current asset		39 667 611	24 512 575	5 543 587	18 814 103	24 973 615	17 568 741
Total asset		**60 031 943**	**57 399 769**	**12 679 388**	**36 805 149**	**34 575 325**	**24 409 325**
EQUITY AND LIABILITY							
Equity							
	Paid-up capital	11 875 000	14 560 000	1 170 750	3 780 000	4 725 000	1 050 000
	Own shares	0	0	0	0	0	0
	Other equity instruments	0	0	0	0	0	499 695
	Share premiums	0	0	0	0	0	0
	Legal reserves	1 263 095	1 712 158	571 535	740 153	2 697 710	224 455
	Other reserves	753 582	16 894 568	511 128	90 687	18 340 473	8 758 849
	Profit / Loss Carried Forward	-1 305 288	2 486 292	1 844 828	8 551 908	4 654	946 618
	Adjustments in financial assets	0	0	0	0	0	0
	Revaluation surplus	1 442 474	1 208 512	158 089	912 471	0	64 666
	Other equity variations	0	0	0	0	0	25 150
	Total	14 028 863	36 861 530	4 256 331	14 075 220	25 767 837	11 569 433
	Net result for the financial period	-728 160	8 319 279	229 015	1 644 320	2 349 856	2 725 427
	Prepaid dividends	0	0	0	0	0	0
Total equity		13 300 703	45 180 809	4 485 346	15 719 540	28 117 693	14 294 860
Liability							
Non-current liability							
	Provisions	0	0	0	56 466	0	0
	Financing obtained	2 399 512	2 400 000	1 161	5 233 388	1 439 346	5 502 302
	Post-employment benefit liabilities	1 886 638	0	0	0	0	0
	Liabilities by Deferred Taxes	2 962	39 113	8 273	252 311	0	16 839
	Other payables	1 052 195	605 040	0	0	0	0
Total non-current liability		5 341 308	3 044 154	9 434	5 542 164	1 439 346	5 519 141
Current liability							
	Suppliers	16 852 389	2 222 197	3 251 864	1 633 814	3 062 118	1 298 588
	Advances to customers	0	0	0	132 395	0	0
	State and other public organisations	1 165 284	2 464 377	413 874	801 695	1 545 983	552 357
	Shareholders	0	0	0	165 343	0	10 500
	Financing obtained	20 694 129	0	3 443 174	12 316 272	0	1 684 712
	Other payables	2 678 130	4 488 233	1 075 695	468 849	410 185	1 049 166
	Deferrals	0	0	0	25 077	0	0
	Financial liabilities retained for neg.	0	0	0	0	0	0
	Other financial liabilities	0	0	0	0	0	0
	Non-current liabilities retained for sales	0	0	0	0	0	0
	Other current liabilities	0	0	0	0	0	0
	Total current liability	41 389 932	9 174 806	8 184 607	15 543 444	5 018 286	4 595 324
Total liability		46 731 240	12 218 960	8 194 042	21 085 609	6 457 632	10 114 465
Total equity and liability		**60 031 943**	**57 399 769**	**12 679 388**	**36 805 149**	**34 575 325**	**24 409 325**

APPENDIX 2.6 - ALFA'S INCOME STATEMENT, YEAR 0, 1, 2 AND 3

ALFA'S INCOME STATEMENT	YEAR 0		YEAR 1		YEAR 2		YEAR 3	
Income and expenses (Euros)	**Euros**	**Sales %**	**Euros**	**Sales %**	**Euros**	**Sales %**	**Euros**	**Sales %**
Sales and services provided	79 613 782		83 056 000		89 758 124		100 023 765	
Operating subsidies	0		0		0		0	
Gains / losses credited to subsidiaries. assoc. and joint ventures	0		0		0		0	
Changes in production inventory	-238 723		0		0		0	
Works for own company	64 531		0		0		0	
Costs of goods sold and materials consumed	50 554 710	63.5%	51 494 720	62.0%	54 931 972	61.2%	59 214 069	59.2%
Supply and external services	14 059 838	17.7%	13 787 296	16.6%	13 463 719	15.0%	14 487 167	14.5%
Personnel expenses	12 537 518	15.7%	11 627 840	14.0%	10 860 733	12.1%	11 302 685	11.3%
Other income	92 857		0		0		0	
Other expenses	110 445		0		0		0	
EBITDA	2 269 937	2.9%	6 146 144	7.4%	10 501 701	11.7%	15 019 844	15.0%
Expenses / reversals of depreciations and amortisations	3 019 585	3.8%	2 823 904	3.4%	3 051 776	3.4%	3 400 808	3.4%
EBIT – Operating result (before financial expenses and taxes)	-749 648	-0.9%	3 322 240	4.0%	7 449 924	8.3%	11 619 036	11.6%
Interest and similar income obtained	0		0		0		0	
Interest and similar expenses covered	251 188		249 168	0.3%	269 274	0.3%	300 071	0.3%
Results before taxes	-1 000 836	-1.3%	3 073 072	3.7%	7 180 650	8.0%	11 318 965	11.3%
Income tax for the financial period	-272 676		0	0.0%	718 065	0.8%	1 697 845	1.7%
Net result for the financial period	-728 160	-0.9%	3 073 072	3.7%	6 462 585	7.2%	9 621 120	9.6%

3. The 7 Types of MUDA Model

All organisations have waste in their activities. We define waste as all those activities that, when carried out, do not add any value to the customer. The customer can be internal (next operation in a process) or external. Triggering tasks that do not generate value consumes resources - time, labour, energy and/or cost - that must be properly applied, in order to achieve results aligned with the objectives of each team.

Created in Japan, this model originally identifies the 7 types of MUDA in an industrial context. The same model is applied to logistics and services, with slight adjustments.

1. Overproduction:
Production of quantities greater than necessary or before they are really needed. Overproduction represents the main type of MUDA, since it can generate all the others.

2. Transport:
Transfer or transport of information or material between processes, generating increased costs and search time as well as loss of information.

3. Material waiting:
Stationary material does not add any value and is usually referred to as stock (which includes finished products, semi-finished or parts). Higher inventory levels imply more floor space and additional features.

4. Movements of people:
Usually, when employees are moving, they are not carrying out their task. The causes of this type of waste are mainly due to an incorrect sequence of tasks, misaligned layouts, non-ergonomic workplaces, and materials search.

5. People waiting:
This represents the time during which employees are stopped without performing their task, waiting for materials, equipment or people. Waiting is consuming resources without generating results.

6. Over-processing:
Usually associated with tasks unnecessary for the final output, or repetition of activities due to errors or inefficiencies in the process.

7. Errors and defects:
Error production is usually associated with rejected items. Time and cost associated with wasted products, reprocessing and reverse logistics causes obvious inefficiencies and customer dissatisfaction.

4. Product Development KAIZEN™ Methodologies Applied to ALFA

APPENDIX 4.1 - SET-BASED ENGINEERING

The current paradigm of a typical product development process consists of the following phases:

1. Perceive an opportunity of differentiation in the market.
2. Think about winning concepts for a product.
3. Select the most promising concept (performing pilot-scale tests).
4. Draw the product in detail.
5. Produce on a large scale (industrialisation).

In order to achieve a speedy product launch, most companies try to accelerate the first four stages to their maximum, so that the product is being produced as soon as possible, and thus meet the customer's promised date.

However, what normaly happens is (multiple) changes in the design of the product or the means of production, usually when the process is already in a large-scale production phase.

This is due to the way new knowledge is generated and communicated. Generally, simultaneous learning of the various departments throughout the project is not done, i.e., while Product Engineering is thinking about the interesting features or forms the product may have, Process Engineering is not concerned whether current product on means allow them to accommodate these requirements at a reasonable cost. In this way, many interesting initial product concepts turn into products that are impossible to manufacture and launch, or products with very low margins.

On the other hand, learning is not effectively transmitted from one project to another and errors recur.

Set-Based Engineering consists of developing products in a simultaneous learning environment within various areas of the company, all being involved from the very first moment. This not only allows better alignment among teams, but also mitigates the potential design and industrialisation problems of a product at the preliminary stage. In this way, a more linear development process is obtained, avoiding the high costs of internal rework or recall of products, with a consequent impact on the company image.

APPENDIX 4.2 - STAGE GATES MODEL

A project is a set of successive steps toward the final delivery of the product on the market. Several organisations have already identified that it is beneficial to use the same set of phases in every project (also called the Stage Gates model). The main benefits of this model are:

1. Everyone within the organisation works on the projects in the same way, fulfilling the defined sequence of steps, ensuring uniform performance in the management and execution of the projects.
2. By defining the rules that allow them to move from one phase of a project to another, they are ensuring the same level of product maturity at the end of each phase, minimising the risks.

APPENDIX 4.3 - LEAN PROJECT MANAGEMENT TOOLS

Lean Project Management refers to the use of Lean concepts in project management. The main waste in product development projects is "dead time" (waiting for decisions, for materials to be delivered from suppliers, for information, or completing a task from other project colleagues). Lean Project Management tools aim to eliminate these inefficiencies. At the core of Lean Project Management is the use of Visual Management in planning and monitoring project performance. Good Visual Management coupled with planning that clearly identifies the dependencies and timings of each task, ensures that each function knows what to do, when to do it, and who to ask for the information needed. It is in the room where the project is visually generated that the project team's meetings are held (with a minimal weekly frequency), where the situation is shared, critical aspects and actions are discussed to recover delays.

APPENDIX 4.4 - VERTICAL STARTUP CURVE

In the production start-up phase, it is essential to standardise the performance of all players (Production, Logistics, Engineering and Quality) to ensure that all the correct components are assembled, in the correct sequence, within the defined operating time and without stoppages. This is the only way to ensure a vertical production start.

5. Brief description of the purpose of the KAIZEN™ Events planned for the first year of Hoshin

Pull Planning (PULL): Implement a planning model based on real customer demand, in which consumption triggers the replacement of the finished product stock.

Mizusumashi (MIZU): Concentrate all operations not adding value to the process with one or more employees and standardise all those tasks into a repetitive logistics cycle.

Standard Delivery Lead Time (SDLT): Standardise the lead time for each finished product reference.

WIP Inventory Supermarkets (WIP): Size and implement systematic replacement of the products in progress stock, through the installation of supermarkets.

Theory of Minimum Inventory (TMI): Reduce the raw materials inventory by implementing Kanban systems with suppliers.

New Product Development (NPD): Standardise and accelerate the development and industrialisation processes of new products.

Lean Line Design (LLD): Design and implementation of a new production line using Lean concepts.